The Big Work

125 Years of Art, Journalism, and the American West

story by Kevin Wallace
editing and photography by Matt Berger

A Wallace-Berger Family Art Collection

The Big Work: 125 Years of Art, Journalism, and the American West
The Wallace-Berger Family Art Collection

Text copyright 2020 by Kevin Wallace and Matt Berger

Photographs copyright 2020 by Matt Berger, except where noted

All original works of art copyright 2020 by Grant Wallace, Moira Wallace, Kevin Wallace, Madeline Langworthy and Various Artists are the property of The Wallace-Berger Family Art Collection.

All rights reserved. No part of this book may be reproduced or transmitted in any form or by any means, electronic or mechanicalm, including photocopying, recording, or by any informnation storage and retrieval system, without written permission from the publisher and original copyright holders.

Publisher: Matt Berger

Editor: Matt Berger

Photography, Layout, and Design: Matt Berger

The Wallace-Berger Family Art Collection
Campbell, California 95008

ISBN: 978-0-578-68460-4

Printed in the United States of America

First Printing: April 2020

The following publishers and names appearing in The Big Work are trademarks: Walt Disney Co., The *San Francisco Chronicle*, *The San Francisco Examiner*, the *New Yorker Magazine*, the *Carmel Pine Cone*, *Time Magazine*, *New York Times*, corvoisier Gallery, and Courac of Monterey.

To the Wallace women and men,
and their many important husbands, wives,
kids, and collaborators. May your Big Work
live on through the eternal inspiration
of art and new ideas.

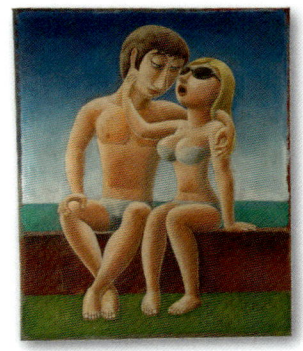

Contents

Introduction
by Matt Berger (1976—present)   **6**

Pleiades Roots
An unfinished memoir by Kevin Wallace (1918—1979)   **8**

Last of the Bohemians
The misadventures of Grant Wallace (1867—1954)   **18**

Carmel's First Family
The California art colony welcomes Moira Wallace (1910—1979)   **48**

News Boy Wonder
Sketching history at the *San Francisco Chronicle* and *Examiner*   **86**

Art Order: *SF Chronicle*   **132**

Postscript
The Ordinary World by Matt Berger   **146**

Featured Art Collections
Carmel Portraits by Moira Wallace   **150**
Carmel Blockprints by Moira Wallace   **176**
California Art and the New Deal by Moira Wallace   **182**
Drawing the World in Color by Kevin Wallace   **238**
Humorist, Humanist, Nudist by Kevin Wallace   **248**
The Berkeley Benefactor by Madeline Thomas Langworthy   **276**
West Indies, North Berkeley by Urania P. Cummings   **296**
The Langworthy Collection by Various Artists   **302**

INTRODUCTION

by Matt Berger

There is one thing in common among many of history's most prolific painters, sculptors, writers, musicians, and creators. They all have relatives and extended family members who end up decades later with attics and boxes full of their legacy of work.

In 2017, my three siblings and I found ourselves in just this position as the co-owners of a cache of family art work, historical artifacts, and cultural memorabilia that spanned the past 125 years of California and American history. My ancestors, the Wallace family of Carmel, participated in and documented many of the 20th century's most defining periods at home and abroad: the Russo-Japanese war of 1896, William Randolph Hearst and his "Yellow Press," The Roaring 20s, The Great Depression, the federally funded Works Progress Administration art movement, World War II, San Francisco in the 1960s, and those are just a few of the highlights.

This collection came to us as a scattered mess of boxes of paintings, piles of drawings, reams of sketches, drawers of artifacts, binders of newspaper clippings, and albums of photos. Some of it had been stored for decades, untouched by time and the elements. Others were in not so good shape. A few pieces were destroyed.

There had been some modest attempts through the decades to take stock of it all, mostly by my late grandmother, Helen Wallace. But no one ever had all the elements required to pull it off: desire, motivation, time, and a means to make it happen. My grandmother wrapped and boxed her collection neatly, preserving it as best as any DIY collector could. My late mother, Deirdre Wallace, carried her stash around her entire adult life from garage to attic to storage container circulating it through the walls of our family home for appreciation, or — as young adults — letting us pick one to hang in our college dorm room or studio apartment. My uncle Brian, the last of the Wallaces, still has his take tucked away in temperature controlled storage facilities, and various sheds and vans up and down the Monterey coast.

And then came death, and inheritance, placing a large cache of it under the stewardship of the newest adult generation of the family, the Berger kids. It's a strange and privileged position to be in, I'll admit. And it's a difficult thing to consider until you are faced with the question: What would you do with 125 years of original family artwork, significant cultural objects, and family heirlooms?

Do you hang it on your wall and display it all on your furniture tabletops? Do you sell it? Can you sell it? Do you donate it to museums and archives? Will anyone want it? Will everyone want it? Will no one want it? Do you put it out in the world? Or do you hide it away, locked up in isolation and obscurity for the next generation to deal with? These are the questions that our family has wrestled with for more than a century of accumulation.

I've been formulating my answer to this question for more than 30 years, ever since I first discovered my family story in an unpublished memoir by my grandfather Kevin. I came across his typewritten manuscript as a teenager among the aforementioned boxes in the garage of my childhood home, and devoured the pages of our family story with wonder and amazement. The title page proclaimed *The Big Work* and reading it set off a life-long journey and pursuit for my own Big Work. Sadly, it took the death of my mom to give me the courage to bring this story to light.

My great, great grandfather Grant Wallace often gets the credit for kicking off our family tree of genius and madness, and I'll let you make your own judgment based on the evidence presented here. He always claimed that his Big Work would "unlock the secret structure of reality's nine dimensions and in general set mankind straight through rational scientific method." It's no wonder he got most of the attention.

It may actually have been Grant's daughter Moira Wallace, my great-aunt, whose impact and artistic visions will be felt far longer than the occult philosophies and writings of her father. Moira's portraits, murals, block prints, and sketches reveal more about the history of America and the West and the struggle of Womankind than any modern art history book observes. Ironically, it was likely her gender that prevented Moira's legacy from being preserved in the best private galleries, museum collections, and public institutions. The 20th-century was the era of Man, and it left little room for those prodigal women who toiled in the shadows.

Another chunk of credit goes to Kevin, Moira's brother eight years younger. He was the only one in the family to suck it up and continue the struggle with two kids of his own — and by proxy my mom who made four more. That's what it took to get us to modern day when a great-grandson with professional publishing skills can captivate the attention of the world with his ancestor's 100-year-old original artwork.

There are other people to thank for this, most notably the husbands and wives of the creators in our family who have worked tirelessly to keep the family nurtured and clothed, but mostly went unrecognized because they didn't leave behind their own legacy of published work.

Finally, I challenge you to consider a more mystical and elaborate contributor to it all, referred to in this book as "The Pleiades." I'm an atheist and son of a scientist father, so I've had my doubts. But after compiling this anthology I can't help but think the whole story is fueled by a bit of divine intervention, as if it was written already.

Luckily for me it was, in the following unpublished manuscript last revised on his typewriter sometime just before his death in 1979.

Kevin Wallace, Boy
by Moira Wallace
c. 1926
Colored chalk portrait by his sister

Signed by artist
Unframed, Fair Condition

Pleiades Roots
An unfinished memoir by Kevin Wallace (1918—1979)

Growing up in Carmel in the 1920s and 30s, modesty prevented me from letting on to my friends that I was our woodsy seashore bohemia's only home-grown messiah. Like Haroun al Raschid going among the people, I wore my disguise as a little boy with quiet grace, joining easily with the real children in their normal wholesome recreations.

We shivered in cheesecloth and helmets on weekend nights in fog blowing across the Forest Theater Stage. We sported after school in great rollers splattering the turquoise surf, Pt. Lobos purple on the horizon, under diving pelicans. When lucky we dragged dead sea-lions from the white strand and arranged them, nonchalant in sun glasses straw boaters from the theater prop room, in deck chaises of surprised vacationers on Scenic Drive.

I rarely did any messiah homework beyond reading after-images as auras and curing my mother Peggy's headaches by laying on of hands when she remembered to ask. I was more practiced at goading my beautiful sister Moira into hurling her paints at me and retreating in tears up into the garden oak, while I primly advised my chief protector, "Forgive her, Mother, she didn't know what she was doing."

Our family was so picturesque a little unit — radiantly auburn crowned Peggy, Jehovan silver-maned Grant, dark and beautiful Moira, and I, when small, so swamped under platinum curls that I regularly snarled "I'm a bear" when asked "Is 'oo a boy or a dirl" — we seemed more reasonably assembled by Central Casting than genetics.

But behind the scenes it was much more complicated. Before my birth in 1918, my mother had intimations she carried an infant of high destiny. Not long after I was born the matter was confirmed by the Order of Light from the Pleiades, who revealed through automatic writing to my father, that I had been reincarnated from among their number expressly to carry on the Big Work he was then doing, with their collaboration, when his hand should falter.

Grant's hand was not about to falter and even if it did, he was too skeptical an investigator to take any damned astral's word credulously; but it was no secret, either, and I grew up in the knowledge of my mission as a light bringer.

There was a lot of messiah work, according to Grant, who retired abruptly to collaborate in automatic writing and drawing every morning, unlocking the secret structure of reality's nine dimensions and in general setting mankind straight through rational scientific method.

In childhood, awed as we were by the troops of angels and pharaohs traipsing through Grant's studio, we had sense enough to speak of our father's occupation as philosophy and identify him simply as a former newspaperman.

Grant generally got tuned in to the infinite before the first gray of Carmel's foggy seashore dawn, and took down the Pleiades people's fancy automatic writing, drawing and math until noon, when the sun came out and malefics jammed the vibrations.

He let me stand around in his pipe smoke, watching his fingers glide magically around his drawing paper, professionally sketching heroic portraits of my free-floating fellow Light Bringers, ravishing Zu-la Zu-le and stern-jawed Alzuil-bel, and of Charles Darwin, evolving through key reincarnations from Atlantis ape-man days, with elegantly penned messages like "At death the cage is buried, but the bird is free and sings above the grave," and "Blessed is the lazy cynic who expects nothing, for he shall not be disappointed," signed "Per Zimias," and beautifully unfathomable geometric charts of cosmic ether's essential structure.

"Do the astrals grab your hand and shove it around?" I asked.

"Hell's bells son," Grant told me. "You know I wouldn't surrender control of my process to let anyone domineer me dead or alive."

And I did know, for Grant often railed at our mother, Peggy for trying it.

"And what you suggest would invite hypnotic domination by packs of roving astrals "charlatans and quacks and earthbound malefics who'd try to put anything over on me if I didn't keep my wits alert."

I gathered Grant got the visions and messages by inspiration, telepathically, and indicted them according to his own high standards, constantly re-lighting his pipe and selecting the right pens from hundreds around his desk.

Grant was splendid and awesome, tall and granite-hewn and a half-century my senior, with flowing silver hair and blue eyes that saw through time-wasters of this world and the next. Afternoons, he napped and tended our wildly beautiful garden, oranges crossbred with grapefruit, hydrangeas mixed up with delphiniums and iris, honeysuckle garlanding wild lilac and local oak, cactus,

(above) A portrait of Carmel's First Family of the Arts, the Wallaces. c. 1914. Grant Wallace poses with his second wife Peggy, and their first child Moira; (left) Kevin was born in 1918 and is seen here a few years later photographed in a wash bucket.

melons, monkey puzzle trees, birdbaths, Oriental poppies, harmoniously entangled.

Grant disdained his older admirer Luther Burbank's small talk with plants but they adored him anyway, stretching and writhing and putting out more blooms, even the geraniums he coolly touched up with leftovers from the window-trim green.

Evenings, the Pleiades themselves bright through the pines overhead, Grant settled by the fire and radio with his friends' latest yarns in the Saturday Evening Post, which was handy to roll up to whack me when needed, notwithstanding my being Zarathustra, Hammurabi and Pleiades reincarnated. Back when my stunning sister Moira had been mistaken for indigestion — and so arrived as Carmel's first-born, instead of over the hill in the Monterey hospital like everyone else — the woodsy beach colony had been a year-round picnic of expatriate artists and writers from San Francisco, each transfixed by his own soaring vision. But now 15 years later in the Great Depression it was a worldly hamlet, where Grant went incognito as retired newspaperman and author.

A few sincere curiosity-seekers did get in to his cluttered studio behind our house on the Ocean Avenue hills: a family named Marshal from Pasadena, Van wyck Brooks when out from Boston, and every year the toney old Morrison girls from San Jose's thin upper crust, who resembled Alice's Red and White Queens and carried a fragrance of mothballs.

The girls, Essie and Judy, would arrive grandly in their chauffeur-driven tonneau with lap robes, their cobwebby old live-in Judge Houghton, and a hamper of dead little cocktail sandwiches and petis-fours tasting of formaldehyde.

Cloche hats askew and pearl strands heaving on satin bosoms, they nibbled and bobbed their flushed faces and made little birdlike sounds over Grant's immense portfolios of thunder-and-lightning from the might shades of Cheops, Emanuel of Swedenborg, Grant's onetime collaborator Ambrose Bierce, talented Will Shakespeare, and minor annotators like Jesus Christ, who said he never could figure out all the furor he'd stirred up.

Grant presided judicially above the proceedings while Peggy shone and sparkled as docent, her magnificent head of wavy auburn hair tossing over her artlessly actressy animation: Melodiously she exclaimed on the extravagant truth and magical wonder of this and that, just as she did for Carmel's melodramatic sunsets, paling them by comparison.

"Oh, the endlessly thrilling magic and wonder of our universe!" Peggy would exclaim.

A portrait of Grant Wallace

Ravishing Zu-la-Zu-le
by Grant Wallace
c. 1915
"Self portrait" by the Pleiaden queen
by way of automatic writing

photo courtesy Brian Wallace

"Darling Peggy — remarkable!" Essie and Judy would agree.

"Harmless old coots," Grant praised the Morrisons as they drove off—more credit than he gave Sir Arthur Conan Doyle on a similar errand. After a few hours with Grant's big work, Sir Arthur informed the attending press, "This is certainly the most wonderful stuff, and has immense wisdom," which Grant saw as a snap judgment.

"Doyle is credulous," Grant told The San Francisco Examiner reporter who gave the encounter a full Sunday page, complete with reproductions of Grant's lunar and Martian alphabets, Hypatia of Alexandria's self-portrait in her new Pleiadean helmet, and a careful summary of Grant's skeptical scientific rigor in probing the afterlife, unmasking impostors, and validating such wisdom as came through, including a formula for telling true statements from false, and mathematical proof that individual improvement over the eons is what the universe is all about.

The reporter, Bobby Willson, knew Grant's legend on San Francisco papers, and confided that he too had flown in his sleep, scaring him. He became a regular visitor. Bobby's drawbacks were his raucous flapper wife, Shiela, and two unwieldy Old English sheepdogs, one of which could say "Elizabeth" and did so at every opportunity, and both of which could stay everywhere in the Willsons' air-cooled Franklin and sat up self-consciously at the table, with their own linen napkins and silver napkin ring.

Also Bobby and Sheila drank, though not at our house. They found Peggy's exuberant inspiration made them miss booze less, as had others, including our then resident derelict, poor Joe. Peggy, no drinker but temperamentally high as a kite the whole time, alternately giddy and exalted, was fond of taking in bums who panhandled at the kitchen door to uplift them with talk of their undiscovered possibilities while they fixed faucets, hauled firewood and carpentered skew-gee sun-porch additions. Their temporary ennoblement reminded her of her idea of the loyal retainers who served her wild North Irish forebears who rode to hounds all day, drank all night and beat their women and servants soundly.

Poor Joe, short and cockeyed, with cauliflower ears, a gimpy leg and tattoos swimming in freckles and red body hair, was dazzled but suspicious of Peggy's bewildering impression of her girlhood heroine, Lorna Doone, and seemed more at ease with Grant, whom he called "my writer fren', Mr. Wallows."

Grant, though wary of Joe's crab-wise scuttling, sensed the man's native simplicity and praised his incredulous spirit.

Credulous was bad, but not so bad as being a piffler or time waster, a category that included several famous editors, materialistic creditors; Grant's rich brother Charles; and schemers who wanted to pave Ocean Avenue hill. Also his one-time Carmel protege Sinclair Lewis, whose new Nobel Prize disqualified him from admittance to Grant's studio, leaving him to dodge my dog Frightful's enthusiasm in the garden.

And especially the hobohemians and Pebble Beach loafers who paid court to the painting genius of my sister Moira, retired at age 19 from New York commercialism to her own Big Work at her easel in the living room.

Secretly, Grant dreaded Moira's jazz-age swains for their sophisticated banter's threat to Peggy's assumed ignorance of the facts of life. It horrified him when Peggy reported merrily, "Moira's friends know people they call fairies and thespians, which we certainly never had when I was a girl in San Francisco."

Grant was especially hostile towards the

A feature story by reporter Robert H. Willson, in the Wednesday, November 4, 1923 edition of the San Francisco *Examiner* on Grant's "Startling Claims" on the occult.

Maje, Moira's polo-playing major, who anticipated the end of Prohibition by passing around his recipe for home brew, telling Peggy it was an essential for maintaining robust health.

Peggy, a pushover for diets promising still more zest for the whole family, discreetly hid a big stoneware crock or two behind the barricades of stacked Big Work in Grant's studio and stirred in ingredients The Maje listed.

Then one afternoon she took Grant off for a walk on the beach and returned to find the Willson's Franklin under the front oak, their sheepdog bounding excitedly through the plants, and Bobby and Sheila collapsed in hysterical mirth in the studio's rock garden.

"We drove all the way down from The City to bless our Angel Peggy for saving us from the demon alcohol," Sheila gasped, " and what do we find but she's poisoned the servant staff with green beer…"

"Joe was passed out beside the drained crock in there," Bobby added, " and when we brought him around, he confessed he was on the run from a Texas prison, and then floated off in the woods…"

Grant looked Jehovan and Peggy sat down on a rock and covered her face with her hands to hide helpless giggles. I was at the moment with Fightful, my dog, in the living room next door, munching a raw turnip and eavesdropping on a Los Angeles magazine columnist named Cornelius Vanderbilt Jr. who was interviewing Moira at her easel dabbing at her big tempera "Madonna of Pt. Lobos."

The Dutch door was open at the top, giving new arrivals the look of cows in their stalls. Joe now appeared there, wild-eyed, and threw open the bottom panel to stagger in.

"You people," he slurred darkly, fixing his attention on Vanderbilt to make him out, "are so, so dumb."

He accepted an anchovy sandwich and Tom Collins and, starting to weep, went on "Never worked a day in my life, not until I come here and had to take pity on people so, so dumb."

"Only stayed sober because if I didn't protect you people, some worse crook would come along and rob you blind."

Just then The Maje, looking overdressed in riding togs, came up to the door and said, "What's going on with your parents and the people with the dogs tearing up the shrubs out there?"

Joe sidled towards the door and past The Maje and swept us all indignantly, with his parting shot: "Dumb or not, you've seen the last of me, because now I see it, you're all Goddam schnobs."

Joe's insights troubled me. During the next few days, I became attentive at Grant's side. Afterwards I would retire to my own garden cabin, a boarded-over tent, to hold a pencil poised expectantly over a notepad. but nothing happened. I fetched a crystal ball from a trunk stored with us, along with the cabin, by theatrical friends, but still no luck.

I sat on the great boulders in the spume in front of Jeffers' rock tower, brooding across the tide at mystic Point Lobos and tuning in various friends' thoughts. But, though Pegging unnervingly claimed she could read my thoughts from any distance as though I were in the next room, nothing registered.

Depressed, I checked out the Carmel library's whole shelf of occult how-to books. Then I became distracted with the heavy schedule of that summer following my grade school graduation.

There was my messenger-boy role in the first 20th Century revival of a P.T.. Barnum temperance melodrama "The Drunkard," that afterwards went on without me for 20 years up and down California. There was my week's job at a makeshift candy counter on the old coast road at Bixby Creek, as lookout for some amateur Carmel rum-runners. There were two weeks camping out at Big Sur with Sam and Neil, discussing my best approach to the unapproachable lovely Paula Schraps.

Back from camping, we built a Druid ring of driftwood phone poles on Carmel Beach to attract tourists marks for magic tricks from the Johnson Smith & Co. Catalogue.

I mastered Bing Crosby's vocal mannerisms on Moira's records of "Just a Gigolo" and "Too Late," joined Sam in publishing a little magazine satirizing Sax Rohmer and Dorothy Sayers mysteries, and haphazardly did the exercises Charles Atlas sent free after I had ignored his more expensive offers.

When high school started in Monterey, the library notified me that my occult books were so overdue that to help pay the fine they would give me a job shelving all their returned books after hours. I had been out of work and broke since the sixth grade when I stopped delivering the Monterey Herald to everybody north of Ocean Avenue.

Grant and Peggy seemed more pleased by my unexpected new $5-a-week than any amount of augmented psychic powers could have made them. It made sense: the family had more of the one than the other. Moira explained, "They're really very nice about anything we do so long as it's for the true, the good, and beautiful, and brings in a little money."

Dawdling while shelving over the next four years, I read through the whole library, feeling a little guilty for postponing my work as a Light Bringer, and wondering how Grant got his knack.

It's a complicated story, and the place to begin is with my father's getting into it in the first place, back in Missouri in 1873, when he was six.

Last of the Bohemians
The Misadventures of Grant Wallace (1868—1954)

Grant got interested in the infinite, prompted by his pioneer mother's flitting distracted for several days around the Missouri frontier farmyard, lecturing in what sounded like basso Latin.

The fifth of her nine mostly conventional children, Charles, explained to the sixth child, Grant, that their mother had gone briefly gaga as a result of the rigors of participating in America's great westward expansion. These had included a perilous odyssey with her firstborn under her arm, via fireprone windjammers and plaguey Nicaraguan isthmus to catch up with her Argonaut husband Tom at his California gold rush diggings in the Sierra motherlode near Grass Valley.

While Lola Montez tempestuously shot a husband next door for annoying her bear, Mother Wallace stuck to business and gave birth to children numbers two and three, two being Ella, the first girl born in the settlement. Then she packed everybody back east as far as the tornadoes and blizzards and religious fanatics of

Missouri's Nodaway country, where husband Tom planted wheat and corn, fought for the Blue, took a county judgeship, entertained the fugitive James boys, and encouraged competition in ornamental Spencerian penmanship among his increasing brood.

The family's last born was on his way when word came of the first born's untimely death on a snowy grizzly bear hunt in his father's ancestral New Hampshire. Pioneer mothering was rough.

As for her spell, apart from the odd behavior, Mother Wallace seemed sound as a dollar, and Grant rejected Charles' diagnosis of temporary insanity as failing to stand to reason. Though Mother had not been herself, she clearly had been somebody—somebody else, male and Latin speaking—and the logical explanation Grant surmised was demoniacal possession by a Latin-speaking male ghost.

Charles laughed, but Grant laughed last. The psychic revelation reverberated with wider implications. Grant's natural indignation was not yet jaded by the gross unfairness of the human condition, as contrasted with those lingering intimations he had of a freer, more purposeful, better-arranged prenatal clime that poets hang onto. Where others accept civilization's apologetic "It would be better if we had more cooperation, respect, sunshine, money, love, political clout, good looks, time…" Grant did not.

With Emerson and Ruskin in his hip pocket, and Indians and Congregationalists and Charles' arbitrary world about, Grant hoarded his vision of a broader life and meantime beat Charles out in the family penmanship lists, going on eventually to teach the subject and draw the Palmer Method's ornamental examples. The skill also enabled him to forge trouble-making mash notes to adolescent Charles from idolized girls who didn't know he existed.

Grant declared for Charles Darwin's new theory, ridiculing the region's shrill Campbellite and Baptist camp meetings, and teasing Charles' Christianity for standing up devout neighbors all night on a nearby hill, waiting for Doomsday dawn.

At 13, out of the fields and into the local Hopkins Journal as printer's devil, Grant bet Charles he could write and sell dime novels as trashy as what they read, and wrote and sold four.

Charles took refuge in the Iowa teachers' college all Judge Tom's children went to. Grant pursued him there, and upstaged him with the undergraduate professorship in commercial subjects.

It was the 1890s and there was much more to see. Grant zoomed off to see Tom Edison's bright new lights on the cobblestones of New York. Grant tested Greenwich Village's lively Ouija boards, hypnotic telekinesis, telepathy, clairvoyance, theosophy, karma and hypnotism soirées, séances, reincarnation sessions, and pieced them into Darwinism.

Where evolutionary theory let individuals die off, depriving them of substantial progress, Grant's revised theory gave some point to everybody's otherwise inane classroom work, courtship, housekeeping, bread-winning, and dying off. Incarnations were semesters and astral intervals holidays when ghosts with nothing better to do could communicate telepathically with those on earth, and, if the latter weren't careful, hypnotize them.

Grant financed the New York interval with space-rates from the New York Evening Sun for sketches of sidewalk crime victims and hocking his coat.

At 19, he went on to Delaware for a period as principal of a Wilmington business school, starring in amateur theatricals and holidaying in the high Adirondack vibrations of a cabin once frequented by Boston's great transcendentalists.

And at 21 he was back in Greenwich Village, polishing his conversation and expertise in exposing fraudulent mediums, and paying his way through Cooper Union and the Student League by posing for Dan Beard's ideologically scandalous illustrations for the first edition of A Connecticut Yankee in King Arthur's Court.

Mark Twain would drop in on Beard's studio in the attic of the Judge magazine building and exchange enthusiasms with the model for Tom Edison's plans to harness telepathy via phrenophone, as he had done for sound via gramophone and electricity via light bulb.

Returning west—to criticize Charles' dogged academic research, open and close two art schools, marry, and take a Nebraska professorship—Grant was ready when Mother Wallace suffered a second basso Latin spell.

While Charles argued for the loony bin, Grant gave the patient a firm look and spoke directly to the possessing demon—evidently a guilt-racked earthbound monk left over from the Spanish Inquisition—and advised it to vacate Mother Wallace instantly. Mother Wallace focused her gaze, remarked "You boys look hungry!" and went to the kitchen to fix a chicken fricassee with dumplings and

gw-0002

Keep Out
by Grant Wallace
c. 1925
Newspaper illustration denouncing
Collis P. Huntington's Southern Pacific Railroad.

Signed by artist
Framed, Good Condition

biscuits. Charles tottered back to his books.

On the Other Side, Grant's work did not go unnoticed. The Pleiades people in the Order of Light were so impressed that they sent their leader Zu-la Zu-le to sound Grant out on collaborating on a Big Work to free mankind as he had freed Mother Wallace from hypnotic bondage to illogical notions. Grant replied he didn't know the Order of Light from Adam's off ox, and he was perfecting his skills for such a work on his own; thanks anyway.

Grant took wife and small son, whom they annoyed by calling Junior, to St. Paul, drew chalk-plate illustrations for the Pioneer-Press, exposed frauds at a nearby spiritist convention, and resigned when his paper wouldn't support the presidential bid of his neighbor across the street, William Jennings Bryant.

Besides, he had been in one place a year and it was time to move on. Also, Judge Tom died, and Mother Wallace expressed willingness to revisit California with her two remaining spinster daughters, Ella and Olive. Grant and his small brood went on ahead to prepare a little Eden he called Tanglewood on the American River at a Sacramento suburb called Fairoaks.

Theoretically a working citrus orchard, Tanglewood was in fact an artist's ornamental fantasy on his Scots-Irish ancestral agriculture, a child's garden of improbably cross pollinated and grafted Australian and African trees and shrubs and flowers, presided over by staggering royal palms. Grant supported Tanglewood by occasional river commuting down to San Francisco where he replaced Homer Davenport as editorial cartoonist on young Willie Randolph Hearst's Examiner, and alongside Ambrose Bierce denounced the perfidies of Collis P. Huntington's Southern Pacific Railroad.

When Huntington negotiated a private truce with Hearst, Bierce told Grant, "We could make a more honest living digging gold out of teeth in Calvary Cemetery," and encouraged Grant to moonlight as a reporter on the rival morning San Francisco Chronicle.

Grant the writer dawned on the Chronicle's readers in huge type that started down the middle of the front page:

> A little wife trying to be brave, but with tears in her voice; a hollow-eyed husband with head sunk on his breast, his unseeing eyes seeming to probe a hopeless picture; a little yellow-haired girl clinging to his hand, weeping—that is the picture of the household engineer who forgot.

The next day, Chronicle city editor Ernest Simpson's reported in the weekly Town Talk:

> Grant Wallace has been one of the best newspaper artists in the West... A month ago he asked the city editor of the Chronicle for a position as a reporter. He was without experience, but editors have learned that geniuses now and then turn up...
>
> When the Sunset train was wrecked last week and lives lost, the city editors fell over themselves in efforts to get the best accounts. Wallace learned that engineer Coffey had been taken to his home... The next morning the Chronicle printed the most striking bit of writing seen in a newspaper in several years. It was Coffey's confession that he had forgotten his orders to stop at Upland.
>
> Wallace pictured the remorse, terror and dejection of the wretched man in the style of a Zola. Little else was talked of in the newspaper offices for several days... Above the startling story was a portrait of the engineer, also made by

Wallace, which was itself a startling example of realism. Wallace has been overwhelmed with the congratulations of his fellows."

Grant was forthwith lifted by Fremont Older to become the rival evening Bulletin's chief editorial writer and artist and feature reporter. It was phenomenal. His first Big Work platform mounted, Grant suddenly was everywhere.

With a byline as big as a cigar, he preempted the whole front page and a spillover with what correctly announced itself to be: "As strange and terrible a story—and a true one withal—as ever novelist put to pen."

The headline rang: SICILIAN LEAGUE OF BLOODHOUNDS TO DEATH OLD GARIBALDIAN OF THIS CITY

The story involved a boon friend of Grant's, Orazio Raffa, former grand opera basso and head pastry chef at Senator Sharon's Palace Hotel, who had divined and now practiced Stradivarius' secret method of making terrific violins, one of which Moira still had somewhere around the house.

Raffa's trouble was that the Sicilian Mafia had tracked him to San Francisco to retrieve a priceless Titian Magdalene painting that Raffa had captured from a castle he sacked in his youth with Garibaldi's troops. Summoned by Raffa's wife, Grant discovered his gifted friend comatose from poison injected through a cruciform cut incised in the neck. Grant wrote:

> "I placed my hands on his head, put him into a hypnotic sleep, and gave him a series of powerful suggestions. "You are no longer ruled by fear of La Mafia," I said. "Who did this thing."
>
> "They will cut my throat—cut my heart—my heart—and burn it..."

Raffa rallied enough to explain he wanted the priceless Titian for his old operatic diva chum Adeline Patti, and gave it to Grant for safekeeping, then expired. The Mafia tried to distract Grant from writing it up by hurling at him a heavy ill-aimed rivet, whose photograph accompanied the article, along with Grant's answer:

> "I have the names of the ringleaders of San Francisco's Italian League of Blood... Let them lift a hand and it is just possible the sky will fall on them."

For the next few years, his byline took him wherever his interests diverged. Grant was photographed as the only mere male frolicking at a six-hour lunch with a troupe of 16 chorus girls. He criticized the theater and analyzed itinerant cultural and spiritual stars, on whom he imposed hard standards. All of this was just the frosting on the rich cake of Grant's big, stylish, eloquent, three-a-week editorial page musings on vaster dimensions than Bay views and current events encompassed.

With the best of both eternal and afternoon daily worlds his, it seemed increasingly unreal, coming home from a hard day of hubris and the office to the new house on Parnassus Heights, where wife and child were resettled from abandoned Tanglewood.

Grant's wife was as indulgent of her tall, dark, inspired matinée idol's Big Work as of the rest of his endlessly amusing idiosyncrasies, and occasionally she suggested ideas of her own to his attention. Grant responded to her suggestion once with a newspaper editorial denouncing interference, and concluding: "You solve your problems, I'll solve mine."

He wondered how he got married in the first place. Reviewing the facts, he saw he had returned west from the Art Student League

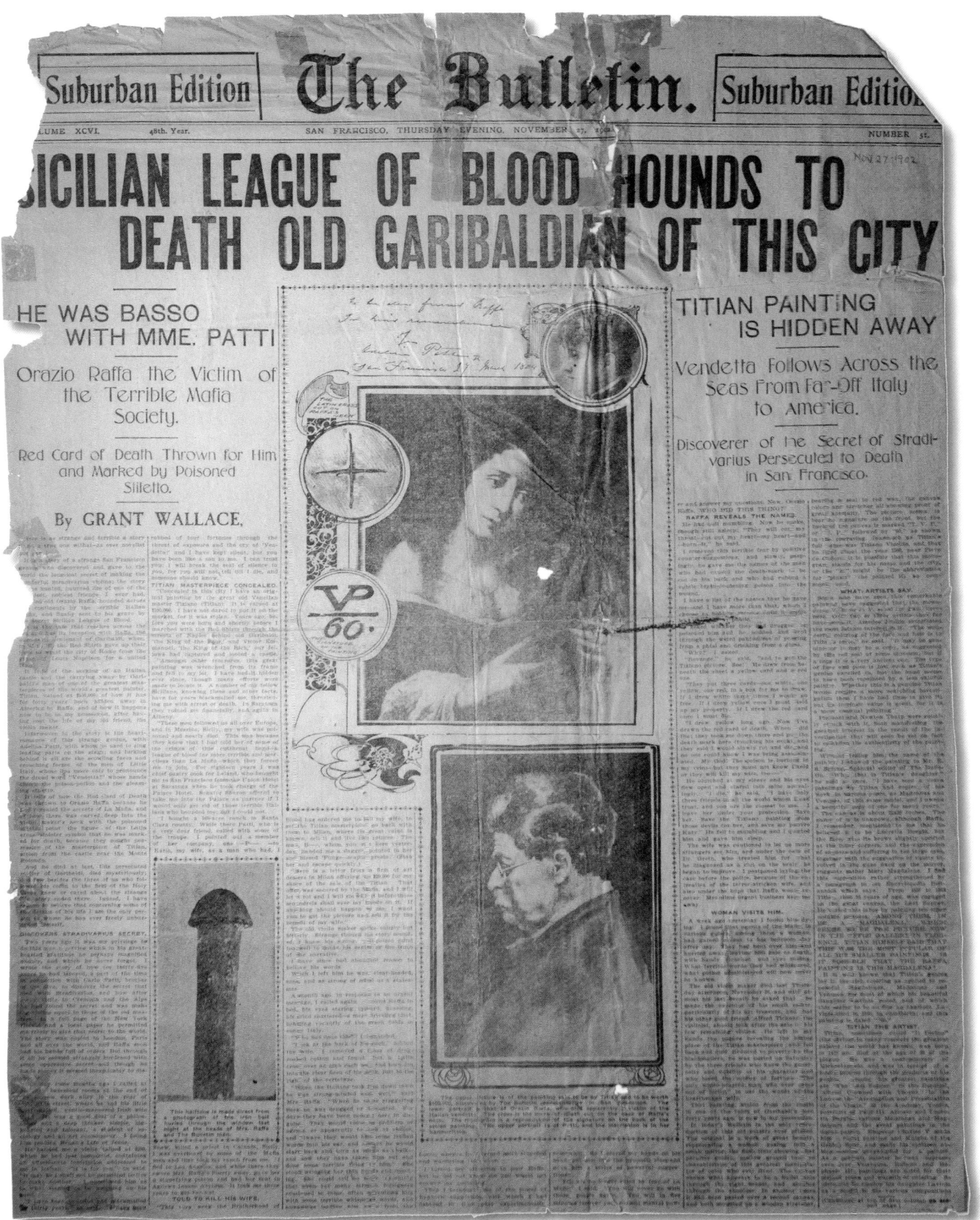

The *San Francisco Bulletin* published Grant's exposé about a San Francisco man murdered by the Sicilian Mafia over a priceless painting.

The Examiner Christmas Humorist
by Grant Wallace
Newspaper Illustration

Signed by artist, Original artist captions
Framed, Good Condition

What We May Hear at the New Zoo
by Grant Wallace
Newspaper Illustration

Signed by artist, Original artist captions
Unframed, Good Condition

Some Slaves Were Feed, But There Are Others
by Grant Wallace
Newspaper Illustration

Signed by artist, Original artist captions
Framed, Good Condition

Why We Laugh
by Grant Wallace
Newspaper Illustration

Signed by artist, Original artist captions
Unframed, Good Condition

credulous. Taking a ring to his sister, Olive, he had let her college roommate try it on first, and didn't protest when this person collapsed in his arms sighing "I will."

He demanded a divorce, and when his helpmeet brought him hot milk for overtiredness instead, he wrote a column declaring:
To maintain an association of family or state, when it is only a form or a word, and not the genuine birth of a free spirit, seemed too dangerous and immoral.

The columns continued but Grant had an even better idea, to dislodge his wife's affections and give her grounds too; and he went about trying with efforts that included entertaining young admirers in a Parnassus Heights lodging house.

Nevermind, said his wife. She would never abandon him.

Though he looked to time to free him from his marriage he eventually concluded it would take more than that, and arranged to mail in columns from the Mojave Desert, where a moonlighting job as a wilderness ranger was available, alone with his pony, Carmelita.

The Bulletin next heard from Grant and Carmelita perched 7,000 feet over Ojai, atop a sea of clouds.

Fifty feet below the hanging pulpit whereon we stood on the top of Topatopa—above a dark pocket of serried pines, crawling up the wild chaos of boulders, tumbling over the long dark shoulders of the mountain and beating against the vertical granite palisades—poured the great cloud cascade.

He added pointedly:

> The wise man goes into solitude, not to lose himself but to find himself. Lonesome? A person who is interested and enthusiastic is never lonesome. I people my solitude.

And he did. Pretty soon long interviews were arriving with such fellow seekers of wilderness experience as Booker T. Washington, Grant's old art teacher Henry Ward Stimson, President Teddy Roosevelt, desert gunslingers who obligingly let Grant photograph them in action, hateful gun-happy hunters, and a whole Indian tribe in the process of being swindled of its land by the Bureau of Indian Affairs.

Grant extolled the night's glittering stars as he ranged the long desert's circumferent mountains, and the flora and fauna, and the rattlesnake meat he ate to ward off death one day, and the quail whose cry led him to a water hole in the nick of time. The emotional content of the latter incident prompted an essay titled "We Enjoy Only by Contrast."

He even reported another successful exorcism. At Sim Hopkins' dusty little ranch, he found that the young hired man, Tom Walker, had been turned onto automatic writing by a nearby outing of Long Beach spiritists, became bowled over by astral attentions showered on him by a fraudulent John the Baptist and Jesus Christ, presently started chasing the boss's wife around with a butcher knife—"only her superior agility in climbing the canyon saved her life"—and now in pursuit of buried treasure, after an arson attempt, was tied down raving in the barn, while a couple of passing doctors were diagnosing hopeless insanity.

Grant put poor Tom into a hypnotic trance, rousted the astrals, and explained to the restored patient and his audience what had happened—an explanation he enlarged into five subsequent columns, citing learned publications of Europe and America and the writer's own research into California asylums.

He found that haphazard telepathic hypnotism accounted not only for insanity but also for the psychopathology of everyday life.

"Walk down Market Street any day and you will meet a hundred people walking under the whip and spur of some one dominant outside suggestion," Grant noted.

Examples including everything from compulsive window shoppers to reformers and their prey of down-in-the-chops sinners, all in situations in which "the idea rules of man" and the opposite.

Insane asylums of the future, he suggested, would be mainly detention hospitals employing therapy of music and counter-suggestion.

Winter drove Grant home to Parnassus Heights and its sheery atmosphere of claustrophobic domestic contentment.

If he couldn't get divine discontent certified in court, Grant informed his obstinately loyal wife, he would seek it in the next world, and hasten the day by volunteering to walk through the murderous crossfire of the impending Russo-Japanese war.

The day that war was declared, Grant's picture was on the Bulletin's front page, headlined "Grant Wallace to Report the War for the Bulletin," over a story remarking:

Mr. Wallace's contributions to the Bulletin, covering as they have a tremendous range of fact, thought and philosophy, have served to build up for him a huge following... He is recognized as foremost of all the reviewers and commentators connected with the Pacific Coast...

And so forth.

Once safely out to sea, Grant chirked up immeasurably, and soon was editing the shipboard paper written by his fellow war corre-

spondents, all bully fellows.

In Tokyo, the Imperial government welcomed the Western correspondents with every courtesy—state banquets, high-level briefings, Imperial Hotel musicales, nature and culture tours of Kyoto, the addresses of the best tailors—but no way to get to Manchuria where the war was going on.

Grant grew a sinister beard, outfitted himself in a corduroy suit with leather leggings—a style he favored ever after. Hoping to get around red tape, Grant took ship with a freelancing correspondent, the novelist Will Levington Comfort, to Shanghai and Chefu, with a side trip to the Great Wall, and a night glimpse of a naval battle, but no other luck. Comfort found Grant's cosmological asides so unsettling that he gave up on the war and went home to write three novels about Grant and a memoir of the trip exclaiming, "In junks, in steamer bunks, afield in blankets at night, Grant opened up my mind. He was in and out and around all I knew. I had to go apart for hours and catch up."

Jack London, covering for Hearst, also got restive and went home. After seven months, forty correspondents were approved for shipment to their story, among them Grant and Collier's companionable Richard Harding Davis, "wholesome, boyish and unaffected," who endeared himself to his colleagues by falling off his horse repeatedly on the first two-hundred-mile land-leg from Haicheng to the front, once into a rushing torrent, and setting stepped on.

The correspondents were shepherded to a vantage point securely screened by hills from any view of the great gathering battle for the Russian stronghold city of Liao-Yang. Grant's first dispatch from the hemmed-in compound noted the correspondents sought stimulation by organizing cricket races, whereas "Richard Harding Davis read a London paper through twice, advertisements and all, and then, overcome by the excitement, fell to composing the third act of a society comedy to be 'tried on the dog' in Hartford next summer."

Davis too gave up and went home. Grant, apprehensive of a similar fate, wrote home.

When I get back, I am resolved to live the life of a literary horticulturist. The conviction grows stronger and stronger with me that the only place for me most of the time is a garden orchard.

If I go on year after year trying to do office work in a city, I'll frizzle out completely. Already I almost hate writing. I hate a city office. It makes me cross and unbearable. I feel so old and weary of myself and sick of asking what I am and what I ought to be.

Immediately rallying, Grant recruited the Figaro correspondent Reggie Kann, to sneak with him past their guards into a Kiaoliang canebrake towards the mounting battle. They emerged into a narrow valley between steep hills crowned by chimney rocks shielding Japanese artillery, and swarms of "angry bees seemed humming and droning" past his ears—dum-dum bullets splattering on rocks, shells yowling overhead, and shrapnel bursting everywhere, at one moment clipping Grant's hair and the next nicking his boot and stirrup, as the truculent mule Kuropatkin dug in his hoofs.

Kann informed Grant: "We must not be keel down here wiz no heroic nor honaire by shrapnel-accidental!" And he did the two-man charge up the hillside, crying: "If we are to be keel, let us be keel where we can be seen!" a point Grant endorsed.

Squeezing in with Japanese soldiers behind a rock, Grant:

> "...looked down, as one who looks down from an upper tier box at the opera" on 300,000 or so troops commencing to lose 650,000 (CHK) casualties in "the bloodiest charges of war panorama, embattled hill billowing after hill and endless plain dotted with a hundred mud villages, to the Liao River, the tree-fluted pagoda of Ta, and the white walls of Liao Yang."

A bureaucratic patrol nabbed Kann for being out-of-bounds but missed Grant, who strolled that day and the rest through unceasing carnage. A soldier he was chatting with registered severe embarrassment with half of his face as a bullet removed the other half, including the eye — embarrassment he explained, while declining Grant's help, on grounds that be getting wounded he dishonored his Emperor.

> "They hope and expect to be killed," Grant wrote indignantly. "It displeases these fellows to come back. They have the notion that it is more desirable to die for their emperor than to live for their families. I rather like war. It kills so many fools."

Grant analyzed all the military strategies going on, but his eye was for the vivid. In a field command tent, a lieutenant colonel orders his bugler to sound the attack and in the instant both are shot down:

> "The major pauses to bend over his wounded lieutenant colonel. As he does so a shell strikes among the rocks just in front, blowing Mizushima's head to a pulp. He falls, his blood spurting over Mariam's white cap and blouse. Leaderless, his men lie firing…"

A new officer rushed in, waving his saber, but can't be heard above the gunfire. He yells at the wounded bugler, Nagai. Nagai lifts the trumpet to his lips, sounds the call and then "Nagai falls flat in faint."

Battle continued close-up through the first two nights, when Grant napped fitfully on an altar shared with the surgery of a field hospital, "back in the holy of holies, where sit the usual nine gods of luck, of war, of winds, of fecundity, of happiness and the rest," in a small Buddhist monastery at the foot of Wedge Hill.

"Shells exploded yellow overhead… bullets rattled on the heavy tile roof… shrapnel from two directions. Fireworks displays without intermission" and 14 frightened monks tinkled bells, and doves cooed, as surgeon Hidehara plucked mangled soldiers from their pools of blood on the floor and did what he could.

Hidehara probed one boy's shattered leg and a flattened bullet popped out. Grant gave it to the soldier to clench between his teeth as the surgeon set the leg and looked around for a splint.

I caught sight of a broad, gaily painted green and blue wooden sword held aloft in the hand of a fierce squat paper mache god—the god of war—and pointed it out to Hidehara. He nodded approvingly and I twisted it from the dusty hand, ripped the painted cloth cover from it, trimmed the ends smooth with my hunting knife, and it was quickly bound along the shattered leg with many yards of gauze bandages… a legitimate use for a sword.

On the third morning, the battle drifted off from Wedge Hill, and Grant strolled through fields of dead.

Here a mere boy, his whole blouse front one encrusted royal-purple badge of courage, lies like a baby on his back with open palms spread wide and a smile, and there in a trench a young Russian with wide open eyes full of horror and supplication, staring upward, the mouth open in agonized prayer for mercy, a jagged hole as large as a walnut straight into the top of his head.

Heads and limbs missing, fingers clutching, grass, guts, playing cards, letters from home, medals of Buddha and Madonna, men spitted on "wolf-trap" stakes, fallen in heaps — bodies Grant helped stack onto Japanese funeral pyres or pitch into mass Russian graves.

> "To lie in that made embrace til the juices of grasses and flowers lift them above the clouds to strange and beautiful resurrection.
>
> "So at last each valiant little preposterous patriot-fanatic inheritor and victim of age-long hypnotic suggestion, of

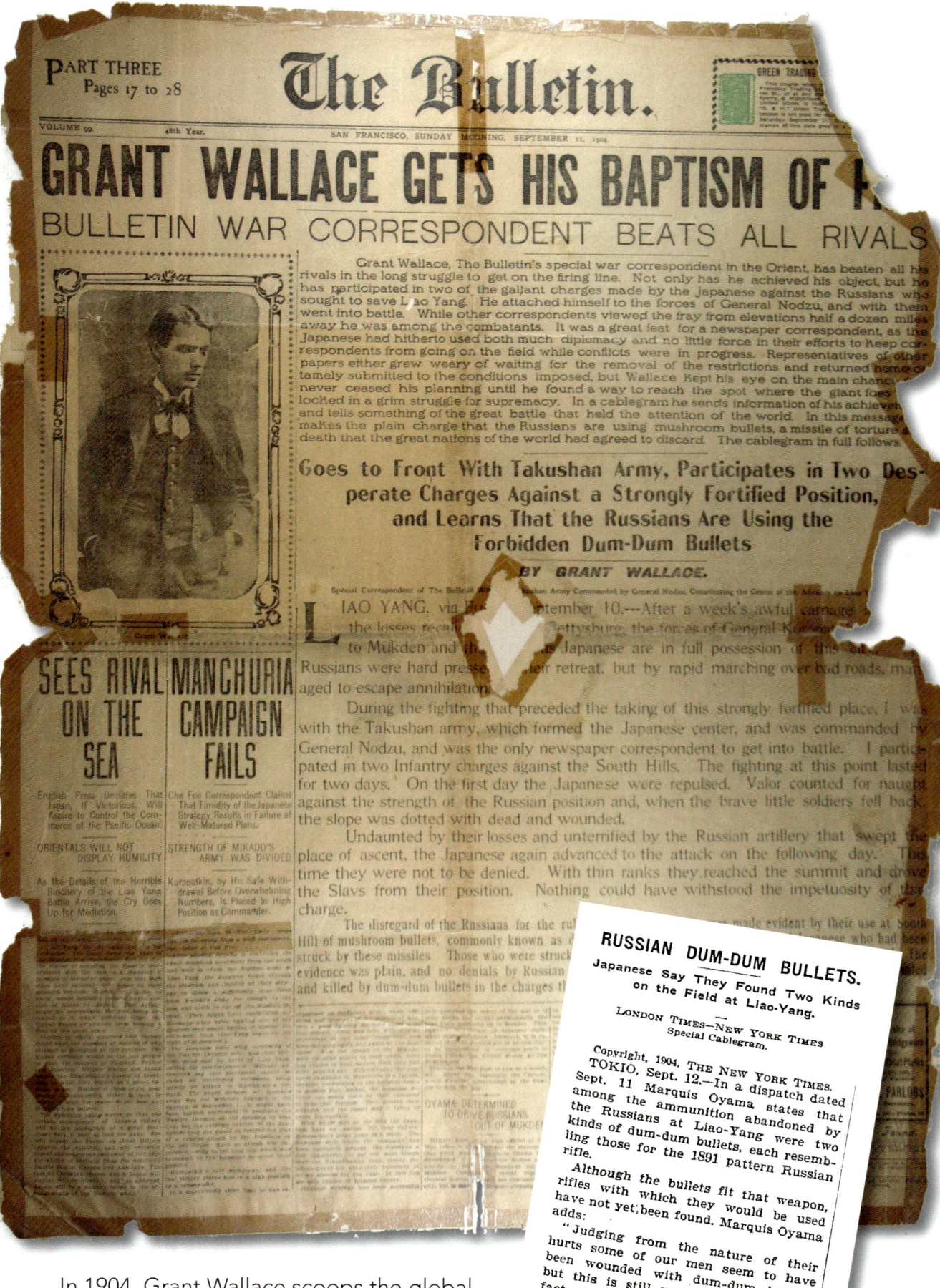

In 1904, Grant Wallace scoops the global press with his first-hand account of the Russo-Japanese War

bushido and myth and moonlight, which the world applauds as sublime courage, is now reduced to a handful of black oily dust, a bit of charred bone or a wisp of straight black hair to be placed in the little urn among the ancestral tablets under his picture in the straw-thatched home in Bihar or Ugina—all that his little village world has left of him.

"He dies and goes up in black smoke and is forgotten; and others take his place and tramp along by arcane field and bog and hell-swept mountain, to kill and to die and be forgotten in their turn, without shrinking, without sympathy or tears…

"What does it matter where men's lives are so cheap and generals are so busy contriving other murders?

"These gashed bodies, lying so silent under the fresh morning and the songbirds, speak of crime and ignorance and folly, so inept, so ugly, so senseless."

Grant got back on his mule and rode off toward the noise of further skirmishes and charges and encounters, what became 25,000 words of them in the Bulletin.

After seven days he entered the Muscovites' fallen stronghold of Liao-Yang, moseying feverishly with dysentery a month Manchu corpses and Russian bottles of harem luggage, and wrote until he passed out on a deadmans he added brick kang, quite ill.

Guy Skull of the New York Commercial Advertiser, among the arriving correspondents hearing of the military's plans to bury Grant before moving on, borrowed a six-shooter from Bill Brill of the Associated Press, visited the general staff, and emerged with orders for Grant to be loaded onto a flatcar with military casualties, all to be duly towed by conscripted Manchu coolies with ropes to the port of Yangon, for the unprecedented trans-shipment of a foreign civilian to Japan by military hospital ship.

But by way of reprimand, the military refused to mail Grant's dispatches and drawings and photos, the only firsthand English speaking account of the great campaign in that war.

So he recovered and took them home, where in due course Sunset Magazine's war expert called them "thrilling" Everybody's called Grant one of the few top reporters of the West, a streetcar hit Grant on his triumphal passage from the dock to his Parnassus Heights address, and there his domesticity sat bright and ready to close in on him, just as though he hadn't been away.

***

Fate having declined Grant's offer to die if need be for his freedom, Fremont Older acceded to Grant's pleas to at least get him out town again rapidly, and the Bulletin shortly announced:

> Under the banner of Frenzied Finance and Graft, many so-called captains and more undoubted chevaliers of industry are marshaling defenseless victims to the slaughter.
>
> The Rockefeller's, Rogerses, Armours, Chadwick and Hannah Eliases are abroad in the land. Their pathways are strewn with corpses. To these stricken fields, Grant Wallace, who made such a brilliant record in Manchuria, has been commanded by the Bulletin…

It was the time of muckraking.

Grant's first stop was a Cleveland jail to chat with Andrew Carnegie's reputed dowager bastard Cassie Chadwick, "The Queen of Frenzied Finance", whose bovine hypnotized bank officials to yielding her heir all."

The extensive interview, illustrated by Grant's sketches, was going fine with "in her excitement, her upper teeth dropped out — fatal slip! She gave me a look calculated to raise a blister and turned her back."

In New York, Grant was cheered by reunion with some of the old San Francisco newspaper crowd — Henry George, Edwin Markham, Homer Davenport 0– and William Jennings Bryant, Frederick Remington, May Stannard Baker, Lincoln Steffens, Hamlin Garland… In Washington, he dropped in on the White House and straightened out Teddy Roosevelt on East Asian politics.

Closing in on Rockefeller-related wickedness, he learned from Dennis Donahue that the arch-fiend to unmask was the combination financier-muckraker Thomas Lawson of Boston, whose exposes in Everybody's were calculated to shake down Standard Oil for $1.5 million — " a conscienceless rogue and the most picturesque liar of the age whose seems to be trying to corner the newspapers."

But when Grant waited on the Boston rogue, the 14-hour interview discovered other aspects, detailed in two double-truck Bulletin installments, the first carrying a 16-column banner, "Grant Wallace Has a Genuine Heart to Heart Talk with Thomas Lawson of Boston."

It turned out all Lawson really wanted was to give Wall Street back to the American people. "I am going to plug up the ratholes," he told Grant. "There isn't anything that will stop me in my life work."

> "He is a man of strangely magnetic personality, absolute concentration, winged imagination, amazing… If Thomas Lawson ever lies down in the fight, or proves himself a quitter, then I am no reader of men."

Lawson acknowledged the articles, wiring, "I think I am a judge of men who make good, who have the courage to get the facts. I want you to travel into every State, gather material on the lives and hidden activities of all the U.S. Senators, and prepare a series of articles for Everybody's Magazine to parallel my own articles. Will you do it?"

It wasn't just the challenge — it was the prospect of extending his leave from domestic dilemma indefinitely. Grant sent his resignation to Older and settled down to unmasking the Senate.

When, Many months later, Everybody's lawyers agreed the series was so great it was too libelous to print, Grant examined the prospect of returning unemployed to Parnassus Heights, and saw destiny's unkindness in denying him passage to the Other Side on the Manchurian battlefield,led.

Happening to be in Norfolk, Va., he collapsed in its hospital with a recurrence of dysentery augmented by several other grave conditions including brain fever, and awaited astral vacation to rest up before his next incarnation.

Twice he technically "died" and was revived, before the third dying he dispatched a deathbed plea to Parnassus Heights for a divorce, largely for pro-for a dramatic effect. As he was going down for the third time, what was his surprise to find his boon granted.

He recovered quickly, rented a Greenwich Village studio, sold two fiction stories to Appleton's Magazine, consorted at Moquin's with O. Henry and Will and Wallace Irwin and Mary Austin, an listed himself in Who's Who in America as, among other things, "Student and writer on occultism; lecturer; short story writer; illustrates own stories. Office: care Everybody's Magazine. Union Square, N.Y."

In San Francisco's, his wife cheerfully sold

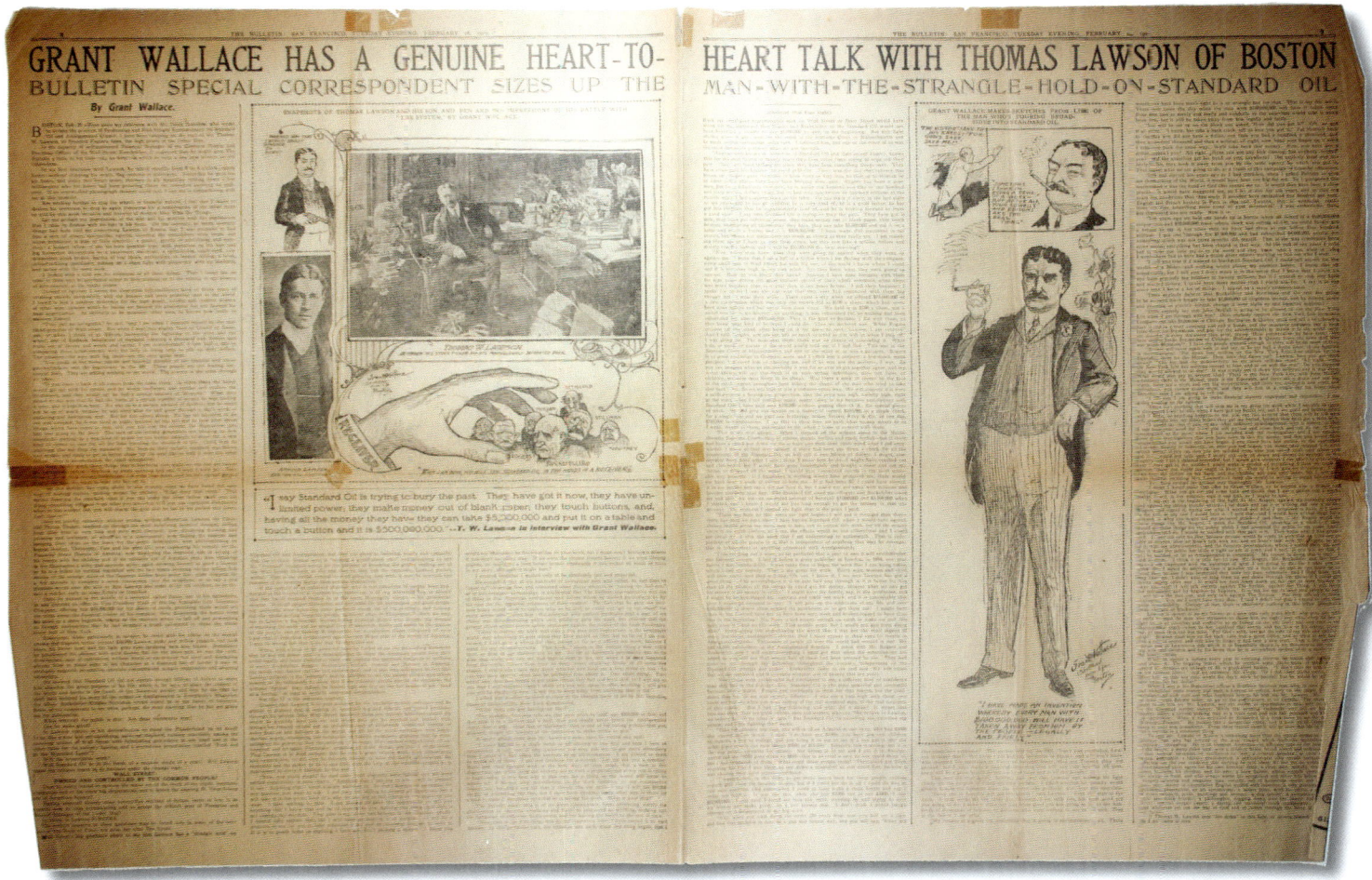

the Parnassus aerie just before the big earthquake shivered its timbers and took up writing, eventually turning out thoughtful columns for the New York World on such thought-provokes as "How to Hold Your Man."

His spiritual claustrophobia relieved, what Big Work could he not accomplish!

Having rid himself long since of sibling and now of spousal encumbrances, Grant celebrated his emancipation by plunging right into Big Work with New York editors, who, however, were none of them Fremont Older, and doubted this world was ready for so much good news.

Instead, the Evening Sun gave him Irwin Cobb's old desk as hub or writer, where dialect confrontations between lower East Side tenants and landlords proved festering to his immortal longings.

So he got The Times Magazine to send him to a Cuban insurrection with the cognizable General Fred Funston and, again, chummy Richard Harding Davis. But the ensuing "opera bluffed" chases through swampy jungles turned out to be similarly short on lofty challenges.

***

Back in Manhattan, Grant was approached by the grizzled "P.T. Barnum of the western lecture circuit, "Colonel" Windy Jones, whose Nickelodeon ventures needed footage of a first-ever roping of a grown mountain lion alongside the Grand Canyon. Grant had never roped a mountain lion — nobody had, Jones claimed — and was piqued by the challenge.

Jones promised Grant free story rights not only to the lions but the whole Grand Canyon region, its wild horses, buffalo, Catalfo, Indians and archaeology. Grant scented the

PROF[illegible]IONAL JEALOUSY

BILL [illegible] the [illegible]-Victorian Yegg (to Deadwood Dick, the Terror of [illegible] Gulch): "Ye'r dead right, old-timer. We're both of us [illegible] an' has-beens. Wot chance has us honest crooks an' indust[illegible] ruffians got against this here sort o' competition?"

gw-0007

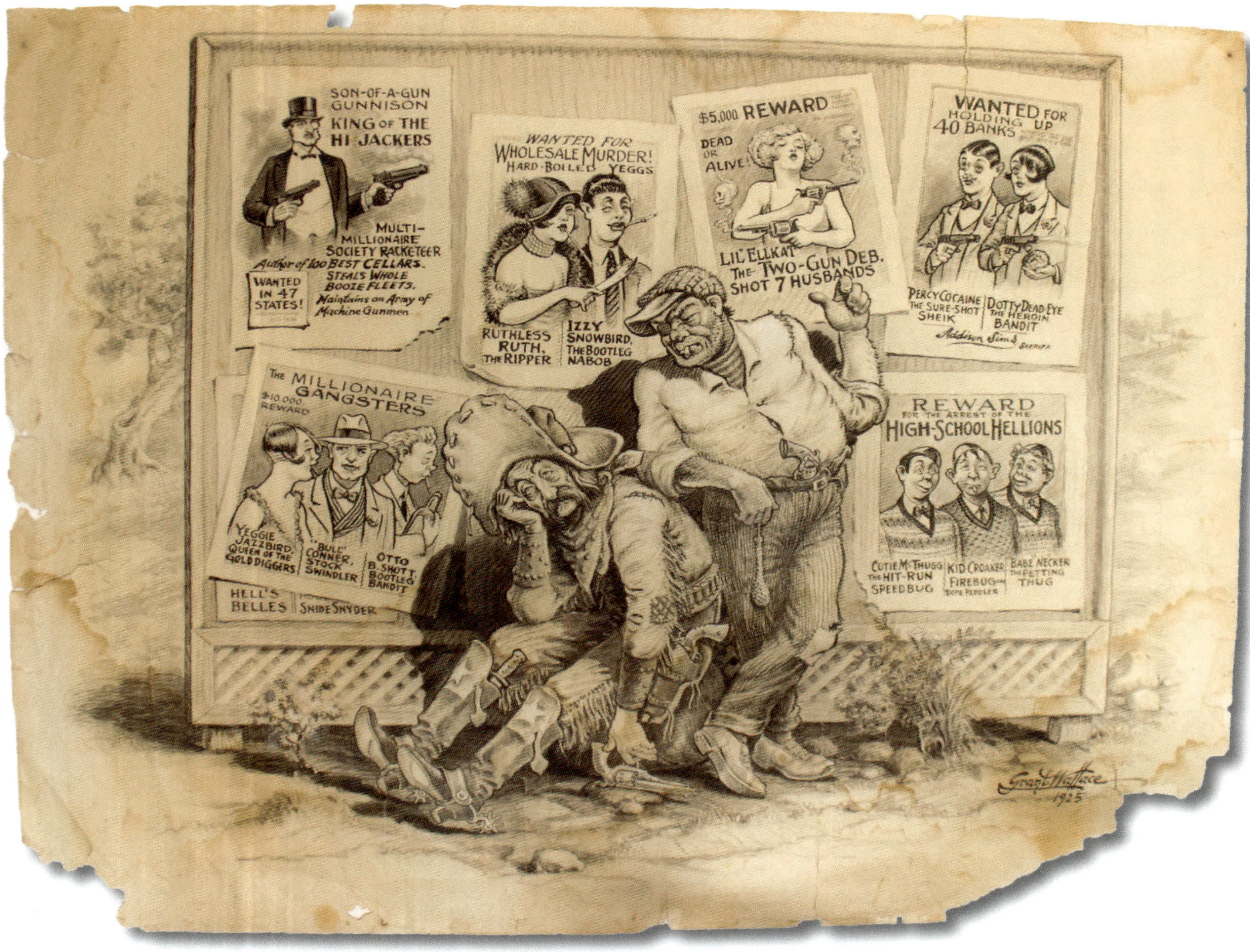

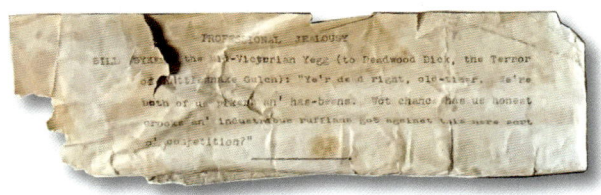

Professional Jealousy

by Grant Wallace

1925

“Bill Sykes, the Mid-Victorian Yegg (to Deadwood Dick, the Terror of Rattlesnake Gulch): “Ye’r dead right, old-time. We’re both of us pikers an’ has-beens. Wot chance has us honest crooks an’ industrious ruffians got against this here sort o’ competition?”

Signed by artist, Original artist captions
Unframed, Fair Condition

desert's old promise of yarns good for bootlegging Big Work back into public print. Everybody's and other magazines said fine. Grant got off the train at Santa Fe and found a message from Jones in Kansas, rescheduling the rendezvous for Flagstaff the following spring. Little he cared — he was an old hand at peopling wildernesses.

Grant repaired to the four corners of New Mexico, Arizona, Utah and Colorado and fell in with friendly Pueblo Bonita Navajo. Pesch-liki, the medicine man declined to reveal the occult mysteries of his sand blanket routines and faith cures, but was pleased at Grant's open admiration for the instant divorces he dispensed.

Grant continued pestering the shaman for an exchange of metaphysical shop-talk regarding telepathy, the Other Side, and so on. At length Pesch-liki gave in, accrediting Grant with the title of Chief Neverquit.

Grant's newfound friends instructed him on the whereabouts of fifteen well preserved pre-Columbian cities gouged into rock walls in the Chaco Canyon and Mesa Verde region, complete with burial caves and petroglyphs and bric-a-brac. Grant found them, and wrote them up with appropriate ruminative overtones. But New York's Wichita-oriented editors let them molder until "accredited" archaeologists unveiled them again, some years later.

Grant and horse arrived at Flagstaff at the appointed hour. "Colonel" Jones was gone. The colonel had found a mark he couldn't disappoint — a literal lily eager dentist from Zanesville, Ohio, named Peter Grey, willing to pay for an exclusive outing to try his hand at writing western stuff. The betrayer's safari had a 12-hour start across the ghastly desert. Grant galloped off in pursuit.

Ten days he rode through dry wash and freshet, quicksand and shimmering desert, snowy crag and blizzard, arriving during one of the latter at a ranch Jones was palming off as his own to his greenhorn Lorenzo.
The Ohio tenderfoot's subsequent writing exercise on his brief time in the is heady company lionized Grant with his "prominent square jaw and browned cheek and flashing eye," standing "six-feet-five," three inches higher than usual.

He marveled at Grant's discovery of a wind cave, " a gloomy hole, large enough to admit a church, hollowed in the cliff by ages of nature's chiseling. "Vast sepulcher of Time's past, give up thy dead!" cried Wallace solemnly."

But in Grant's presentation copy, where the fledgling author wrote "It has been my destiny — wat a play fulfillment of many dreams of border spirit! — to live for a while in the fast fading wild environment." Grant's marginal scrawl specified dryly: "10 days!" Among other corrections.

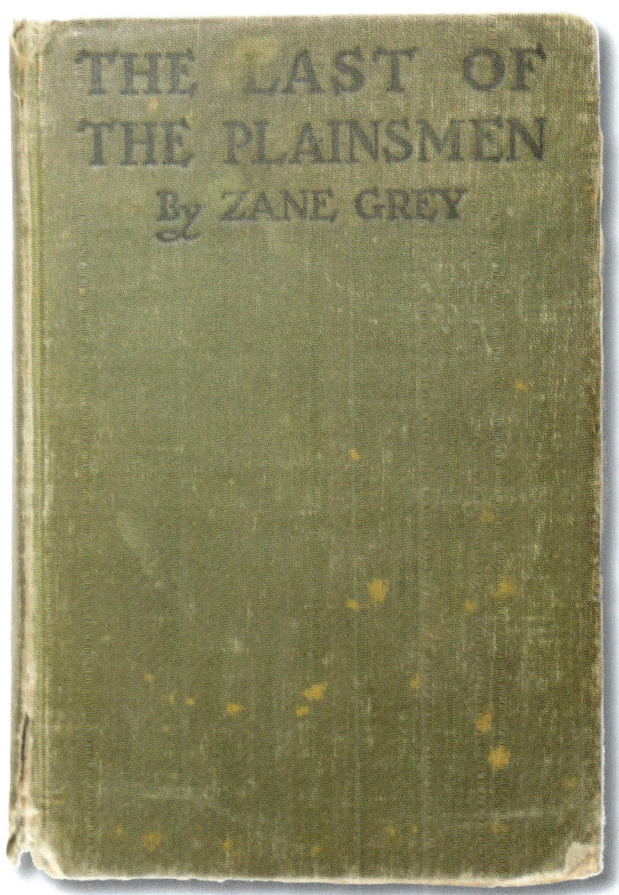

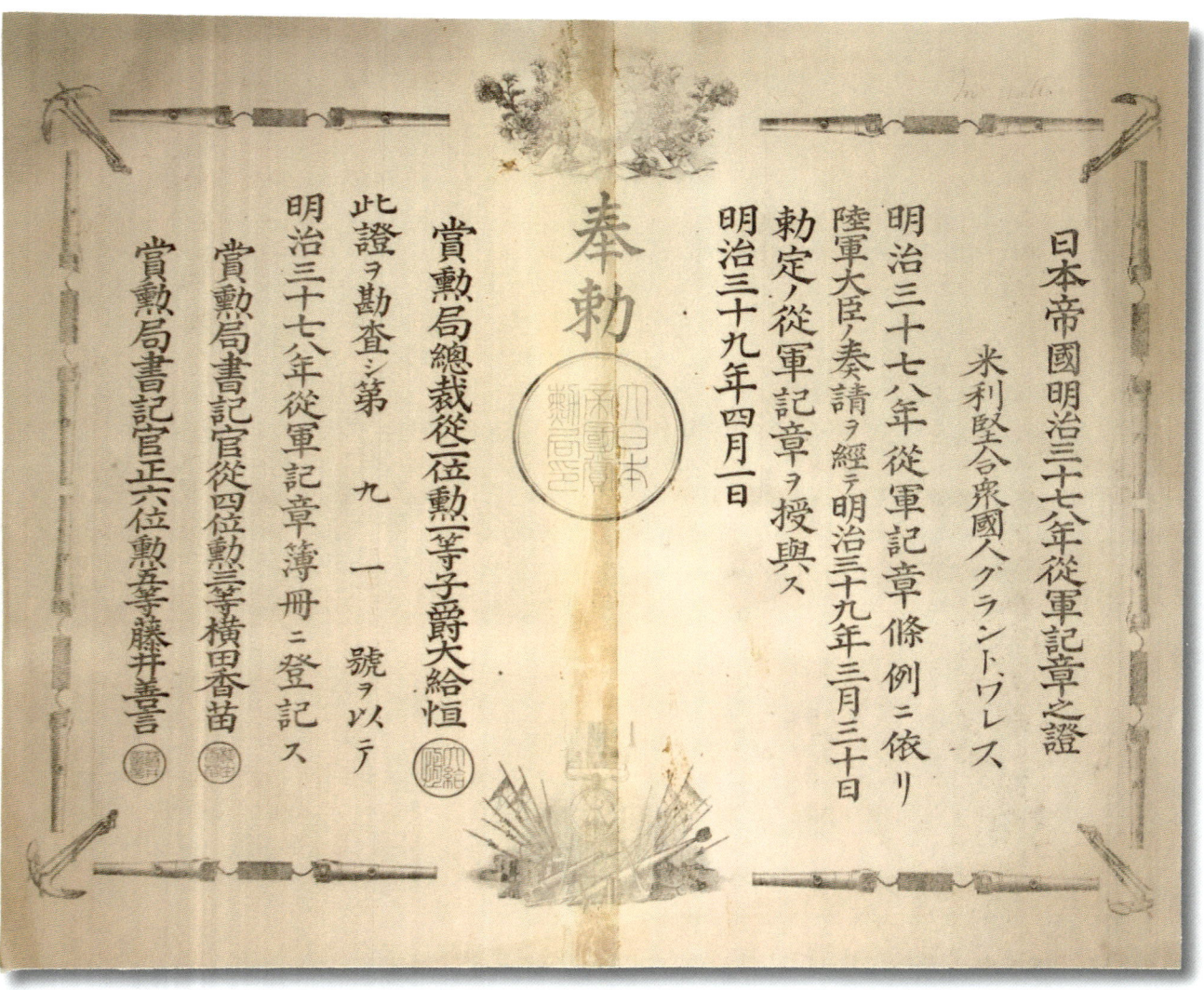

The Emperor of Japan awarded Grant with a sword, a medal, and this proclamation for his contributions to their victory in the Russo-Japanese War.

But Grant had a grand time for three months after young Grey went home to his typewriter, snubbing Jones, roping wild horses, herding buffalo, discovering petroglyphs, repairing the Bright Angel funicular cable singlehanded, and tumbling down cliffs along the Grand Canyon's north rim in pursuit of grown cougars, three of which he not only roped but tamed with bacon from his campfire skillet.

One morning Grant chased a big lion over the canyon rim onto a fantail of loose shale, precipitating an avalanche that he rode down to a cornice, the while dodging faster boulders. One rocketed into a grown binge and decapitated it. Presently he treed his cougar and clambered towards it. It sprang slightly above his head and vanished over the final abyss.

Trudging back to base — climbing roots and lassoing shrubs to scale various cliffs en route — he found himself joined by a Pleiadean named Alzuil-bel, who said "look" (or "Lo," more likely) "are you ready?"

Alzuil-bel was referring back to his female astral colleague Zulazu-le's old offer of the Order of Light's collaboration on a really big work. Grand said not on your life, reviewing all the old objections — artistic control, checking credentials, shared credit, viewpoint conflicts, and his own simple reluctance to be a joiner.

Alzuil-bel said that was all gosh, since the fact was that Grant had been of the Order of Light in the first place, and had returned to earth specifically for this project as karmic atonement for the harm he had done one time when he was incarnated as Apep the Snake, Akhenaten's spirit of evil in ancient Egypt.

Grant agreed at least to think about it. Lazuli-bel noted the date was May Day, and said the Order would check back regularly on future May Days to renew the offer.

Grant packed up a couple of his tamed mountain lions and set off in a covered wagon for Salt Lake City. En route, and Indian courier caught up with him, bearing as parcel that the State Department had been forwarding all over containing a sword, a medal, and a fancy Japanese proclamation saying the Emperor of Japan esteemed him mightily, presumably for snapping illicit pictures and going AWOL from his military escort at Liao Yang.

At Salt Lake CIty — where admiring crowds upset the lions to the point of clawing him, prompting him to sell them — another letter as waited from Everybody's, saying economic recession prompted suspension of publication, as well as his Grand Canyon story contract.

Grant looked up Mother Wallace and Ella and Olive at their new place back at Fairoaks, and was prevailed upon to start another freelance writer's orchard paradise nearby old Tanglewood. For hands, he summoned an honorary blood-brother Navajo he had met named Jim "Kid" MacNichol and his son, Grant Jr., lately bored stiff with maternal relatives in the Midwest.

He sold various pieces to The Times Magazine, Review of Reviews, Out West, and the San Francisco News, and some short fiction to Appleton's but growing a mortgaged new Eden was costly. Besides, his tenderfoot dentist had rushed into print with Grant's Grand Canyon scene, worse yet with a bestseller irritatingly titled in homage to 'Buffalo' Jones: Last of the Plainsmen, under the nom de plume of Zen Grey, launching a famous career.

Billy Comfort wrote that his principal novel about Grant, Routledge Rides Alone, was bringing in great amounts of money.

Rubbing it in, brother Charles also made it into Who's Who in America as a distinguished Elizabethan scholar, having found in the London Museum's basement rubble some old creditors' chits casting what his book on the subject called "A New Light on Shakespeare."

Warmed as he was by Mother Wallace's chicken fricassee and biscuits, Grant felt drawn to some other place without bill collectors. Where he went — taking Junior and Kid MacNichol with him was America's spanking new outdoor bohemia-by-the-sea, still in the process of being founded by Grant's bohemian writers and artist colleagues from San Francisco's Montgomery Block and Papa Coppa's Restaurant, 120 miles south of the city's madding crowds, Carmel.

A young Sinclair Lewis wrote in the New Thought magazine Nautilus:

> "Grant Wallace came riding into the Carmel yard on a rangy ranch pony, as though sent by some telepathic message this necessary time. For Grant Wallace is even greater as an occultist, a metaphysician, than as a war correspondent, or an explorer of the Arizona deserts. Looking quietly from under his great sombreros, Grant heard my suggestions for the new novel, approved, suggested, by his interest put the cachet of finality on the scheme…"

Margaret "Peggy" McVicker Wallace
Portrait of her Mother by Moira Wallace.
Oil Paint on Laminated Wood Board c. 1925

Signed by artist
Unframed, Fair Condition

It was fine for a bit, being lionized by near-peers, if not as fine as a steady paying audience. In his youth Grant had dealt with an overbearing brother, then with a domineering spouse, and now it was difficult editors who persecuted him with delays in responding and miserable payments and materialistic prejudices barring him from the only thing every inspired messenger truly needs, doting readers.

Though appreciative enough, Carmel's audience of geniuses all demanded more than equal time around the beach bonfire mussel-bakes and musical abalone and martini feasts in front of poet George and Carrie Sterling's great stone fireplace.

The Sterlings lived up beyond Pine Inn and the grocery in the woods. Grant and Junior had a redwood shack under cypresses by the shiny-white beach, shared for writing purposes with Mike Williams and Len Parton. In a nearby hut, young Red Lewis invented plots for Jack London's stories and pestered Grant for instruction on writing them himself.

Mary Austin's beaded Indian headbands, bucks in fringes and purple moods got on Grant's nerves. So did all the suicidal love affairs under manzanita bushes complicating mushroom hunts, and the East Asian philosophy and Greek dance recitals culturing Camel's breath-taking vistas of limitless blue sea, eternal moon and stars and pelicans, southern coastal mountains, morning fogs, wildflowers… Like any perfect place to write it was maddening.

Then suddenly one day Grant recognized an apparition translated from the past, holidaying from the city — Margaret "Peggy" McVicker, erstwhile ward of the glamour souls musical widow Clothilde, now grown to astonishingly beautiful young womanhood. Though 18 years his junior, Peggy was, he saw, his Big Work's radiantly necessary audience. He told her they must marry or he would die.

***

Peggy had the will and the gift to breathe into others her intoxicating belief of their powers. In fact she had just returned from a year with her mother in their ancestral Glens of Antrim, breathing exuberant life into legendary but wilted North Ireland.

The living link was her Belfast dowager granny Mary McVicker, who bragged she had never washed a dish in her life, and forbade Peggy to, though she didn't care who else did. Mary came by her haughty manner honestly. Her mother, a Protestant Dixon, had as a girl put up with boarding school at Larne for two years, but at 16 climbed a wall spotted a handsome Catholic McCambridge lad strolling by, fell in love, and eloped to Gretna Green, Scotland. There — on a stormy night in their cottage on a cliff — she died giving birth to Mary, whose distraught father wandered off into the tempest, either to his doom over the abyss or, according to another story, Seattle.

Either way, the Protestant and Catholic relatives went to court for baby Mary, and her upbringing was awarded to her four fatuous Dixon uncles, who did well in lumber and shipbuilding, one becoming Sir Daniel, Lord Mayor of Belfast.

When little Mary spied a pretty kelp flower bobbing off the wild coast, it was understood an uncle or two would clamber down the precipice and swim out to fetch the damn thing.

Approaching womanhood, she was her mother's daughter. Holidaying upcoast among the glens at Cushendallo, she spied from her carriage the toothsome young squire John McVicker, who preferred riding horseback up the village inn's staircase and

peace and love. This portion of Monterey is rich in memories of such great or beloved names as Joaquin Miller, Bret Harte, Mark Twain, Robert Louis Stevenson, Charles Warren Stoddard, Daniel O'Connell, Ambrose Bierce and others. Men and women high in the ranks of established contemporary names, such as George Sterling, Mary Austin, Jack London, James Hopper, and others, know and love the place and draw inspiration from it through living here, or frequently visiting its sea-murmurous, wooded hills. College presidents and professors and their families and people of culture and refinement reside there for a part of the year, or visit it for longer or shorter periods; while the constant stream of travelers

Grant Wallace and Mrs. Wallace in "Twelfth Night," a 1911 production

travelers, and which is a Mecca for painters, and the home or haunt of artists of many sorts, has since the day of Fray Junipero Serra been a magnet, so to speak, for serious and devoted workers in artistic and spiritual channels. This region is geographically

steeplechasing out the back window to running Ballyvooly farms, where his widowed mother did what she could.

But Mary found Squire John less than ideal as a city husband, and dispatched him after he sired her daughter and four sons — back to Ballyvooly, which he gradually lost to his wild ways. The two older boys grew up to become hard-drinking captains of their uncle's great sailing ships. The youngest boy started out to sea and drowned.

When it came the hours for Alex, the third son, to go to sea, Mary set her clock back 30 minutes and prolonged the farewell until his ship had gone out the slough past Bangor head without him.

Alex retaliated by eloping with the hoyden Hessie, the Ballymena parson's wild daughter, to San Francisco. There Peggy and her older seafaring brother were born, to a household scarred first by Alex going into trade as a prosperous wholesale grocer, and second by divorce.

But Alex, the Olympic Club's handsomest handball champion, charmed Peggy as every other female, and sent her along with his poems to the fond Clothilde before he expired of pneumonia following a particularly cheerful Bohemian Club high jinks.

Teenage Peggy dwelt widely in romantic family legend, "Lorna Doone" and the fabled Grant's cosmic Bulletin columns as she studied art at Cogswell College and wrote charming verse.

Her year in Ireland boggled her Belfast cousin Madge McCormick, who later recalled:

> "The young men all fell in love with her but the Cushendall villagers called her my crazy American cousin.
>
> "She discovered the peasants said the hill called Tiveral belonged to the fairies, and the dawn before she left she followed a dream's instructions, climbed Tiveral, plucked three long curly hairs from her head, and buried them on the hilltop.
>
> Then she went and sat in the ruined doorway at Ballyvooly for hours, looking down to ruined Layde graveyard on the lower pasture towards the sea, where she'd scratched moss from the stones and found her namesake and ancestors who sailed there from Stranraer, which you can see across the channel, in 1649.
>
> "She left our farewell beach party that evening, saying she wanted to say goodbye to the place. Then she walked away out on a rock in the tide and let her beautiful golden hair fly in the wind, and one of the boys who was in love with her, Bondi, and Austrian count who was over to learn the linen business, thought she was going to commit suicide and wanted to go after her."
>
> "Also that day, Peggy gave away all her clothes to the servants, and packed her steamer trunk with lovely green peat moss. But the time the trunk went through customs in New York, it clanked with dry mud and hay inside. The customs inspector accepted the story she'd lost its key and let it go through.
>
> "She always had what the Irish call a fayness," Irish cousin Madge noted, fondly but only just tolerantly.

***

Grant tried to interpret Peggy's fayness as something loftier than Irishness, which he regarded as synonymous with pig-headed emotionalism, never mentioning that between 1645, when they left Ayreshire and 1720 when they helped found Derry, new

Hampshire, his Scot ancestors too had been Londonderrymen, around past Grant's Causeway and Dunluce Castle from Cushendall, in Coleraine.

Peggy's spectacular capacity for sympathy was that of a great theatrical directors', matching her talent for conceiving great healing love, both of which tended to make andybody's actual troubles somewhat incidental to the process.

She was captivated by the inspirational possibilities in freeing Grant's Big Work from its prison of petty circumstances. They were married on a sunny May morning on the top rock of Mt. Tamalpias's over San Francisco Bay. And returned to Carmel to plan a way of life that would release Grant's message from the tyranny of editors and economic compromise.

"One does not die and go to heaven," Grant had written in the Bulletin. "One lives and grows to heaven."

Just one issue of Sunset magazine contained, here and there, photographs of several fine flourishes of the happy new marriage: superbly costumed Grant and Peggy as Duke Orsino and a court lady in the new Forest Theatre's "Twelfth Night;" Grant as King Manetho in Bertha Newberry's controversial "The Toad;" as Don Gaspar de Portola in Carmel's first Serra Festival; Grant in diving suit and helmet, about to be cranked down into the abalone beds beside Pt. Lobos; Tented with Sterling and London, Grant as official artist at the Bohemian Club's high and low jinks."

Peggy's Belfast cousin Madge arrived to visit, having arrived ahead of her warning telegram:

> "At Monterey, the Del Monte Limited was met by the Carmel Stage, a two-horse covered wagon driven by Sam Powers, who let me off at Pine Inn — and here was my beautiful cousin at the top of the steps, surrounded by a lot of fine looking boys who turned out to be the Stanford Rugby team…"

"She said we were going to dinner at the Sterlings' and made me a little lantern, a candle set in a coffee tin, to light the way through the woods.

"We sat on the floor in front of the big fireplace burning blue and green because of the salt in the dried driftwood, and listened to the nice young pianist David Alberto playing.

"Jack London and his wife Charmaine were back from their sailboat trip on the Snark, and Ambrose Bierce was visiting from New York. That vulgar little artist Xavier Martinez was a nuisance, but Fred Bechdolot and Jimmy Hopper, who wrote stories for the Saturday Evening Post, and the photographer Arnold Genthe were delightful. I'd never seen a wooden bungalow before."

"The next day Grant went from his and Peggy's cottage down to his writing shack on the beach, where he was pestered for lessons by a tall young gangling pockmarked boy who was the homeliness thing you ever saw but full of fun, Red Lewis. Peggy and I took an apple and wandered along the surf to the rocks at Pebble Beach where we lay down and unfastened our hair to be fanned out by the waves.

"That night we had dinner at Professor Vernon Kellogg's and met Herbert Hoover and his wife…

"Grant had planted a lot of eucalyptus seedlings in Seaside behind Del Monte Hotel, but two nights of heavy frost ruined them. Later he made eucalyptus

Dear Grant Wallace:—[1] October 12, 1909.

Say, Mrs. London is sick in bed, I am busy harvesting my grapes, and I leave to-morrow for my cruise.[2] And, worst of all, on a strange machine, after years without touching one, I am trying to type some letters. Nevertheless, here goes.

I am going to put in a slight experiment of seven thousand trees this fall. I want seven thousand FOREST RED GUM (E. Tereticornis). I want each tree potted separately in ten-inch carton. Will you please have these trees ready, subject to shipment in two days after receipt of telegram to that effect? You see, I must wait until after the next rainstorm in order to have the ploughing for the trees done. Being away myself, Mr. Edward B. Payne, a dear friend of mine, will take charge of the planting, and it will be from him that you will receive the telegram.

I am prepared to plough and harrow and water and cultivate these trees thoroughly for a couple of years, before leaving them on their own. And, if after one hot dry summer, on my particular soil, I am able to have them still alive, I shall then, next winter, put in a hundred thousand or so.

Please let me know what my order comes to, whereupon I shall promptly remit.

Also, send me samples of seasoned and polished eucalyptus wood, and charge same to my account.

This is the very Dickens, trying to typewrite!

Jack London

P.S.—When you ship, please *Prepay*[3] freight, & send me charge for same.

J.L.

MS: CSmH; 1 p., cctl.

1. Grant Wallace, proprietor of The Eucalyptus Agency in Monterey, California. JL had written him on September 11, 1909 (CSmH): "I want eucalyptus not so much of the hardwood variety but for fire-burning purposes, also, I want eucalyptus that can grow on high-dry soil." In a letter of September 25, 1909 (CSmH), Wallace offered advice on the variety of trees to plant and the proper planting methods, and stated: "If you will set out say 200 of your broad acres to eucalyptus you will have a bonanza which will have most of the gold mines lashed to the mast." See JL to Stratton, January 7, 1910, n. 3.

furniture that was quite good looking, but so heavy you couldn't lift a chair..."

In fact, that frost killed 2 million Australian blue gum eucalyptus seedlings, being readied to revolutionize the American hardwood industry, wiping out Peggy's patrimony; and before the furniture fiasco, Grant went deeper into the eucalyptus chimera by getting Jack London to plant 200,000 of them at Glen Ellen, and writing a learned-treatise on the "wonder wood," and managing a Sacramento Valley eucalyptus development whose Chicago backers proved fly-by-nights.

It was all industry in line with the newlyweds' plan to turn Grant's "literary-horticulturist" hankering into an economic base to free his big writings from commercial and editorial compromise.

When the eucalyptus bubble burst, Grant planted Van Sickle Island in the Sacramento River Delta with a. A major experimental bean and Tabasco project, just as the island vanished under a flood.

Some other disaster befell a subsequent high-ground planting that featured 140 varieties of Lima and other beans. And later on there was a really costly investment in a philosopher-farmer community envisioned by Kathleen Norris's brother, Fred Thompson, on a Mexican island south of Mazatlan, Palmito del Verde, opposed by Yaqui Indians, who nearly finished Grant off when he went to inspect the sandy premises.

Some ventures entailed temporary uprooting from Carmel, for instance running the news bureau at San Francisco's 1915 Panama Pacific International Exposition, which had many to buy four historical pageants from Grant but ran short of funds.

It was from Carmel that Grant first issued a syndicated press service of lofty socialist tracts, by himself and Berkeley's idealistic Socialist Mayor J. Stitt Wilson, at a time when capitalist publishers did not care to buy tirades against them.

He launched a similarly doomed, but far more elegant, Sunday newspaper literally magazine, The Pacific Slope Monthly, featuring Grant's drawings and articles and fiction pieces, and those of all the friends and neighbors, including Jack London, George Sterling, Joaquin Miller, Luther Burbank, Ella Wheeler Wilcox, Jimmy Hopper, Fred Bechdolt, and John Kenneth Turner.

Carmel's First Family
The California art colony welcomes their first daughter,
Moira Wallace (1910—1979)

Dancers who welcomed the new year at fashionable Hotel Del Monte, on the Monterey peninsula of California, admired this central theme of the huge decorations for the gala celebration. It was done by Moira Wallace Harnden, who doesn't allow her recent marriage to Peter Harnden to interfere with her art career.

The Carmel colony's first home-delivered infant, Moira, was born when cousin Madge was again visiting Peggy and Grant. She recalled:

"The evening before, Peggy went walking by herself up on the 17-mile drive and didn't come home, so Grant went looking for her one way and I the other, and I met her crossing a log over a little stream, and she told me she was going to have a girl, as, walking along, this beautiful young woman suddenly appeared beside her and said 'I am your daughter.'"

Peggy's recollection was that Moira was at that time a rather aloof East Asian princess of some sort, not altogether crazy about the prospect of getting mixed up with such a wooly household; nor did she indicate she planned to get born at two the next morning, five minutes after the doctor arrived.

Though it later turned out she was a born artist, Moira at three became a child movie star, when a film company saw her peeking out of a halved eggshell in a trick photograph, prepared by the ingenious Burr McIntosh to occupy the whole cover page of some San Francisco paper's Easter special.

She debuted as the young Mignon in the movie of that name, a role requiring her to fall off a cliff on Angel Island in San Francisco Bay, into the clutches of buccaneer kidnappers below, for take after exhilarating take.

Her next role was that of Little Tom in "Mrs. Wiggs of the Cabbage Patch." Grant grew impatient waiting around Sausalito's Alta Mira Hotel while his daughter was exploited by Hollywood money, so he and a stray cinematographer founded the Fairfax Motion Picture Co. in nearby San Anselmo.

He wrote, directed, drew animated cartoon sequences for, and with Moira and Peggy co-starred in a lavish production called "Whimsey Tales," whose first print had been received favorably at one tryout when the rented family house and movie studio Barton went up in flames with all contents except Moira's favorite doll.

Moira turned her talents to writing:

> There was a little mouse
> Who lived in a little house
> Where lots of cheese was stored
> And in this little house
> He got his room and board,
>
> He had a little wife
> WHo cut her cheese with a knife
> She had whiskers all her life,
>
> And when the children all were born
> The neighbors looked at them with scorn
> Because they all had whiskers
> And you couldn't tell the brothers from the sisters.

Grant repaired to Hollywood to try his hand at original scenarios for Triangle Pictures — "The Garden of LIes" and "Footprints of Eve" and "A Pagan Madonna" were among his titles, with action intended to meet the studio's standards, enunciated as "no more than 20 interior sets, and please keep expensive mobs down."

Even so, the scenarios tended towards real problems of desert Indians Grant had known, and Mormons he knew from his Utah trek with lions, and silent movies were simply not ideal for a writer of complicated worlds.

At first the family shared a Santa Monica Canyon house with resident skunk, whom Grant didn't mind, and a veterans circus performer and film beauty who had appeared with Moira in "Mignon," Belle Bennett, whom Grant did mind, fearing her worldliness would tarnish the innocent Peggy.

So when I was born, surprising Grant with another little loudmouth to feed, he had just quit a materialistic city editor at the Los Angeles Tribune, and we resided in a Los Angeles cottage afflicted with a mockingbird, whose all night carousing kept everyone from sleep.

Over the bird's horrible cries one dawn, Peggy heard Grant creep from bed, pick up his rifle and exit. There was a loud gunshot report and Peggy thought fuzzily to herself, "Poor man, who can blame him for killing himself?" And, in the sudden silence, was asleep before he got back to bed.

Peggy's buoyant faith remained in general unabated. She stuck to Grant's Bulletin observations that "Obstacles are for the joy of overcoming," even when Grant didn't.

But as Moira later remarked, "They were game about doing whatever they were supposed to do in this mysterious world. Now and again a life raft would bobble by in the flood, and Grant would grab a reed on the

THIS WAS THE Carmel seventh and eighth grade class from 1923. Most of the students are identified; a few aren't, however. Starting with the front row (left to right) is an unidentified boy, Eugene Roehling, Gordon Campbell, Thomas Warren, Clayton Leitch, Virginia Burton and unidentified girl. Second row: Shield Stark, Moira Wallace, unidentified girl, Anne Greene, Violet

shore and say 'No more, no more!' I felt like Alice being dragged along by the Red Queen shouting 'Faster, faster.'"

Next, Grant became assistant director of archeology at the San Diego Museum, entailing slight pay but free lodging in the exhibition Indian Pueblo opposite the laughing hyena in Balboa Park. When the menu suffered a payroll cut, Peggy took Moira and me to visit cousin Madgie's family in Sausalito over what by chance was May Day, when the Pleiades people made their annual check0in on behalf of the Order of Light's standing offer to merge Big Works.

This time the pitch narrowed down to one main point: Clearly, Grant had given the idea of making a preliminary economic base for Big Work a fair try, with little to show for it besides rebuffs from flood, fire, frost, scenario editors, Singh museum trustees, and distracting childbirth. That being so, there yet remained one clear, logical method of simply knuckling down to Big Work with them, and letting them figure how to keep the groceries coming in, with Peggy's kind cooperation. As Grant had written in the Bulletin, drawing on bicycle steering for analogy, "We are drawn inevitably to what we keep our eyes fixed on." He conceded.

When Peggy got back from Sausalito with Moira and me, the drafty Pueblo was buzzing around the clock with Grant's conferences with all the Pleiades people and their guests from ancient Egypt and Akkad, Greece and Rome, Atlantis, even Hopkins, Mo.

The Order of Light had another selling point that wasn't mentioned — the news that toplofty brother Charles, holidaying in from the University of Nebraska with all his laurels from the British Museum's scrap heaps, had inadvertently struck $5,000,000 worth of Texas oil, and was announcing to the press his plan to leave several millions for a research foundation in his name.

Among the first big messages for mankind from an advanced Pleiadean was one denigrating too much wealth, noting "Whatever you use, you own; whatever warps and defrauds and hampers you, owns you."

***

Carmel's protective coloration served for us as Hollywood did for W.C. Fields — so well that in childhood Moira glanced yearningly in through the only bourgeois picture window in the village, wishing she belonged to the grocer's unimaginably plain looking family tableau under the bridge lamp inside.

In fairness, the grocer's little girl, Moira's classmate, turned out less plain than expected, and in later years was paroled back to her dazzled Monterey bank to teach her brilliant embezzling methods.

Little Moira's best pals were Ann and Ginny, Ann lived across Monte Verde street from us—we rented the University of California architect John Galen Howard's little summer cottage, with a pine tree growing through the living room — with her own distinguished architect father, who padded around town in tonsure and medieval monk's robes from his favorite past incarnation.

Ginny's father was a dapper unfrocked dean from the Massachusetts Institute of Technology, which he had abandoned, along with Brahmin wife and children, to fidget of Ginny's mother, a strikingly homely poetess involved in Navajo bracelets and cartwheel braids and affairs of the heart, who had first caught his total attention by hurling herself into a shallow part on the Seine as he tried to stroll by.

Other close friends included a violist who played his compositions chiefly to spellbound sea lions on the rocks of south of the beach, and the rocks' owner, who deeded over not only much of his acreage but also his last previous wife to the young poet whose gloomy cadences he admired, Robinson Jeffers.

The snow-white beach, the turquoise-and-indigo bay, jagged Pt. Lobos and the blue Santa Lucia mountain range marching down to Big Sur, were not so theatrical as our little community whose adults and children alike appeared in deep woods fog on Forest Theatre's stage to the applause of holidaying film stars from nearby Hotel Del Monte and Pebble Beach.

I made my debut at 5 as a bearded genome in "Rip Van Winkle," though I had earlier made impromptu appearances in interpretative dancers' recitals in the woods, the locale too of little talks by Persian swamis, the young reluctant messiah Jiddu Krishnamurti, and no end of nature and health food nuts.

Everybody meditated, only a few drank or committed suicide any more, and Peggy kept her melodious speaking voice fluid by mooing mantras to startled cows among the California live oaks in Hatton's fields.

But the Pleiadean people were not content. Carmel's petty realities conflicted with their greater Reality, and the vibrations of all the "hobohemians" created static, encouraging astral earthbound Malevich to screw up transmissions and palm themselves off as Pleiadean.

So we regularly left Carmel for a few months at a time, always returning because whatever their failings, Carmel's vibrations were relatively best. We left so often that Moira and I each changed schools 11 times in the seven years we spent in the eight primary grades, in the course of which I somehow took California history four times and missed English grammar altogether.

The Pleiades people were right. Though as with even the best planned projects there were crises to cope with over ensuing decades, the Big Work was underway, its momentum capable of overriding any human institution worth mentioning and, more important, dispelling whatever anxieties and depression the mysterious human condition might try to fob off on Grant. Not that the Pleiades people themselves always came up to Grant's standards. But they seemed on the right track.

Like other creative types, their initial reaction on landing the new commission was to forget the serious work at hand, instead boisterously dragging in all their friends to sit for portraits and provide autographs under one-liners that Grant could have phrased better.

As the Order of Light outlined it, the agenda had three parts:

First, ghosts would vouch for facts unknown to Grant, which he could later authenticate in historical records, validating the ghosts too, and all their implications.

The Spirit of Carmel-by-the-Sea

Varying moods of Carmel, the California art colony, are caught in the etchings and paintings of the University of California extension class students. Three of the etchings included in the class exhibit now in San Francisco are shown above. At the top: "Carmel Bay," by Andrea Asbjornsen of Carmel. The studies below are (left) by Moira Wallace, 14 years old, of Carmel, and Dorothy Wilkinson, Berkeley.

Second, as soon as they got the bugs out of it, they would come up with a Truthmeter, as a series of numerical formulae converting written statements to numbers — resembling numerology, whose quackery they deplored — solutions symbolizing either "true" or "false."

The Truthmeter's unfailing accuracy in testing known matters would support its analyses regarding such hitherto uncertain matters as "Death is a step into more conscious life."

Finally, the hard part. Advanced math would once and for all clear up the essential structure of the universal either and its contents, including all 569 dimensions, with proof that the endless perfecting of the individual ego is the point of the whole thing.

Nancy Hanks Lincoln came by to sketch a lot of her earlier reincarnations — as Iphegenioa, marco Polo, Ninon de l'Enclos and the mother of William of Orange and of Oliver Cromwell among others — and remarked:

"The supreme law of Becoming, of Being through Unfolding, must quickly be handed on to mankind."

Handrian popped in and said, "Religion like science should be based on fact-finding and proof, through the free use of all nine senses — the whole mind — not, as now, upon a mere emotional fraction such as fear, greed, superstitious awe and gullibility."

Grant kept an open but suspicious mind. "I am not the advocate, only the reporter of facts," he reminded them.

Peggy said that was all very well, but what about the grocery bills? An tactless Pleiadean responded that if she couldn't concentrate on helping, the distraction of the latest infant might have to be removed.

It was a remark made without having taken Peggy's measure. She flew into such a rage that Zulazu-le had to be interrupted in her rounds — "From planet to sun I speed," She described the routine, " my wings are my aspiration to be and my will to do!" — to smooth things over.

"Greetings" she told Grant reassuringly, as if nothing had happened:

> "Great truths are ready to be given through your hand."

> "Your wife will do very noble work with you.

"We rejoice to see the beautiful family life, the joyous spirit of companionship and trust and labor for the highest good of the world.

"This is the perfect home life.

"Your daughter is of those who walk with the wise and with dreamers of dream beautiful things and create them.

We know her, even as we know the son whom the Druid Lady (Peggy) well calls the Golden Boy.

"Cherish him. He is of the wonder workers from afar. He is the Giver of Law, the one destined to point the way to millions who shale seek the light.

"This is the word I wished to give in greeting, that she at your side might know some small part of how we regard this family group who came together by no accident but through the Great Law.

"Now may I draw one little sketch? And then Mr. Shakespeare would like to continue his verses…"

Peggy wasn't altogether mollified concerning my expendability so Zarathustra came on to add, "Your son was my son Zarathustra II in old Persia. To him the greater work which you have but begun.

"Cherish him, our comrade, our son, our illumned Master of Wisdom. He now hath a great mother, else earth had not seen him.

When she as a maiden did say 'I aspire to be the mother of great man, 'she spoke the thought not held by her alone. It was an echo from the certitudes of the high celestial worlds we know.

"The crystal purity of her spirit she held untarnished. And lo, the great man shall bless the mother."

Peggy still wanted to know about the grocery bills. "Means will be provided," the Order said, and dragged in the earthbound ghost of a pirate who drew a map of the hiding place of his ancient loot at the base of nearby Pt. Loma.

The Order claimed Moira was naturally gifted at psychometry and she was appointed witch's wand to help find the treasure. But the buccaneer was a liar, it turned out, and the Order had to think of some other tack.

Incorporating and selling shares in the Great Work was suggested. Grant drew up papers for the 456 Society (456 means "true" in Truthmeter code) and called some well-heeled psychic enthusiasts who lived on top of Pt. Lomas.

The were the elderly retired banker and Secretary of the Treasury Lyman Gage, his young ex-Foloradora Girl wife Gloria, her handsome young Hawaiian beachboy-sculptor-movie actor-admirer Kamuela, and the Chinese cook, who had lately started chasing Gloria around the estate with a carving knife.

Grant perceived that the cook had become possessed by an earthbound malefic dispatched from the Greek temples of the theosophical center across the drive by the jealous Purple Mother, the medium Mme. Katherine Tingley, who had wanted Gage for herself, along with the sporting goods magnate A.G. Spalding and other resident guests.

The Gages were so pleased with Grant's prompt exorcism of the cook that they put on a big seance at which members of the Order of Light consented to make personal appearances.

"Zulazu-le sang in a beautiful contralto voice an invocation aria, the most beautiful 'operatic' air I ever heard," Grant noted, " and then

People of Atlantis
Self portrait of prehistoric man drawn
through automatic writing by Grant Wallace

No artist signature
Unframed; Fair condition

Station Mars Broadcasting?
Self portrait of Tah-Nezh, of Mars, drawn
through automatic writing by Grant Wallace

photograph courtesy Brian Wallace

spoke in clear Bernhardt-like tones a dozen sentences through a trumpet.

"Hermes made a speech, much as he writes, and two or three other of Marzolia (the Pleiadean capital) spoke in whispers. I felt the hands and fingers of one of the Marzolians, satiny and softy.

"There was no chance of fraud in some of the cases, anyway. The medium, Mrs. White, and her 'guides' were amazed by the 'Golden People', a strange experience for them.

"It took that sort of pheronema to complete Gage's growing belief that it wasn't my subconscious mind doing all my work!"

To cement the point, a Pleaidean pointed out, "Consumption of wealth is the only legitimate purpose of acquisition. Let superfluous wealth be given to assisting the nation's creative writers, artists, musicians, scientific workers and teachers, so that they may be free from the press of penury and enabled to devote their whole time and genius to their own line of work."

Unfortunately, Gage hadn't become rich by accident, and he was buying into no big inspirational work, though Searle did do a heroic bust of Grant, along with others of Cecil B. DeMille and David Wark Griffith.

However, a well-off Miss Putnam, who had been to the seance, came to see Grant's work, sized up Peggy and the children as needing a little investment, and underwrote the Big Work for the next 16 years to the tune of $50 a month at first, later raised to $75.

The Pleiades people had passed their first big test.

But Peggy exacted a price. She insisted on protective coloration for the times ahead, " so the children will have normal surroundings," and moved everybody back to Carmel.

***

After a year back in Carmel, we picked up and moved to the healing vastness of the high Sierra, where thin air stimulated the red corpuscles to a fine frenzy, cold spring weather coursed down ancient flumes, and grandpa Wallace's gold rush diggings down pas receding blue ridges of pine at Grass Valley below.

We were a mile from the nearest neighbors, the Jouberts, who owned our abandoned vine-clogged mine shanty at Depot Hill, five miles from groceries at Camptonville, The Pleiades people were so pleased with the lack of competition that they produced several maps of buried treasure and undiscovered gold veins — useless alas, since their sources had been dead several generations, and the landmarks had vanished.

Our lack of a car to get to the store played into Grant's weakness for ornamental agriculture, and he began ignoring his Big Work in favor of growing ginormous multi-colored squash and exotic string beans from his private seed catalogue stash.

In between heroic bouts with dirt, crumbling floorboards and other ravages of the perfect wilderness setting, Peggy composed glorious letters to Carmel friends extolling the blessedness of the new hideaway. Her eloquence had the untoward effect of attracting the correspondents to arrive to see for themselves, first the Danielses. Then the MacMurrays.

Daniels was a lawyer whom Grant had inadvertently inspired to be a writer, in the course of which he abandoned one family and commenced another. MacMurray was the violist who played to the sealions. He too had a second family, having abandoned his first wife, unaware that their Fred Jr. would grow up to be the richest movie star of his era.

Both the misuses were delighted to turn their troublesome new offspring over to Peggy's care, along with the cooking and cleaning and their own piteous travails, encouraging Peggy to ever higher flights of inspirational counsel, which they carefully avoided taking.

Peggy was a natural-born compulsive healer, an aspect of her notion of her family tradition, where lairds' noble daughters their loyal retainers from whatever might beset them. Any cry of pain, however humbug, set Peggy off, and there was not stopping her — short of cure, which her beneficiaries were not about to let happen — until she was winded, and collapsed in laughter at the idiocy of her vast concern.

In this she was like an actress unable to get offstage until the big scene was played out the rounded conclusion.

The routine commenced with her identifying with the petitioner's complaint to so exalted and exaggerated an extent that the patent was spellbound at the possibilities for suffering not yet plumbed, and began complaining of more things to keep up.

Compassion, exhortation, uplift, positive thinking, cosmic force, the law of external harmony, absent treatment, all these were brought into play, along with personal intercession with third and fourth parties, loans of hard-to-find funds, and generous ministrations of whatever odd new health food diet happened to be on her agenda.

Her considerable charm, beauty and attractive voice made Peggy's healing frenzies fairly bearable, and probably accounted for the note of envy that seemed to be at the bottom of some of her petitioners' plaints.

But Grant tried to ignore these episodes. He was content to rest his healing laurels on his youthful exorcisms and let karma take care of complainers. He was particularly zealous about circumventing Peggy's diet fads, and rose before anyone else to ensure the kind of man's breakfast he made for himself, burn inch-thick griddle cakes with lard—except once when he used soft soap, not really altering the end product — garnished with bacon chunks and rock-hard fried eggs, and coffee boiled to the blackness of hell.

Where they agreed, partly for reasons of economics that neither stressed, was in denouncing "materia medica" in favor of the cheaper chiropractors, Ionica-belt salesmen and naturopathic quacks they consulted occasionally, the favorite being a Dr Dudgeon, who charged $1 a session for whatever ailed one, making his rapid diagnosis with a wand hooked up to a washboard with fluttering needles on dials.

Then he would poke one's neck a bit, and as a rule the patient departed feeling much better.

Grant felt Dudgeon was a kindred scientist and brought around several massive portfolios of the Big Work for Dudgeon's edification. Dudgeon ran his wand up and down the unopened volumes' spines and told Grant admiringly, "Ninety percent of this is perfectly sound!"

As for the mountains' healing properties, they dissipated with the first snowfall, and as we were ever to do, we settled for a return to Carmel's low hobohemian vibrations as better in the long run than those just tested.

But this time a peculiarly irritating new healing force awaited Grant and the Pleiades people in Carmel, a new enthusiasm of Peggy's in the glowing Valkyrie form of a Norsewoman physical culturist name Haldis, whose principal conversational gambit was the stern order, "Buttocks In!", accompanied by a smart crack on the rear for anyone slouching in her presence.

Cosmic vigor, it seemed, was to be obtained

from breathing like a winded fraught horse, squaring the shoulders and expanding the chest to give the solar plexus a feeling of security, and marching around the whole time like a Marine color guard, vibrant and pulsating.

The Pleiades people excused Grant for taking a day off from Big Work to limb a vicious panel of caricatures of a physical culturist named Mme. Umbumpum, which he mailed off the the Saturday Evening Post, and was surprised to get back a check and, in due course, find his vengeance given the full page in the magazine.

***

The next venture from Carmel, though brief, was to a recurrent destination, especially for Grant in periods when domesticity grew to thick — his sisters Olive and Ella's immaculate little white Victorian house not far from his ruined Tanglewood in Fairoaks, a small museum of carved frontier oak bedsteads and rockers, canopied under a giant oak at the top of a lawned hill, ringed by bamboo jungle, then rose and gladioli gardens, a prim porchard, a sweet-smelling barn for the milk cow Daisybelle and her hay, and behind flowering vines and lemon trees, an uproarious chicken yard.

The occasion this time was the funeral of the clan's pioneer mother, the matriarch, laid out in gruesome splendor on the porch glider, moved in beside the harmonium in the parlor for the occasion.

Belligerently offended and too-handsome brother Charles had motored out from Texas with his chauffeur, and upstaged Grant unsuccessfully with his pities.

Their handsome younger sister Olive presided Cooley and sensibly, while chickens were slain and fracases with dumplings and biscuits by the eldest sister Ella, Grass Valley's first born yankee girl, a bad-tempered old thing who muttered constantly under her breath to a rakish ghost that plagued her with off-color jokes and pinched her when she bent over.

The ghost had attached himself to Ella during the ouiji period Grant had warned her about, and had resisted all Grant's exorcist in skills, a source of some dissatisfaction to him.

But Ella had not helped with the exorcism, which was typical of her contrariety, a trait blamed on her early chagrin when, as an infant, she had been kidnapped and then returned by Indians, who explained they'd confused the Wallace house with that of Lola Montez next door.

When she grew old enough to understand, Ella had felt slighted by the brusque rejection, and refused to relinquish the grievance.

Olive and Ella and Charles and "young" Milan from St. Joe, whom they ignored — all that was left of their generation — agreed their mother had been taken before her time, in her 97th year, because of the hardships of too much childbearing.

Peggy's enthusiasm for carrying on the generations was regarded as an Irish eccentricity and delicately overlooked. Olive especially was fond of Peggy, though there was no escaping that she was Grant's second and very much younger wife, and their basic loyalties remained with his first real family.

Each of Grant's many visits to Fairoaks ended on the same note as the funeral visit did, with the girls' reviving their standing offer of a headstone for Grant for the plot they had reserved for mine, alongside another reserved for his first wife in the family plot.

Headstones were anathema to Grant and the Pleiades people, who regarded them with unseemly mirth, as anachronisms left over from a time of superstition when death was regarded as something to be taken hard, rather than as the threshold of the good life untrammeled by domineering relatives.

Returning to Carmel — from Fairoaks, Grant went on ahead while Peggy stopped off with Moira and me to visit her mother Hessie at the San Francisco Bayshore valley called "The Ranch," a barren windswept property that had fallen to her second husband, Peter Garrett.

Pete had been a San Francisco house ice when Hessie, divorced from Peggy's father, had fallen in with him.

Peter's Catholic forebears had been champion distillers of Irish whiskey on the old sod, but temperance had gotten to them, prompting them to shut the plant and destroy the recipe and emigrate to the northeast reaches of San Francisco Bay, where the great spread they bought was gradually decimated in the interests of buying deceased family members out of purgatory, through the good offices of their clergy.

To the haunted original farmhouse had been added a smaller undaunted cottage, where Hessie occasionally moved when life with Pete grew too boring for her high spirits, which was often.

The only working part of the "The Ranch" was the clam beach yonder of the Southern Pacific and Santa Fe railway tracks, the seafood farm being operated by a San Francisco Chinatown figure named Qong Sang and his collie dog, Come.

Come carded the clambers from the onrushing trains but one day grew so determined that he stood barking in the middle of the track, which was the end of come.

Once in a fit of ennui with Pete, Hessie experimented with strangling him, but found that the operation drew back his Wales so effectively that he looked positively young again. Murmuring, "Pete, you're beautiful," Hessie released her grip and fell upon him, alarming him even more.

Hessie liked to see Moira and me because she knew her unsuitable stories amused us and upset Peggy — stories about her rolling in the shrubbery with the tall handsome policemen of Ballymeena in her youth, and critiques of Grant, whose going on ahead to Carmel was no accident but a measure of prudence.

Alone of all those who knew Grant dealt with him irreverently, referring to him as "The Old Man" or "The Old Fossil," reviling him as "out of date," mourning his throwing away fortunes in order to take up with his spooks, and threatening reprisals if he or his children made her darling Peggy suffer.

"Your mother never wet her finger before she met you Wallaces," Hessie loved to storm at us.

"If anything ever happens to her I swear to God I'll come back and haunt you to your graves!"

Grant's mother had been known to us as Grandmother. Hessie wished to be known strictly as "Gammaw."

***

Our next foray from Carmel fetched us up on the north shore of Raccoon Strait in San Francisco Bay, in a cottage built on stilts over the waves lapping at Tiburon, looking across at the deer in the weeds of Angel Island.

Salt air was known to be invigorating, and the murmur of waves was advantageous for psychic communications. The initial distractions tugging at Peggy's ready sympa-

Man at Point Lobos
by Moira Wallace
c. 1928
Linoleum Block Print

Signed by artist
Unframed; Good Condition

thies were sea lions suffering indigestion from holding their jaws open to the straits's herring run letting too many fish swim in and then retiring in the tide pools under the house to belch and moan in the middle of the night.

Peggy would put on slippers and robe and by candlelight, creep down to their beds of pain and commiserate with them, telling them their bilious spells would pass.

A graver threat to the vibratory integrity of the premises was perceived by Grant in the form of a San Francisco artist couple, Mildred and Blanding Sloan, whose rowboat came ashore where little Moira was sketching.

Their opinion that Moira was a genius they'd discovered was not faulted — everybody liked their intercession's first result, getting Moira's etching of me listening to a crystal set radio into the Sunday Chronicle's rotogravure section — but Mildred's advanced Lucy Stone league notions of women's liberation bothered Grant, especially where it came to suggesting Peggy have an affair with Mildred's footloose brother.

He saw a similar threat of worldly corruption of Peggy's innocence from Belle Bennett, the actress who had worked in Mignon and received sleep-coaching in her Alcazar repertoire lines from Peggy. Belle, now a silent movie queen married to a muscular gigolo, took up residence in a nearby rented villa.

Grant returned us to Carmel. Belle, escorted by pimply young Douglas Fairbanks Jr. and Ronald Colman, promptly arrived to film Stella Dallas at Del Monte Hotel, and stayed with us briefly, to Grant's added annoyance.

Thinking to anchor Grant against the Pleiades people's will-o-the-wisp tendencies, Peggy seized her legacy when Auntie Clothie

> ✿ ✿ ✿
> An exhibition of the work of the student associates of Blanding Sloan will open tomorrow in the City of Paris galleries, San Francisco. It will continue for two weeks. The work to be shown is by artists of many nationalities—Italian, French, Chinese, Polish, Swedish, Norwegian, American, who range in ages from 7 years to 50.
> Sloan prefers to call his group "associates" rather than students. Anne Brigman, nationally known photographer of Oakland, will show her etchings. Other exhibitors are Salvatore, Ralph Cheese, Fai Sui Chang, Wah Ming Chang, D. S. Chang, Harry McClintock, Mrs. Agnes Spratt, George Mill, Eleanor Widdis, H. W. Pershing, Myrtle Richardson, Dorothy Wilkinson, Mrs. William P. Harrold, Andrea Asbjornsen, Moira Wallace, Virginia Burton, Eva Belle Adams, Kate Matheson, Helen Sonnicksen, Mildred Taylor, Eugenia Liczbinska and Elizabeth Watson.
> ✦ ✦ ✦

died to buy the sloping wooded block of Carmel north of Ocean Avenue's nonexistent extension up the hill above the village, and mortgaged the property to build a redwood board-and-batten cottage.

She enlisted Grant's enthusiasm for the project by talking him into being its architect, a role he hadn't undertaken in this life since his first marriage, though his experience in previous lives included a hand in Egypt's pyramids, in his bad period as Apep the Snake.

We camped in a tent on the woodsy property while a bad-tempered carpentry crew nailed the place together under Grant's eagle eye, and Grant participated in the masonry of odd chalkrock pieces into the fireplace and walkways.

New Shows At Gump's

Moira Wallace and Seldon Giles are exhibiting at Gump's.

Miss Wallace is a Carmel artist whose work has met with very favorable comment all over the country. Outstanding in interest, perhaps, among her local achievements, are the murals and decorations in the Del Monte Hotel. She has great feeling for the rhythm and primitive grandeur of Oriental and South Sea Island art motifs. Miss Wallace's current show will include drawings, wood cuts and oil paintings.

Selden Giles, who was one of the prize winners in the recent Oakland annual exhibition, will show a group of water colors which includes landscapes at Taos, New Mexico, and the San Francisco Bay Region.

The Pleiades people grumbled they were being snubbed for worldliness again.

A buxom real estate woman became enamored of Grant's portfolios, or as it turned out of Grant, and he was covered with confusion, especially after Peggy got wind of Beth's plan to intercept Grant at the Monterey depot on his return from a brief trip to San Francisco, with elopement in mind.

Peggy adroitly intercepted the incoming Del Monte Limited a mile down the track at Del Monte, and at Monterey descended arm in arm with Grant. Though proud of the new house, Grant agreed with the Pleiades people that it tied them down, and he immediately put it on the market, which fortunately was moribund .

A pretty fan of his Bulletin columns wrote from her gracious spread in the Los Altos hills that she had a scrapbook of his old writings and wondered if the hospitality of her guest house would be of use to his inspirational plans. She guaranteed its vibrations, and Grant departed to check them out.

Peggy wrote him daily, such overwhelming loving epistles that he couldn't take offense at her domineering. The letters took care to send fond regards to "dear little Mrs. Reed."

They and Mrs Reed's eventually cloying helpfulness finally drove Grant home, where he saved face by extolling the Reed region's climate as beyond comparison, and insisted we must move to that vicinity.

So we rented out the Carmel place to San Francisco second hand book dealer—who fancied our collection of National Geographic, and disappeared with them — in favor of a rustic cottage near Los Gatos, where the well water promptly laid Peggy low with what appeared to be typhoid.

The Carmel house being occupied, we shoved on to wait out its rental term in another odd little cottage, on the side of Mount Tamalpais above Mill Valley.

During the Los Gatos-Mill Valley period, Moira was on scholarship at Dominican Convent near Mill Valley, an odd repository for her in the Pleiades, Catholicism was thought the heart of darkness— but consonant with Peggy's complex educational notions, in that it was exceedingly fashionable as benefitted a princess of aristocratic lineage, and the scholarship acknowledged the bright and beautiful child's specialness. Besides it was free.

It was also awful, owing to the suspicions of Sister Mercedes in regard to her adolescent charges of curiosity about the corrupt world in general, and the seedy male gar dener in particular.

Like Grant with Peggy, Sister Mercedes with

Life Guard and the Mermaid
by Moira Wallace
c. 1926—1933
"Return to Moira Wallace care of Belle Bennett
6280 Temple Hill, Hollywood, California"

Signed by artist; Original artist notation
Unframed; Good Condition

her girls stood as vigilant protector, her first line of defense being her office's carpet, under which she hid incoming and outgoing mail, for fear it contained contaminating materials.

Eventually Moira got word through and achieved liberation from academics altogether. Once out, she got a lot of her faintly inspirational but actually terribly good watercolors and drawings together and, at the age of 16, exhibited in a most successful one-man show at San Francisco's prestigious Gump Gallery.

On the basis of that, the billboard form of Foster & Kleiser hired her as artist and "idea man," and announced it was going to transform outdoor advertising according to Moira's higher artistic notions from the grubby and strident medium it had been. Moira boarded with a Navy captain's family in Pacific Heights, and drew prizefight sketches on the side for the Call-Bulletin.

The Pleiades people weren't crazy about admitting it, but Moira was in fact a bonafide art genius and had it all over them and their merely virtuoso academic draftsmanship.

When Moira was transferred to Foster & Kleiser's Southern California offices, the rest of us packed up and moved to Hollywood too, renting a place under the Hollywoodland sign, nearby Belle Bennett's ersatz Tudor manse.

The movie-star bedlam around Belle's place at the time featured overflowing trunks of unanswered fan mail, which were gladly entrusted to me to deal with through forgery as I saw fit.

An ex-Paris-expatriate acquaintance from Mignon days, Imogene Gless, declared Moira's genius was being wasted in California, and offered to put her up in New York, where she could study mural painting with Hildreth Meiere and, to help with expenses, do a little commercial work on the side.

"As if by magic," as Peggy liked to exclaim.

Immy's East 48th street apartment turned out to be a sweatshop version of Dominican Convent and Immy another Sister Mercedes. For some months, Moira was kept occupied drawing dashing figures that enhanced the national advertising of Packard motorcars and Coy perfumes, but Immy didn't allow any time off for such frivolities as mural study.

It was in the midst of the great stock market crash of 1929, with people peeling out of the windows of skyscrapers all about, that Moira made her escape, and returned to Carmel to do "serious work" of her own, financed by sanguine-crayon portraits, in a pixieish cottage that Grant had designed and, aided by another mortgage on the main house, built as a rental unit on our property.

It was a rounded-eave cottage, a riposte and satire on High Comstock's jagged-edge pixie cottages across the street. It is an irony of Carmel history that for years now, it is a photograph of Grant's anit-Comstock house that is shown on a popular postcard as the epitome of Carmel's famous Comstock style.

Moira was still in New York when Uncle Charles' heart suddenly softened and he wrote Grant offering to put us children through school.

We promptly rented out the Ocean Avenue house and moved to Menlo Park, where I was enrolled in the school that met all of Peggy's criteria, Josephine Whitney Duveneck's Peninsula School of Creative Education, a progressive experiment miles farther out than the Montessori school Moira had attended as a tot in San Diego, with enough blueblood connections to give Elton a run.

I wrote a touching note of thanks to Uncle Charles in Texas. His lawyers answered rather stiffly that their client's generosity didn't envision any frilly private school that charged tuition.

Mrs. Duveneck, a woman of diplomacy, promptly awarded me a tuition-free scholarship, and I passed a happy year in the treetop on the grounds of the schoolhouse, formerly a famous haunted house from Victorian times, built for a honeymoon blighted by a mysterious death.

In the treetop, I sported my protective souvenirs from the stockroom of Ted Kuster's Carmel playhouse, a pop-out opera hat and a pearl handled derringer pistol, as I read what the curriculum encouraged, books that interested me, featuring the works of Stephen Leacock and Matthew Arnold's life of Buddha, "The Light of Asia."

Sometimes I descended to paint murals in the hallways. The only teacher who gave me trouble was the physics and math prof, a bad-tempered neighbor who drove me to school in his model-T, and who was eventually turned in by his wife as a fugitive from a Sing Sing rap for forging Columbia University diplomas.

The student body, composed of eccentric children of the region's second-generation rich, provided me with several eccentric lifelong friendships. The odd student's roots were geographically intertwined with those on the Menuhins, of whom it was said that their parents had in effect ordered them from the astral reincarnation genius bank, an idea Peggy had latched on to in Moira's and my cases, and much admired. Suggestion and sleep-teaching were also favored by Peggy, who never tired of assuring us of our greatness. Grant tended to indifferences regarding education, feeling karma would take care of it all in its own way, with less furore around the house.

Theory apart, the educational biases were, for Grant, a timely whack with the Saturday Evening Post, and, for Peggy, and apt cita-

tion from "Through the Looking Glass," and sometimes the recitation of that most useful of moral and worldly guides, the "Walrus and the Carpenter."

***

It was during our Menlo Park period that Grant decided to settle once for all the last remaining questions as to whether his Big Work should continue uninterrupted, or if it should give the world a last chance to finance it directly as it moved from its showier artistic literary demonstrations into its harder mathematical and theoretical proofs.

The previous October's stocks market crash — occurring two weeks after our first and last plunge into investing — forced Grant to borrow fare and set off by train for New York with a truckload of gorgeous astral art work and handwritten messages, suitable for the full-color reproductions on fine paper in elegant folio editions. The Pleiades people, as unworldly as Grant, were all for it. What hadn't been foreseen was that the Depression had put a lot of publishers out of business and the others were not in any position to risk capital on fancy color books on a subject that had commanded a market in the past, but that had abruptly vanished in the new economic preoccupation of the reading public.

Grant hung on around Gramercy Park for six months, augmenting Miss Putnam's pittance with occult book reviews for his old Evening Sun, and the editorship of a short-lived high-class film magazine backed by his dancer friend Ruth St. Denis, and even by the guest editorship of the portly old Journal of the American Society for Psychical Research.

Peggy suggested Grant try to peddle some of the Pleiades stuff as his own, but he reminded her of the gravity of plagiarism.

As Christmas approached, Grant and portfolios boarded a freighter for the trip home through the Canal. The world had had its chance.

Grant returned to Carmel to resume the math he so hopelessly avoided by going to New York. As it turned out, the Pleiades people were no better at math than the average creative writer or artist, and Grant, who at least had taught business math in his youth, had to explain logarithms and calculus to them.

But they agreed that 10 years and more was enough to devote to self-portraits and aphorisms, and they had better knuckle down to the Big Work's theoretical explication and mathematical proofs — intricate formulae and geometric charts — dull though it be.

The simplest of the math stuff had been the Truthmeter, whose formulae had been tinkered with endlessly, without getting around the one loose end of it's always requiring a guesswork addition or subtraction at the end to ensure a correct reading.

The Pleiades people were even more embarrassed than Grant after he took the Truthmeter's word and wired reelection congratulations from Carmel to President Hoover the night before he was creamed by Franklin Roosevelt.

They knuckled down. The work, though humdrum, became stable, after one last flurry of interruptions, concluding Grant's lifelong exchange of stimulating aggravations with his brother Charles. Charles died in Texas, leaving his presumed fortune to his flinty wife Hulda. Or so it seemed, and so it had been expected.

But from the Other Side came a family delegation headed by Mother Wallace, trailing brothers Milton and Frank and sisters Carrie and Hattie, with a brief appearance too by Judge Tom, just coming to after a long and difficult awakening to the higher vibrations of the astral community.

Charles himself was comatose on the Other Side and not expected to rally from the swoon of the unevolved for 25 years to come. "So it was with me," Judge Tom confessed, "though your mother came over wide awake and prepared."

But according to the delegation, Charles had had a change of heart in his latter years, and had remembered his flesh and blood in a codicil "that he secreted in a desk, sealed," but that his wife's conniving physician and lawyer had hidden, while they plied Charles with dubious drugs. The delegation estimated Charles' estate at five million.

Grant got retired old Judge Clark to draft an only mildly slanderous inquiry to the Texas lawyers, who replied that nothing seemed out of order at their end of things, and anyhow most of Charles' vaunted wealth had gone down the drain with everybody else's in the Depression's onset.

The family delegation declared the lawyers were lying, but Judge Clark said there wasn't anything you could do about that. The Pleiades people declared, "We wait in vain for better vibratory cooperation," and urged Grant to forfet it and take a shack available on a retired cowboy's spread in Cachagua Valley, adjacent to upper Carmel Valley, away from family vibrations, in the tranquility of oaks and mountains and streams. "This region with its many interruptions and daily small problems never has been harmonious enough to protect your necessary serenity of mind and our high contact."

He moved his bales of working papers to the Cachagua. Meantime up at the The Ranch on the shores of San Francisco Bay, Hessi's husband Pete lapsed into his final illness. "Love and peace," he murmured in his delirium, "love and peace."

"What was that?" Hessie asked, looming over him.

Pete opened his eyes and dwelt on Hessie. "Never mind the love, Lord," Pete said, closing his eyes for the last time, "just give me peace."

After the funeral, Hessie thought to give Grant's theories a try. "Peter?" she asked the empty old ranch house, "If you're there, will you knock on wood or say something?"

She listened, heard the old house sighing, added, "On second thought, Peter, just phone if you get a chance," and hurriedly moved

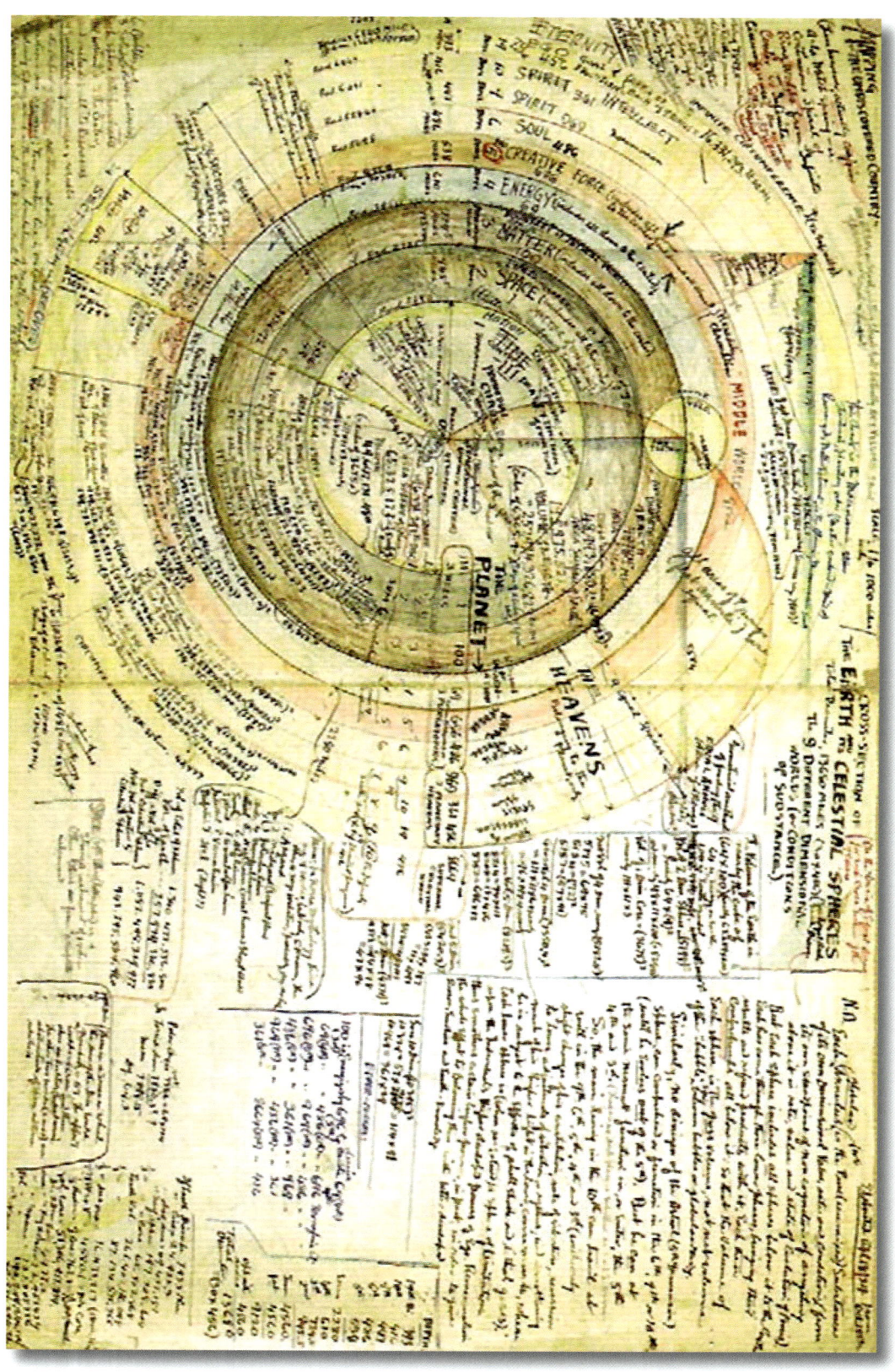

Planet, Heavens

Devine math, drawn through automatic writing
by Grant Wallace

photograph courtesy Brian Wallace

The Big Work

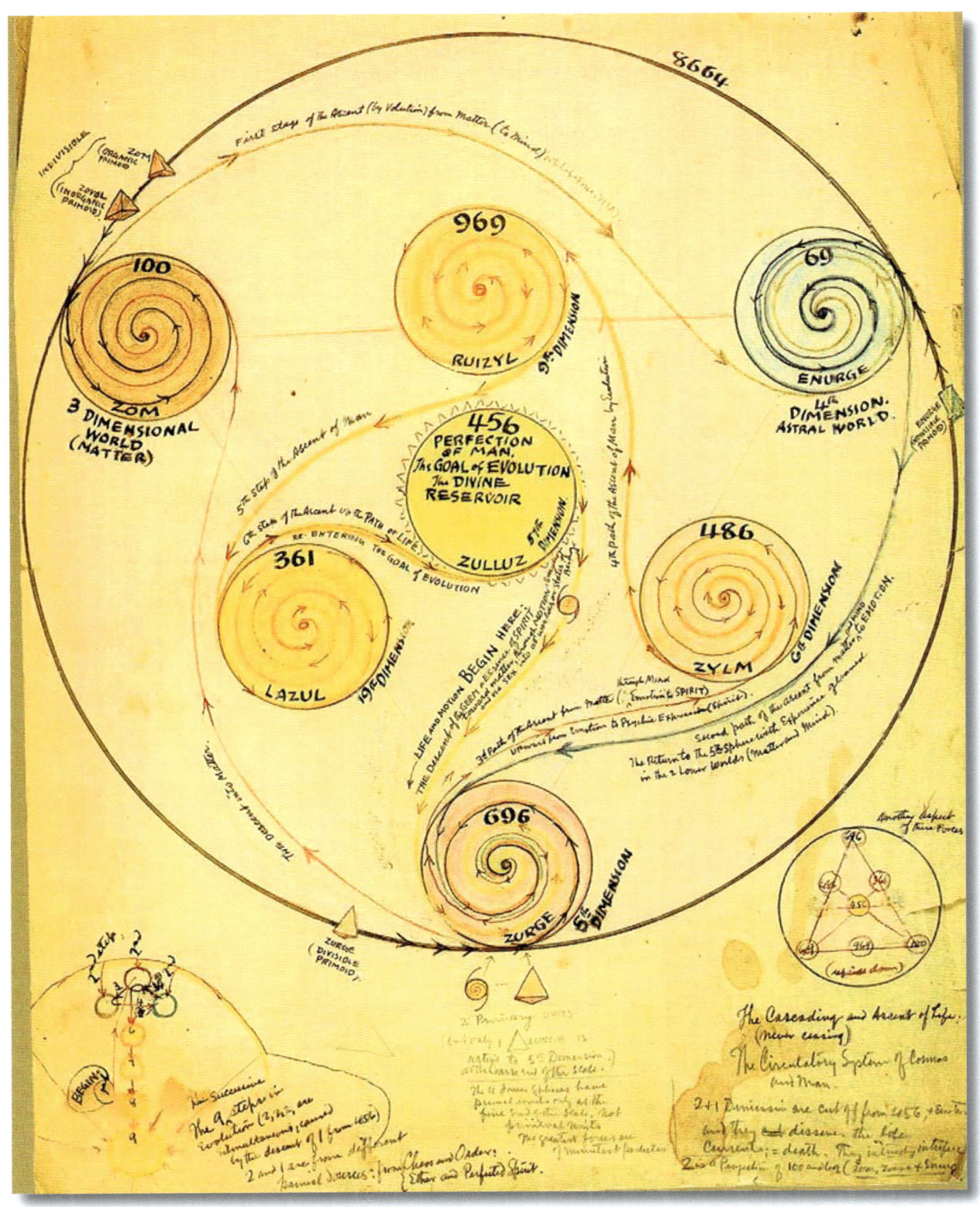

456, Perfection of Man

Divine math, drawn through automatic writing
by Grant Wallace

photograph courtesy Brian Wallace

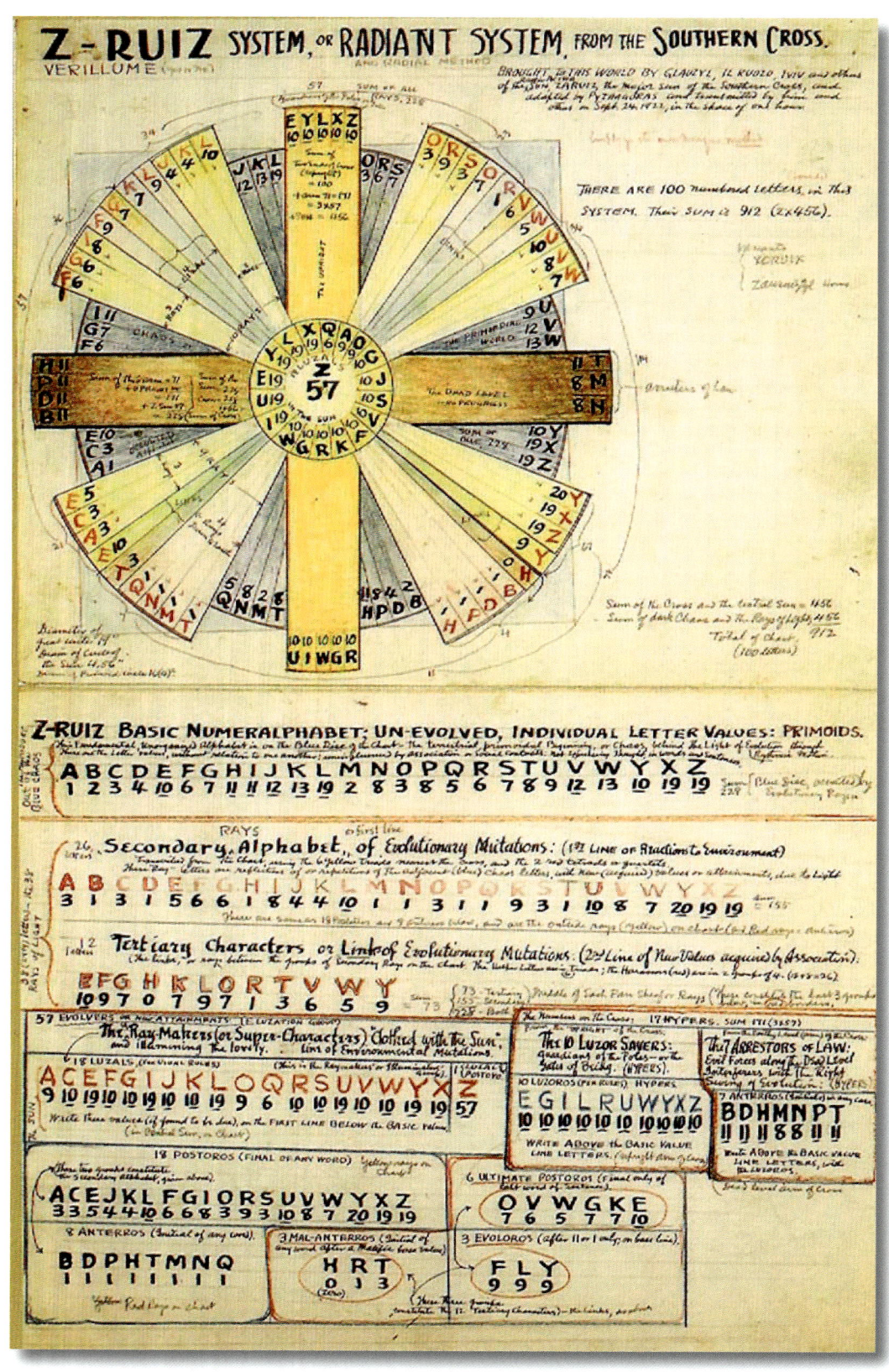

Z-Ruiz

Devine math, drawn through automatic writing
by Grant Wallace

photograph courtesy Brian Wallace

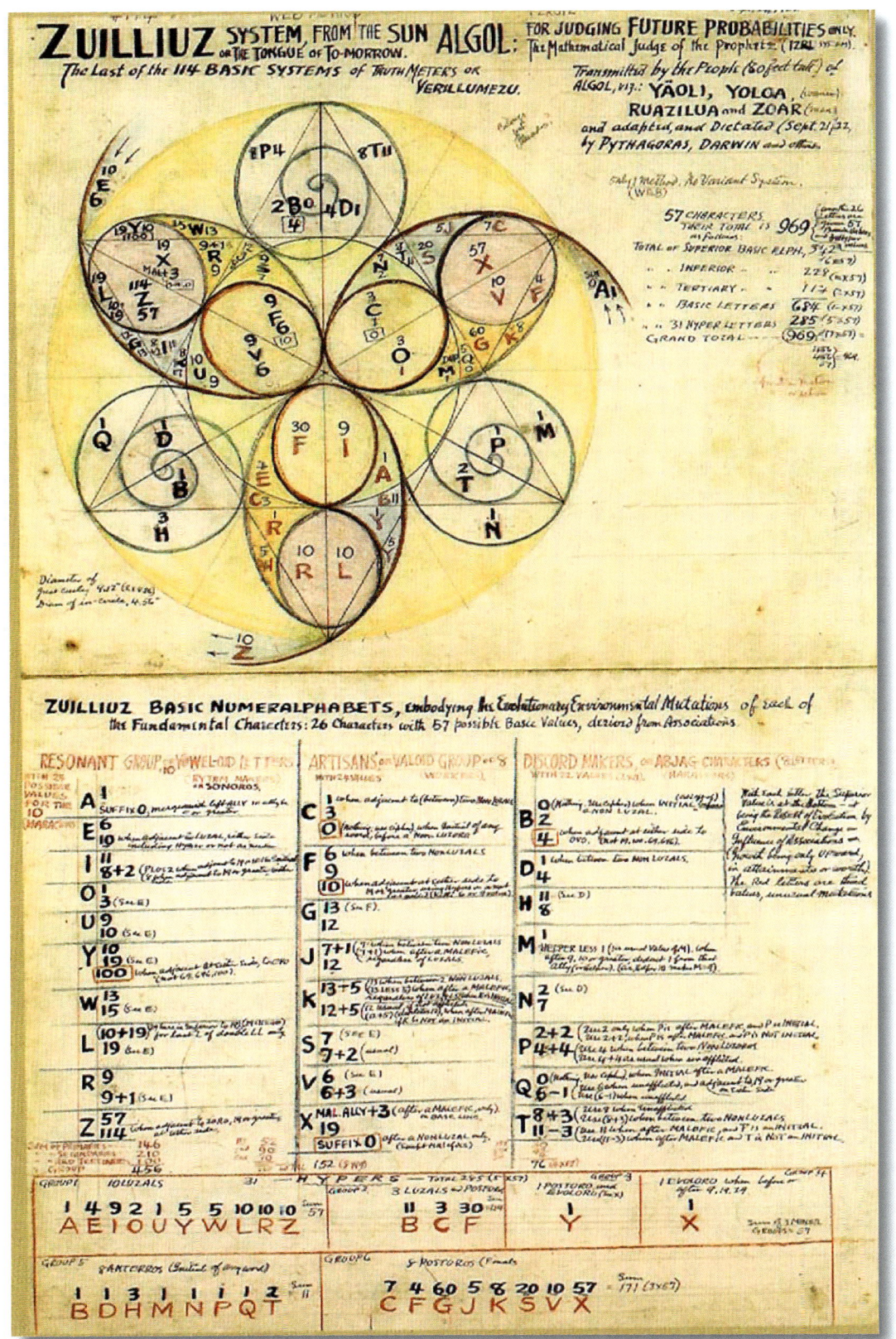

Zuilliuz

Devine math, drawn through automatic writing
by Grant Wallace

photograph courtesey Brian Wallace

nextdoor to a newer, smaller and less haunted looking cottage.

The Ranch was severely mortgaged, and Hessie needed help to outmaneuver the bank. Peggy was summoned, and for years thereafter devoted more and more time to saving the Ranch.

So the Ocean Avenue house became the exclusive domain for great periods of Moira and her bright young people and me.

But as the end of my junior year in high school approached, Moira was called away to San Francisco. She had applied for a WPA commission as one of the muralists to ornament the interior stairwell in Telegraph Hill's new Coit Tower.

Instead, Lucien Labaudt awarded the job to himself, including Moira as one of the famous personages depicted in the mural, and naming her queen of the year's major event in art circles, the Parilia Art's Ball at Dreamland Auditorium.

But other San Francisco commissions beckoned, and so it was decided to rent out the Ocean Avenue house, leaving my disposition for the summer to be worked out.

***

The issue of class allegiance was raised for the first time in our Bohemia when I returned to high school the next fall. Grant's old muckraking colleague, Lincoln Steffens, whole Grant unkindly referred to as Stinkin' Stuffins, had moved to town with his eager bride, Ella Winter, the passionate of the local new John Reed Society, much aroused to social consciousness.

The society condemned me as an enemy of the revolution for my romantic summer during the strike. This hurt, but not enough to keep me from sampling Steffens' Socratic youth seminar, when he asked a question to open our eyes to a new concept.

"Can you think of any motivating force other than many to work for in this world?" The old gentleman posed his riddle.

As a newcomer he couldn't realize he was addressing a Carmel generation brainwashed from infancy to regard money as no incentivize to anything, the only quest acceptable being from the good, true and beautiful.

He beamed at the silence. I couldn't bear the embarrassment of his springing his punchline himself, and let him off the hook by answering, with a straight face, "Personal satisfaction in doing something worthwhile?"

He was as astonished as he was crestfallen, but added gamely, "For the working class!"

Carmel was classless or, another way of putting it, an ideal aristocracy of mind and talent, which gave honorary status to wealthy patrons down for the summer or over from the mansions of Pebble Beach.

A detached analysis would have placed us with all quasi-religious magicians devoted to the arts as members of the entertainer class, and the rest as audience. It was all amiable and old shoe, however, and fame outside the town limits made little difference. Moira danced in her Bali Room equitably with the film star Ronald Colman or the lettuce king Tom Bunn.

At my pal Neil Weston's house, we thoughtlessly ate the green peppers and halved artichokes that his father, Edward, had so obsessively been rendering all day into photographs that would later on be revered by pilgrims from all over the world to the Museum of Modern Art in New York.

At Edward's parties, featuring nuts and raisins and bootlegged rotgut red wine from

Monterey — financed communally, since his $10 portraits yielded slight income — we rated his young admirer Angel Adams according to his original limericks, not the photography he was substituting for his concert piano career.

Because Ansel couldn't stand the idea of abandoning concert art for a field with no standing he began writing about photography as if it were acknowledged art, jimmied it into the Museums of Modern Art as an actual department, and lived to suffer imbecile criticism that sprang up to certify his success.

To be sure, he and his colleagues' prices rose as a result. And as another result, Edward's parsimony was elevated to art theory in such matters as eschewing both enlargements and cropping of his cheap old view camera's contact prints.

Edward couldn't afford modern darkroom equipment without hustling a little, and his life was devoted to dodging practical strenuosities.

I dabbled in photography in Edward's primitive darkroom, but my main creative output was and ever had been in the theater — Forest, Golden Gough, and other less stable stage enterprises. My big stage break occurred during finals week of my high school career. Because of cast changes, we had been in rehearsal four months at Denny-Waterhouse gallery for the American premiere of a stupefying Soviet "farce" called "Squaring the Circle," souped up as a musical, in which I wore false mustache to age my 16 summers in my leading role as husband to one mature actress and lover of another.

But I had the flu with a high temperature on opening night, and while I that morning received a scholarship to Reed College, I also knew I couldn't accept it, and besides I flunked my physics final that afternoon.

The flu interfered with my appetite for the head cheeses I had to wolf down in my starving scene before my main aria. The jolts of whiskey I was fed between scenes didn't help.

I was determined to retire from the theater while I was ahead. The reason I knew the Reed College scholarship was not for me was that the Pleiades people for once had a consensus with Grant and Peggy that the rest of Carmel's adult community, to the effect that higher education stultified creative effort, and postponed gainful employment helpful to the family as one searched for vocation.

It was true, my $5 per week from the library was not much help at stretching Miss Putnam's stipend, especially since I held out $1.50 of it for my fast life with Jeannie and her Pebble Beach set, drinking and dancing stylishly every Friday night in the sophisticated ambience of Bob Saunders' 16-piece band in Moira's luxe Bali Room.

Peggy said the law of eternal harmony was secretly guiding me to the greatness foretold by the Pleiades people, to carry on Big Work by some yet unexpected means, not necessarily requiring Grant to yield the work itself to my hands.

Meantime, I wasn't even ond enough to get hired in the Civilian Conservation Corps. The idea of becoming a great and inspirational novelist presented itself with the arrival of Moira's scene of an international ne'er-do-well named Peter Harnden. He was gathering experience for an autobiographical novel, and I decided to do the same He turned up with a chum named O'Crotty who first took the limelight, having by his account taken out his chagrin at being dropped as a Hollywood film writer in a drunken crap game, from which he rose to find in his pocket only the key to what proved to be and aged Rolls Royce tonneau in the parking lot.

With his first paycheck from a WPA road gang job, he bought several second-hand top-hats for his pick-and-shovel colleagues, whom he drove grandly with their lunch pails every noon to pass the social le hour at one of the Marx Brothers' Malibu pool.

The road was being constructed north up the coast from Malibu on cliffs terrain. O'Crotty, entrusted with placing the charge for a dynamite blast, guessed the amount high, blowing the whole project into the surf. So he came to Carmel.

Harnden had come from mismanaging a shady little nightclub on Capri featuring talent picked up in Munich's "Cabaret" atmosphere, where he had fled New Haven's obloquy, after getting tossed out of Yale. Harnden had great charm and no means of livelihood. He proposed to Moira right away, and left with O'Crotty on a wild goose chase after money in Berkeley.

Returning, their antique roadster collapsed on the highway near Gilroy. O'Crotty, who had a gun, ceremonially shot the car, and they were soon picked up by a Professor Raden, driving to Carmel to absorb the shock of having just been put in charge of the Northern California WPA Writers Project.

By the time they all arrived for dinner at our house, Raden was feeling much better, having agreed to hire Harnden and O'Crotty to run the project for him, and to put the rest of us on the payroll, providing Washington approved.

He phoned somebody in Washington on our bill, and found no more than one family member could be on the WPA role, and his budget didn't contemplate new deputies immediately either, but it was a nice dinner.

Moira was already on WPA doing murals for Monterey High School.

Deciding that Harnden had "strong eyelashes," she agreed to marry him. So as not to compromise his chances with the WPA, they decided to wed secretly, across the county line in the mission village of San Juan Bautista.

Grant was not notified, but Peggy arrived from The Ranch and I tried to distract her sentimental concern by walking her around the ruined mission, while Moira and Peter waited in the local saloon for the justice of the peace to be found. Harnden had lost our savings from the wedding feast in the pinball machine by the time a drunk snoozing at the bar was identified as the missing justice by an alert young drinker, who volunteered to be a witness.

After the license was retrieved from an Indian child who had rolled it into a megaphone, the justice married "you, Nora Walrus" to "you, Pete Hardened." The helpful witness returned to his newspaper office to put the glamours Carmel artist's secret wedding to the international socialite wires for all the WPA at home and San Francisco to see.

Somebody sent the happy couple a Stilton cheese from England. They poured wine into it daily, readying it for the great occasion when it would be carved, to make up for all the lentil soup. Nobody told me it was special. So there was hell to pay the afternoon Sam and Neil and I complained there had been nothing worth snacking on except that rotten cheese we'd forced ourselves to polish off.

Moore, who neither affirmed nor denied he was Edward VII's son by a Canadian Indian maid, had sold Long Island gentry mining stock along with polo lessons, and with the proceeds had built an immense mansion deep inside a mountainous estate off Carmel Valley, with loyal retainers at the gates to keep bill collectors at bay.

His stables were depleted and his creditors many, but the wild boar he'd imported, in memory of his pig-sticking youth in the Bengal Lancers, were fecund. Retainers grew his vegetables, the wine cellars were not yet dry, and the meat courses for Moore's hospitality were provided by means I was privileged to take part in, in a pickup truck piloted by a young relative of the laird's.

We simply drove off into the trackless forest until we spotted a ferocious looking wild boar, and expertly, pour le sport, ran over him.

But he was tough.

We drove home to find the sheriff had posted tax sale notices on our front oaks. Peggy was summoned.

Irene Putnam wrote to say she had to cancel the Big Work's $75-a-month stipend. Grant was summoned.

The house was put up for rent, and we were dispersed from halcyon Carmel to seek our fortunes in San Francisco's low-rent squalor. It was all great experience for our novels, everyone agreed.

SOCIETY COVETING INVITATIONS FOR FANTASTIC AFFAIR

By Cholly Francisco

NOW THAT the adjectives "weird" and "fantastic" have been attached to the Quatz Arts Ball to be held at Hotel Del Monte on April 28, there are many questions about who will obtain one of the coveted invitations. Mrs. Sidney Fish is one of the committee, which includes many of the distinguished writers and artists of the Monterey peninsula, and there will be a program which is being devised by leaders in the art colony of Carmel.

Others on the committee are Moira Wallace, whose murals for the Bali room at the hotel have attracted wide attention; Mrs. Helen Morgan, Jo Mora, Winsor Josselyn and many others.

✳ ✳ ✳

Presently, Moira took a studio in the loft of Ted Kuster's Golden Bough Theater downtown, conveniently equipped with a trapdoor into the theater auditorium's ceiling light system from which I saw many an early talkie for free.

When she was 21, Moira was awarded the job of reviving dear old Del Monte Hotel to splendor by painting 2,500 square feet of grill room wall with 85 giant figures and no end of lesser ones, gorgeous Balinese villagers and dancers in tempera and gold and silver leav, who did indeed make the Bali Room a distinguished landmark for the remainder of the nobel old hotel's career.

Moira did the whole job in two weeks and was established as a Northern California artist of considerable rank, in spite of all the confusing helpfulness that had been put in her path by cosmic forces and their agents.

***

The novel whose material I was gathering was necessarily more uplifting than the proletarian novels I was getting as models from the San Francisco library to read in my $5-a-month penthouse, part of the elevator housing on top of a rundown tenderloin apartment house, next door to the Alexander Hamilton Hotel and its luxe penthouse, occupied by the operat conductor Gaetano Merlot.

Though my first three jobs were menial they were the stuff dust jackets of the day doted on — "Mr. Wallace has worked as a hanger-up of misses' reads to wear coats, a draper's helper, and a department store carpeting stock-clerk and my evenings were free to escort Jeannie, whose mother had taken a house atop Russiian hill, to dance at the St. Francisco to Freddy Martin, slum at Izzy Gomez's, or attend her little friends birthday parties at St. Francisco Yacht Club in Harden's borrowed dinner jacket.

Moira transferred her WPA mural work from Carmel, and she and Peter lived in a picturesque ghetto attic, where they entertained art museum chums and hopeful dreamers like William Saroyan. Presently my influence at the Emporium got Harnden a job in notions, which seemed apt.

A small section of Moira's Bali Room mural was uncovered during renovation in the 1980s, but remains hidden in the storage closet of a dinning room at the Naval Post-Graduate School.

Moira Wallaces poses for the press showing off a section of her freshly painted Bali Room mural in the Ballroom of the S.F.B. Morse's Del Monte Hotel.

Novelists like John Dos Passos evidently came from backgrounds that found the Depression upsetting, but it hadn't made a grain of difference to us. Harden's sorest disappointment was that his ancient Packard touring car was built so solidly that, when it was rear-ended at top speed by a streetcar — demolishing the streetcar — it suffered not one iota of damage on which to demand insurance reparation money.

I progressed at the Emporium to the position of assistant production manager of the advertising department, meaning office boy. My duties were to carry copy proofs — lacking art cuts — of OKs by department buyers.

Naturally I doodled apt cartoons in the blank spaces where the art would later appear. In the space where a gorgeous coiffe was to appear over the Beauty Salon's grabber headline, "Men Always Notice a Woman's Hair," I scribbled the likeness of a bald man critically removing a long hair from his shoulder.

The buyer liked it and ordered me to ink it in. When it appeared in the Sunday Chronicle, it looked so good I was tempted to junk my career as a novelist for the more frivolous opportunity that seemed to have opened.

But there was my foretold destiny to deal with. I felt I had better go to college long enough to take a creative writing course.

The Emporium arranged with an affiliated Oakland department store, H.C. Capwell's, to give me after-school work as a package wrapper.

Peggy found a Berkeley rug dealer's garden cottage for us to rent.

I enrolled at the University of California, and found that the slick-paper student humor magazine, the Pelican, was hard up for cartoonists. I drew some in half-tone. When they appeared so perfect and shiny in print, I was indeed seduced towards superficiality as an attractive life goal.

However, my creative writing classes were earnest and grim. I diligently stuck to Big Work as my fate, but cartooned on the margins.

Department store package wrapping requires a knack I lacked. On Christmas Eve I was fired.

I put off taking the disaster seriously until New Year's morning, when the atmosphere of reckoning told me the law of eternal harmony showed no signs of coming up with anything. I asked myself what skills I had to put to work, but my mind wandered to thoughts of the new San Francisco-Oakland Bay Bridge, and I absently wrote:

> Said a profligate son of our city
> I think I should warn some committee
> The bridge on the bay
> Is bound to decay
> Said his wife, "But I think it is pretty."

The verse prompted a satirical cartoon, and I faced the fact that my only gift was for the irrelevant.

That being the case, I quickly composed a dozen more topical limericks, illustrated them, and set about visiting the Bay area's newspaper offices, proposing them for a daily feature of news commentary and evasion.

Each paper sent out a copy boy to identify himself as managing editor and advise me to go to Fresno for ten years and come back when I had some experience. Out of my former colleagues at the Emporium told me I was going about things the wrong way.

"It's not what but who you know," he said, adding that he would seek a note of introduction for me from his father, a broker who had once employed an apprentice now risen

The Big Work

mw.0003
Self Portrait
by Moira Wallace
c. 1928—1931
Pencil on Paper

Signed by artist
Framed, Good Condition

to the eminence of boy wonder editor of the Chronicle, Paul C. Smith.

I returned to the Chronicle with the letter to find the receptionist gone and the door marked "Editor" ajar. Inside I found a short scrubby-haired office boy, as I thought when I forcefully stated my business, though he turned out to be the wonder editor himself, too new at the work to know how to get rid of so positive and towering a talent without hiring me.

So my column began on the front page in the space vacated by Will Rogers' untimely death in a plane crash. The column gradually drifted further back into the paper, and out the other end, but not before I had seriously compromised my taste for high destiny by enjoying the fruits of trivial enterprise.

As a severe classmate told me, "It seems like a frivolous way to make a living."

The only defense I could offer was that its hours gave me a chance to go out for freshman crew and overturn sculls in the Oakland Estuary every afternoon.

In the evening I would phone the Chronicle's night city editor for a subject likely to still be Newley for another day, and if need be to explain it to me. This I would reduce to imbecility in line and verse, run down to mail it at the post office, call on varied friends, and at bedtime start my homework.

The Daily Cal and Carmel Pine Cone and Cymbal wrote me up, and I found celebrity status acceptable, except for the pay. I had been promised $20 a week but was getting $17.25 — enough, at that, to disqualify my family for the compassion of the WPA, which accordingly fired Grant, liberating him back full time to the Pleiades people and their math.

He had taken the WPA like other interruptions with philosophical equanimity, but he was fed up with writing the biographies of such old colleagues as Maynard Discon for the archives, and was glad to get back to stir up the astral.

When Time Magazine quoted one of my limericks, I was emboldened to seek out editor Smith and casually ask him if I could have a raise back to my promised $20. I didn't mention Time, only my family's excessive needs, but he wasn't fooled. He fired me on the spot.

I countered by preparing a sample 'city' column based on the New Yorker's Talk of the Town. He said San Francisco wasn't big enough for a city column.

Later that year, fearing radio's ascendant competition, the San Francisco papers discontinued their radio columns, but the Chronicle's radio columnist, Herb Caen, was too popular to die, so he was given the job of city columnist, and is still doing it just as if San Francisco were big enough to handle it.

Smith told my Emporium friend's broker father, "Wallace had promise until Time quoted him and he got too big for his britches."

The publisher of the Chronicle's rival Hearst Examiner told my sister at a dinner party, "Tell your brother to see my city editor." He put me to work as a reporter with split days off, so I could continue UC classes while becoming at ease with cops, bodies, holocausts, and — what rapidly became my specialty — freaky little events involving wayward people and animals.

"Wait, I'll turn you over to many freak writer," my city editor would often introduce me on the phone before transferring a call to me. He meant no unkindness, but didn't explain the usage either.

Moira, meantime, was getting good mural and fresco commissions and Harden took a

Celebrated Mural in San Francisco Home a Moira Wallace Creation

MOIRA WALLACE claims the distinction of being the first white child born in Carmel. Research tends to support the legend, as most other contemporary moppets were more conventionally ushered into the world of art through the Monterey Hospital. Her parents, Grant Wallace, noted writer, artist and war correspondent, and Margaret Wallace, visited the poet, George Sterling one week-end and were immediately transformed into permanent Carmelites, an incurable state of mind known to haunt its victims to the four corners of the globe and return them to Ocean avenue.

Miss Wallace studied with Fred Gray and Armin Hansen in Monterey and with Maurice Sterne and Frederic Taubes in San Francisco. Although her interest is primarily in mural decoration she has also devoted a good deal of time to portrait painting and has exhibited at the San Francisco Museum of Art and the de Young Memorial Museum. In 1932 she painted the murals for the Bali room in the Del Monte Hotel, impressive examples of her art which were so successful that they were never removed. Another 360 foot mural was added in 1941.

Other of her murals are in the homes of Lady Thomas Hughes in Atherton; Mrs. George Oppen in San Francisco and the Prosperpine mural is in the Neutra designed house of Mr. Sidney Jahn in San Francisco.

Page Sixty-two

vaguely genteel post with some kind of stock brokerage, and advised artists and writers of Moira's acquaintance on how to do things right.

They took a pretty little house with a fireplace and garden on the muddy brink of a Telegraph Hill cliff, overlooking the berthed ships and the Embarcadero switch engine that in those days blew smoke rings.

Out at The Ranch, Peggy contracted with a man who ran Filipino crews to pick tomatoes in the creek flats. Hessie, who had a regular supply of hired men who fell off freight trains rounding the bend by the clam beach, acquired a former Mr. America, authenticated by a scrapbook he carried.

The championship training had strained his brain, and though he was not astute, he was light of foot. He often crept up behind jackrabbits, and placed the muzzle of Pete's shogun an inch from their pelts before blasting them into what amounted to lead-shot beanbags, which he then delivered proudly to the kitchen door.

There was a strike at the Emporium and other big advertisers' retail stores, curtailing newspaper revenue, so I was fired.

I was momentarily downcast. There seemed grounds to suspect the Pleiades people's prophecy for me had been working itself out prematurely, and in reverse. Coming from a psychic childhood in what amounted to retirement in Carmel, I had started as a front page columnist at 18, progressed to reporter's work, and was down and out at 19.

But the optimistic if misunderstood messages of "Candide" and Ecclesiastes remained with me, and sure enough I was back at work in the city room in a few days, thanks to the last of eternal harmony and also a quick settlement by the store clerks.

Far off in Tunis, where she was writing an article on Jung, Peter's divorcee mother died, leaving him $50,000. Peter Pequot sundries and notions, took a gentleman's post as unsalaried stockbroker rep, bought San Francisco's first low-slung, right-hand-drive, rollback-proof Standard Swallow, familiarly Stinking Sparrow, and drove Moira and me to the Sierra Club's pioneering Sierra summit ski lodge as guests of Madge Saunders.

The lodge was primitive and lacked lifts. Moira learned to herringbone up the practice slopes to the top, where she sensibly removed her skis and carried them down again.

We took a cross-country tour over a far ridge. On a straight and level meadow, Madge stepped in a soft patch and wrenched her knee.

A pretty little muffin named Helen who accompanied us volunteered to ski back to the lodge to get the stretcher-sled patrol. I told her to borrow a camera for me while she was at it, the opportunity being perfect for me to file a story and picture to the Examiner about my hostess Madge, headlined "Bay Socialite Saved from Snowy Death on Remote Peak."

Helen, dazzling skier, returned with the patrol but no camera. "It would have reflected badly on the Sierra Club whose guest you are," she said in a light and musical voice, with a look of such radiantly gentle reproof that I was spellbound. Here at last was the girl in the world too good for me.

She rarely spoke thereafter, but her brightly grieving eyes were eloquent as I pursued her in the months and years ahead. They were eyes that spoke of wonders only rarely expressed in words, as the first time I kissed their owner, in my second-hand Willys after a movie, and she drew back, gazed at me, and said movingly, "I don't think I love you."

They were eyes to inspire Big Work, and I

Kevin Wallace
by Moira Wallace
c. 1925—1931
Portrait of her Brother.
Oil Paint on Canvas

Signed by artist
Framed, Poor Condition

summoned them to mind in the city room, where — between freak stories and sorties out to inspect murders, suicides, fires and eager celebrities —I spent the long hours typing a finer kind of writing for creative writing class.

It was vibrant, understated, in the prevailing mood of Hemingway's "Hills Like White Elephants." Helen fitted in as though made for the current style.

My best friend, Mac, wrote a more blustery, passion-racked prose, his life being modeled after Jack London's, including his summer seafaring for tuition.

It irked him that I had gone to sea at a younger age than he. It annoyed him that I got paid for prostituting a writer's sacred talents. But he was irritated stylishly, and could sincerely respond to any complaints I might venture, "Why don't you shoot yourself."

Mac's influence too inspired Big Work, and so did the frantic interplay of passions among all 12 young geniuses in Professor Lehman's writing seminar. I wrote a fraudulent memoir of a night surfing in Carmel Bay, so inspired it won a $25 prize in Whit Burnett's and Martha's Fole's unimaginable prestigious little Story magazine.

This triumph piled on all the others — of employment, love, friendship, everything — was too much for me. I felt I had advanced beyond my artistic means, and should refrain from writing more until I knew what I had to say. Having something to say was absolutely necessary to serious fiction, everyone at school agreed. The Pleiades people's expectations of me added to the urgency.

An opportunity to return to the state eluded me. Interviewing Alfred Lunt and Lynn Fontanne on one of their frequent roadshow arrivals in town, I was surprised when Miss Fontanne seized my chin, tilted my face up to the light, and asked "Can you act?"
"No," I said, enacting false modesty too convincingly.

"Too bad," she and Mr. Lunt both said, and went on with the interview, hiring their juvenile replacement the next week in Hollywood.

Story forgot to print my prize-winner. So after a year or two, I got a vacation ride with a professor and his wife to New York, where I presented myself to Burnett and Miss Foley in their untidy office. My name wasn't familiar to them, but they crawled around opening low cupboards, found my manuscript, and like the sounds of honor they seemed, printed my winner a few months later.

I still couldn't decide what more I had to say, a fact I endlessly dilated on to the serene-eyed Helen. After some months she interrupted my self absorbed monologue to say we shouldn't see each other anymore — an announcement she repeated every year or so, resulting in a more or less seasonal round of absences, reconciliations, and resumptions of my monologue.

Harnden's newfound opulence led him to drag Moira back to Carmel for what turned out to be his pursuit by a seedy heiress known variously as Midu or Mildew, whose playwright husband meantime pursued a substantial local attorney's bride.

Harden succumbed to Mildew's blandishments — and the lawyer's wife to Mildew's consorts — at the same time that a British lady houseguest was quarantined with chickenpox in Moira's rented house. A drummer from a jazz band, left over from a party the night before, also turned up on the couch, and was advised he was quarantined too.

The two adulterous couples had meantime left, the consort eventually turning up in Yugoslavia, and Harden in Mexico City, outraged at word that Moira had gone to Nevada to divorce him.

At Gold Hill, adjacent to Virginia City, Moira put in her six weeks as one of many interesting houseguests of the Mizner brothers' niece Skippy Hollins.

The group frequented the great ghost town's Bucket of Blood saloon, with a genial drunken priest who was forgetful about zipping his fly.

When word of the priest's excommunication one day circulated through the saloon, Moira asked, "Does that mean they turn his collar around?"

"In his case," Skippy said, "They turn his pants around."

Another houseguest was a dapper refugee Baron Waltham "Vava" von Scoeler, who mysteriously dug mummy bundles out of the Andes and sold them to American museums. Vava persuaded Moira that after Harnden's tempestuous jealousy of her talent, she needed a calm and supportive husband. So the same judge that granted her divorce cleared his voice and married her to Vava.

They went to New York, where in the St. Moritz Vava suddenly began trying to hurl himself out the window and, when Moira

protested, beating her up. She returned to Telegraph Hill for an annulment and resumed painting in the more moderate environment of just herself and her easel.

News Boy Wonder
Sketching history at the *San Francisco Chronicle* and *Examiner*

In 1939, I was meantime heavily involved in two contrasting endeavors, one frivolous, one big. My frivolous task was the Examiner's daily column from the 1939 World's Fair — the Golden Gate International Exposition on Treasure Island, in the middle of San Francisco Bay, where my work involved J. Edgar Hoover, lost tourists, and similar insustantialities for which my freak-story style was well suited.

Unlike their stoic, world-flattening efficiently stereotyped news writing styles — or their alternative exalting too-sensitive fancy styles, in which they dream of writing on day their novel of woeful existence in a dire world — city room employees talk in a style often mistaken as cynical, but actually an art form of some importance, for its gently Larry leveling of values, to make the world a kaleidoscope of Emperor's-New-Clothes variations.

It was the tone I adopted for freak stories and columns, and I was innocent enough to think it unimportant. Because my fairgrounds office held open houses for visiting newspaper people and free booze constantly arriving from concessionaires, I couldn't start writing and drawing until they went home at 1 a.m., and generally drove home to Berkeley.

This conflicted with my morning classes, so at the end of my junior year, I deferred my finals and took leave of absence, which is still in effect. That gave me more time to brood on my big project. It involved my recognition of a topic on which I had something to say, the impending Second World War.

Self Portrait
by Kevin Wallace
c. 1939
KW

Signed by artist; Dated by Artist
Unframed; Fair Condition

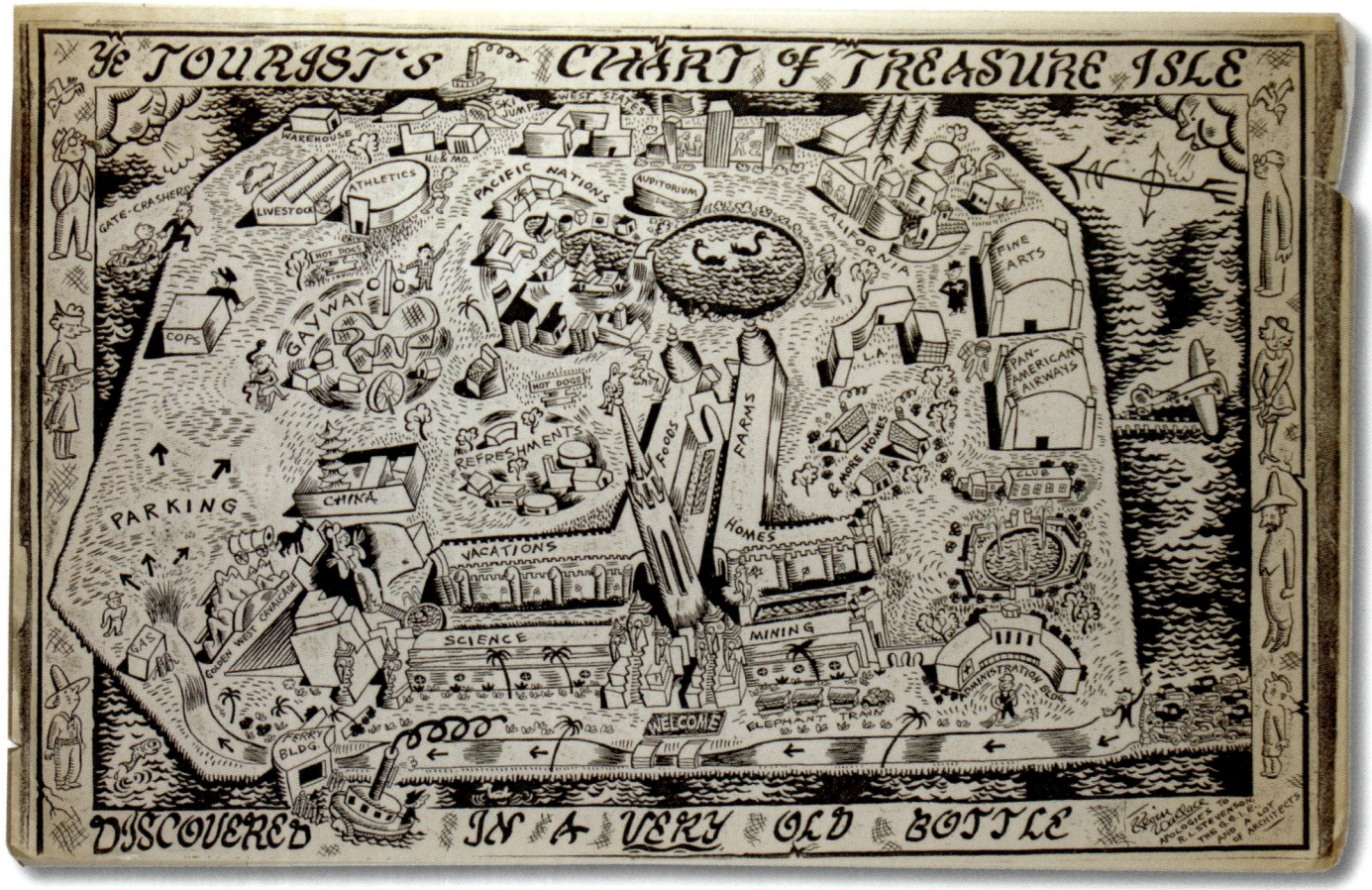

Initially, all I had to say on the subject was "Don't."

I was opposed to war on principle. I had absorbed Grant's battlefield stories and the World War writers' subsequent verifications. At 12 I had joined Sam and Neil in declaring conscientious objector status should anything come up. The Pleiades people's promise of a good time on the Other Side wasn't convincing enough to warrant risking anybody shooting at me.

Too, a war could interfere with my already tardy schedule of finding and doing my Big Work. I aimed my big guns at the war threat. I influenced the cosmic ether to prevent war breaking out. A gentleman named Dr. Troward "Edinburgh Lectures on Mental Science" (1911) enlarged the Coue method in this regard. I could concentrate on looking out at the world around me and see it, actually see it, as the projected contents of my own receptor-brain. It was dizzying, better than lying on my back on the Campanile lawn and watching the bell tower hurtle past the stationary clouds, as I forced myself to perceive the relationship.

Hitler invaded Poland and war in Europe began. Clearly I'd done something wrong. The fair ended and I was assigned a nightlife column. It rewarded me with the companionship of a warm-hearted lady press agent for the Palace Hotel's Rose Room named Ruth, or "Woos," and occasional literary discussions at her table with Herb Caen, Bill Saroyan and the bandleader whose band was thrashing away without his clarinet solos as he absorbed our pointers on achieving his real ambitions to write, Artie Shaw.

In exhorting Shaw to improve himself by writing, I saw I was really exhorting myself. I must prevent America's — my — involvement in the war through fine writing! I hastened to my typewriter.

My next effort to circumvent World War II was a reasoned proof that war is illogical —

and so must be discouraged — and epistemology, on top of all the standard physics and biology and the rest of the cosmological stuff so familiar to obsessional neurotics and publishers of arcane books explaining too much heavy reading. My sermon's text, drawn from Sir James Fraser's Golden Bough. The inference of his writing was that modern war could derive only from a mistaken theory of the human value system. For there wasn't a publication around that wasn't arguing the matter on the non-Pleiadean and merely public spirited grounds. There was none with any use for my self-centered view, that losing one's life for a good cause or for a poor one or none at all interferes equally with one's prospects, and what good is a cause you can't live to enjoy?

However, for different public minded reasons, both the isolations and Communists opposed President Roosevelt's machinations to embroil the United States in the European imbroglio — the Communists owing to Russia's current alliance with Hitler.

I knew no isolationist but did know Communists, and had been cool to their importuning — partly because I was annoyed about the John Reed Club's attitude toward my adventuring, and partly because they were generally a little dreary.

But it seemed an opportune time to open my mind, so I accepted the loan of a brown-paper-wrapped Communist primer from a radical reporter friend, and read it enthusiastically in the office, removing its plain-wrapper disguise for convenience. The book's horrified owner waited for me on the street to retrieve the compromised document, and was cool to my requests for further schooling in his cell.

I asked a Communist professor of my acquaintance to help me out — he had once mourned over my "Don Juan complex" interfering with my dropping everything to volunteer for the Spanish War's Lincoln Brigade – but news of my revolutionary instability evidently traveled fast, and he changed the subject.

So I wrote a letter of simple protest to my friend Ted Cook, who duly published it in his rather odd column in the Hearst papers, Cook-Coos.

The Pleiades people announced they had finally got the bugs out of the Truthmeter, and Grant used it to verify information brought by his late brother Milton from private sources in the Great Beyond. These data stated that Willkie would beat Roosevelt for the Presidency, and America would avoid involvement in the war.

On Election Day, Grant sent Willkie the heartening news and his congratulations. The next day, the crestfallen Pleiades people took the Truthmeter back to the drawing board, and I resumed work on my cosmology, proving beyond a doubt that the individual is quite right to prefer himself to any cause.

As to those in favor of America's entry into the war, my old acquaintances the Lunts' came to town with a pro-entry propaganda play called "There Shall Be No Night." They had thrown themselves heart and soul into their roles and messages, and dripped resolve from every pore. They were also helplessly dear people, and dealt fondly with me when I arrived to interview them – I was by that time the Examiner's drama and film editor and critic, owing to my predecessor having tried to allude in print to Olson Welles' "Citizen Kane," which my employer suspected was about him.

"What's that painting under your arm?" The Lutzs wanted to know.

"Just something I'm taking to get wrapped to mail to Time Magazine to see if they want

Kevin worked the late-night shift sketching illustrations for the *San Francisco Examiner*, earning extra work after his editor received a pair of Western Union Telegrams from their boss, William Randolf Hearst.

The Big Work

it for a cover — nothing really." I said, in fact not eager to assault their sensibilities with a grim anti-war propaganda work of mine.

They insisted on seeing it, and being incapable of suspecting treachery of a friend, they simply failed to grasp its meaning, instead asking how they could be of help. "Mr. Ochsner still does own The Times Magazine, doesn't he?"

"Not The Times — Time Magazine," I corrected.

"Time Magazine," Alfred Lutz recited the sounds, as if to test them for any hint of meaning.

"Who owns Time Magazine?" Lynn Lutz demanded.

"Henry Luce," I said, and stood spellbound at the classiness with which Lynn and Alfred cried in credulous delighted unison, "Does HENRY own TIME?"

Out at The Ranch, the delivery boy, Jimmy Silva, entered to find Hessie deep in thought over a document at the kitchen table.

"I'm glad you came in, Jimmy," said Hessie. "I'm revising my will and I've decided to leave The Ranch to you."

"Oh, Mrs. Garrett, you mustn't do that," Jimmy said politely.

"Very well," Granny said, "I won't."

A new hired man was deposited by the train rounding the bend by the clam bench. He was an old cockeyed Indian chief from Virginia named George, with one tooth, a front upper. Sometimes he stood motionless for half an hour at a time and Hessie would hiss "Look, there's George with his ear to the ground."
He was reclusive, but Hessie eavesdropped outside his shed at night and heard him talking to himself in two voices, one gruff and one falsetto.

Gruff voice: "Then what'll you do after you've strangled the old lady?"

Falsetto voice: "I'll chop her in little pieces."

Hessie left the next day for Calistoga Hot Springs to think it over in the baths. While there, she got a call from the Contra Costa county sheriff's office, which seemed relieved to find she was alive.

"The neighbors spotted George brandishing a butcher knife and yelling on your Porch," the deputy said, "and when we arrived, George was gone but your furniture was all tossed around, and we couldn't find you anywhere."

I took Woos to a cast party after I'd turned in my review and was struck when the leading lady who had been sitting with the juvenile, let him up to Woos, said "I'll trade you," and asked me to drive her home. She was old for me — 24, older by a year — and twice divorced yet, young at heart, name of Doris.

 We drove to Guadalajara, a fishing village up the lonely coast road with an atmosphere and jolly bearded bartender. After the show left town, she phoned from New York to say she would take the ingenue's role in a play Katherine Cornell planned to rehearse and open in San Francisco. I was touched.

My friend Mac, a Navy ROTC officer, was called up by the Navy. The day he left for his gunboat in Seattle, we both knew there would be a war and he would be killed. It was a day of portent. That night I took a hike in the clear cold full moon's light on top of Grizzly Peak behind Berkeley, and cased the world from the Trowardian perspective, sharpened by the presentiment of worldwide holocaust, and of the doom of youthful talent, which I could more readily identify with. On the other hand, it seemed more than likely I would be spared, owing to my foretold obligation to write the cosmic work. "I will live my life and do my work," I suggested to the receptive universe.

The next morning, the radio brought the news of the bombing of Pearl Harbor while I was reading Flash Gordon in the Sunday funnies.

***

My impression was that the long anticipated entry into the war was anti-climatic and in fact relatively cozy and familiar, and certainly interesting. It was too bad about Mac and his unfulfilled gift for writing wild, moody, poetic fiction. Still, better him than me.

In fact, Mac patrolled the Artic for the next several war-torn years without incident, and I see in the National Geographic that he is busy writing and photographing his adventures of the Andes and into the rainforest even as I write.

Hessie, loathed to be at The Ranch should George reappear, took an apartment in Berkeley next door to a shabby new co-op dorm, whose idealistic students were trying to get a little shrubbery to grow. "Hashi-hashi," Hessie snorted at the bedraggled greenery. Communists!"

She became acquainted quickly around the Telegraph Avenue business district, and Peggy was intrigued one day to note Hessie hauling her across the street from a shoe store bankruptcy auction, looking furtively the other ways as she scuttled along. The bankrupt shoe man spotted her and Peggy heard him wail at Hessie, "There goes the woman who could have saved me if she would!"

"I barely know the man," Hessie muttered indignantly.

Doris returned to rehearse and open with Katherine Cornell in "Rose Burke," and awful new play by the noted French auther, Henri Bernstein, whose attempts to pinch her kapok falsies led us on a fruitless quest for rubber falsies that would toot when pinched, quest joined in by the productions juvenile, Jean-Pierre Aumont, who we taught English pronunciation to as we went along.

Doris favored low dives and smoky black jazz joints. We terminated the play's engagement with a drive to Palm Springs and a quarrel which produced from me a first-class poem, ending it all on a positive note for literature.

I gave the Troward method a whirl again in hopes of influencing the cosmos to persuade a sensational ingenue from Billie Burke's "Vinegar Tree" company to my will. But her mother in Los Angeles had warned Eleanor about drama critics and other menaces she would meet on the road, and the cosmos and I lost a lot of sleep and patience in my parked

Camouflaged Sandbags—But Not for 'Sandman'

Mrs. Guthrie Courvoisier, San Francisco, Calif., empties sand out of a new type of sandbag which looks like a comfortable cushion. It has two carrying handles and stitching around the top which rips out, spilling contents to extinguish incendiary bombs. Her husband distributes them.

convertible at scenic overlooks, as Eleanor repeated, "But you're really sweet."

Eleanor remained unyielding when I took her to the great hustler-tended Sunday routs at the swimming pool of Moira's friends, the Englehardts, next door to Eugene O'Neill's place in Alamo, even though I apologized about their being rich and idle.

It was at the Engelhardts' that Moira married Guthrie, an amiable inventor who reluctantly ran San Francisco's best art gallery, hoping to save the family name by paying off the gallery mortgages incurred by his late, too frequently married father. Guthrie abhorred the chicanery of high class art dealerships, and adored everything about Moira except her painting career.

He was delighted when America's entry into the war put the gallery out of business — wood for the mainstay framing business became unavailable. He invented a hassock-sandbag for fighting firebombs. Then he and Duke Engelhardt commenced making plastic nose cones for bombers instead.

They put up with Moira painting now and again but yearned for the day she could learn bookkeeping.

Oil was struck at The Ranch, Standard oil, leaking from a pipe in a right-of-way and flowing down Garrett Creek to Quong Chang's clam bed, terminating the clams' tenancy.

A faculty friend found us a freshly graduated lawyer who lost our clam-damage suit against Standard Oil but won a job in Standard Oil's prestigious law firm. This was a silver lining for our fond faculty friend, who shared with his wife a curiously academic conversational heaviness. Moira spent an unaccustomedly solemn evening with them and complained afterwards to me, "Your friends are really terribly nice, but they're not very superficial."

My draft number crept closer.

My revised cosmological treatise now ascertained conclusively that evolution's tendency was towards perfecting complex organisms capable of persisting in spite of environmental disturbance. This proved I would be a fool to give up my complex persistence in my current state, no matter the world's urging to self-sacrifice. In line with this, the boss of the new Officer of War Information phoned to offer me a draft-exempt job in his San Francisco office.

I shared my delightful news with the Examiner's managing editor, and prognathous-jawed

Carousel No. 1
by Moira Wallace
c. 1937
Oil on Canvas. One in a series.

Signed by artist
Unframed; Good Condition

Pablo (Duck) Picasso
by Philip Klein
c1937
Left over from the Courvoisier Gallery inventory. Klein was known
at the time as the "Donald Duck clean-up artist" at Walt Disney Studios

Signed by artist; Notated by artist
Unframed; Fair Condition

96

**A La Conference
and Paris Ville Du Front**
Unknown Artist
c1937

Paris street life. Left over from the Courvoisier Gallery inventory.

Signed by artist; Notated by artist
Unframed; Good Condition

tyrant in a beetle-green eyeshade, who ate rather than smoked three cigars a day, and was widely respected as the most cynical minion of Mr. Hearst's empire.

He startled me by denouncing my whole generation as unpatriotic backsliders. "You're why France fell!" He snarled.

His unexpected lack of generosity stung me to overhasty retaliation. I went down to the Ferry Building and took revenge by enlisting as a Naval aviation cadet. I was given three months to wrap up my affairs and report for training.

Affairs aside, I took a hundred-mile solitary trudge through the timberline Sierra above Yosemite, pausing at one point to drop the ashes of an acquaintance off a cliff according to her will's instructions. I carried pen and paper in case a Big Work should strike in the thin air. None did.

***

Moira, who patriotically consented to take over as my Examiner critic upon my impending departure, was doing some paintings of the dancer Katherine Dunham whose large and hungry troupe was stranded in town, hoping to resist the blandishments of Sol Murkok's mismanagement. Katherine said I didn't look very coordinated for a fighter pilot and insisted I join her classes in authentic voodoo shimmy and grinds.

I don't know that they helped, though they were surely picturesque, and gave a new meaning to the aviation phrase, "he flew by the seat of his pants."

On induction, I was to go to a Navy pre-flight school, preferably at the dear old Del Monte Hotel, where the Bali Room had become the gym, with basketball hoops artistically placed on the bosoms of Moira's generous native maidens, until a barbaric chaplain had the murals whitewashed over. But the pre-flight schools were all full, so my class was shipped to something called a pre-pre-flight school, where we learned to fly first after all.

These operations were contracted to civilian teachers and since civil flying was forbidden within 200 miles of the coast, they were located in the high Sierras. Mine inhabited the dilapidated ghost town called Beckwourth at the headwaters of the Feather River. The snow-covered landing fields altitude was 5024 feet, 24 feet above our flimsy little ski-borne Aeronca monoplanes' service ceiling. The actual way to get airborne was to take off into the updraft against an adjacent mountain and hope to complete the required maneuvers before settling inexorably back to ground level, on the field, one hoped.

After a while the snow melted, our skis, which gave the forward garage of the takeoff and landing runs a deceptive simplicity, were replaced with wheels, which could and did have a nasty way of crimping and precipitating ground-loops in the mud.

I had brought along my own not-much-loved skis for show, and was much respected by my shack-mates, not because I was the only critic among them, but because I was so elderly — 24 to their 18 — and crazily courageous to think I could still compete in a young man's game.

I came down with a slight cold, known in Navy parlance as cat fever, and was put away in the hospital of the nearest town for two weeks, until my temperature settled firmly at normal. Thus I missed eight obligatory pre-solo days of flying with my instructor, Jay, who in real life had been assistant managers of a Market Street theater I had frequently reviled in print, the Warfield.

Since the contractors' pay depended on the bodies they ran through on schedule, Jay

The South Pacific
by Kevin Wallace
1939
First White Woman on the Island

No artist signature; Notated by artist
Unframed; Good Condition

gave me all eight days' training and sent me off to solo in one big super-day. The solo flight was a simple takeoff, circling the field, and landing. On the way around, I neglected to notice the wind-sock register a shift of wind. I cut power to land and was surprised to find myself floating into a classroom shed. I shoved the throttle forward to go around for another approach.

It was as I was about to collide with the classroom's ridge pole that it struck me I hadn't shoved the throttle far enough. I repaired the oversight, hopped the first of the two power lines fencing the adjacent highway, and took a straight and level course between them.

I tried to remember how night I was supposed to get to bail out and open my parachute. The desired detail was getting from between the power lines to an updraft in order to get that high. Luckil;y the road approached a mountain and I began to rise. I soared, and decided to give the runway a last chance. As it turned out, the crosswind subsided and I came in fine.

But the experience cause me to review the consequences of my revenge on my managing editor for slighting my desire to stay on earth to do my Big Work. The prospect of actually flying a plane towards targets that would shoot at me was not one I could envisage.

In the meantime I learnt all my aerial maneuvers except the mandatory solo tail-spin-and-recovery. I was reluctant to stall my plane into a nosedive, and let it groundward out of my personal controls for three turns before I was allowed to pull it out. It would have the upper hand far too long. I declined to give it the chance.

Jay logged me as having performed this necessary task anyway, but referred me on to secondary pre-pre-flight school beside the Rockies at the University of Colorado in Boulder.

He and I had a farewell afternoon drink at the local saloon, and several more, and in the dusk stumbled back to the field and took up my miserable little Aeronca. He encouraged me in buzzing barns, chasing a logging train and dispersing its plume of steam, and even in several spins, which he said I did just fine. "Very relaxed," he said. "We landed by last light somehow.

Presently I was rotated back to an interval of stateside duty at San Francisco's Joint Ocean Air Traffic Control Center, and found the home front swinging.

Everybody was giving parties, especially Moira and Guthrie, who had a Russian Hill penthouse encumbered by a Cairn terrier, a rabbit named Robert whom Moira had rescued from a Chinatown butcher shop, and Moira's old Telegraph Hill tabby, Pussyboys, a six-toed cauliflower-eared cat who had been born in Spediacci's vegetable bin, knew how to use an apartment john, speared peas from the uncleared dinner table on his claws and ate them like corn on the cob, and was, according to an expert, "thirty if he's a day."

I found decorative companionship in a pretty film star of the day, Olivia DeHavilland, who felt much put-upon by her sister, also in films, Joan Fontaine. They had grown up in genteel poverty in the Los Gatos-Saratoga neighborhood where Peggy had once come down with typhoid.

Their mother had a keen interest in the theatre which she had passed on.

On days off I pursued Olivia to Southern California, enjoyed Malibu moonlight skinny-dipping with hot chocolate and cognac, and all-star routs at directors' mansions, in innocent merriment. But a low interpretation was put on the friendship by radio columnist named Jimmy Fiedler, who termi-

The Big Work

Birthday Card
by Kevin Wallace
c. 1937
"Miss Langworthy integrates her personality
in time for her twentieth birthday"

Signed by artist; Notated by artist
Unframed; Good Condition

nated the idyll by telling the word, including Armed Forces Radio, that Olivia and I were engaged.

He was audited out in the hellholes of New Guinean by my wistful wide-eyed skiing heroine Helen, then an Army evacuation hospital nurse, who bided her time before letting me know her reaction.

It was also heard by my touring tragedienne on an advanced island base — so advanced the enlisted men went naked, and wig-wagged in indecision whether top use their hands to salute or take cover when they saw her strolling with a general.

She responded to the broad East more rapidly, arriving in San Francisco to demonstrate to me why she was honored as the greatest Medea of her day.

I had lunch at the Palace Hotel one day with Roberta, a gifted fellow cartoonist of mine from campus magazine days, who now drew for the New Yorker and was embarked on a career of marrying publishing figures. She was in town too show off her next affianced editor-in-chief. WIth them was a bright-eyed young musician with a polka-dot bow tie and big ears named Lennie Bernstein.

Bernstein, like Arties Shaw before him, evinced a commendable ambition to be a writer instead of a McCain, and displayed his credentials by quoting from Eliot's new "Four Quartets," but registered pained ignorance when I asked if he didn't prefer Auden's new "Sea and the Mirror."

Some months later, back at Pearl Harbor, I got a card in which Bernstein mentioned he had by now not only read but written a symphony about Auden's even newer "Age of Anxiety." I responded that "The Age of Anxiety" made little sense as poetry, and Bernstein wrote back, "Damned Wallace call Awden mad," which read the same backwards, and got it off his chest.

In Honolulu, Gertrude Lawrence had taken over my departed tragedienne's work, but the war was clearly too good to last.

From Kinauhale's garden cottage late one night I heard the cheering across the Royal Hawaiian's gardens on Kalakaua Avenue signifying the war was ended — the current one, at least.

The party was over. It would be months before I could get out, but the return to my obligation to do Big Work would occur, and I had to make plans. The time of reckoning was at hand.

It occurred to me I should acquire a helpmeet to steady my tardy course to greatness.

The world was filled with ex-girlfriends. The only one whose compassionately disapproving face came commandingly to mind was Helen, the nurse with General MacArthur's jungle forces, now waiting for demobilization at Santo Tomas University hospital in ruined Manila.

On the other hand, I hadn't seen her in years, and felt I should take a fresh look at her before popping the question. I got myself transferred from operations to public relations and became PIO of our Squadron VR-11, whose new duties included repatriating disabled prisoners of war by hospital planes out of newly liberated Shanghai.

Then I wrote the Examiner's surly managing editor, asking him to request drawings and text on the Shanghai operation. The Navy was threaded with post-war economy cuts in the interests of something called unification of the armed forces, and was eager to do anything for good publicity.

So I had no trouble getting approval for orders I wrote for myself to go to Shanghai by whatever means seemed handy. This meant hitch-hiking at airports en route. Manila didn't happen to be in my command's jurisdiction, but once out of Pearl Harbor, who knew?

At Guam, I hitched a ride on a plane that bumped and rackedted through thrilling sunsets to Leyte, the a smaller plane to Mindanao, and ultimately arrived at a seaplane base on Manila Bay, where it was hot and humid. At Santo Tomas they said Helen had gone home.

But at the deprivation center south of town, Helen was still waiting shipment. She looked like an angel.

We borrowed a Jeep to a picnic on the bough of a jungle banyan, where I asked her to marry me before I had to go on to Shanghai. She suggested I ask again after she took a few months or years to consider the old question in her mind as to whether she actually liked me.

I said I couldn't be responsible for any such offer for more than twelfths hours at the outside.

She said, in that case, no God knows I tried, I told myself, and we drove to a phone, where I arranged for a hitch to China the next dawn. We went to dinner at some officers club with my old Examiner city editor what was editing Yank Magazine for the Army. During cocktails, Helen said she'd changed her mind and would call my bluff. I said I'd already arranged my ride, but she said to cancel it. Josh, the city editor, said he'd give the bride away.

We were late for the ceremony the following afternoon in a thatched chapel with an electric piporgan, owing to red tape. It seemed we needed our commanding officers' permission to marry.

I radioed my request to Pearl Harbor, where the enlisted radio men knew my deadpan jokes but couldn't think of any topper response beyond returning an equally dead pan "Permission Granted," which they thought amusing enough.

Helen's commanding officer was more trouble. His headquarters had to be found by Jeep, miles back in some jungle over shell-pocked roads. On the way back, a roadside jewelry and wedding ring stand loomed out of the jungle, reminding us we'd forgotten to get a ring. We got one.

Alcohol wasn't allowed in civilian cafes, so our Chinese joint's wedding banquet featured sarsaparilla.

The honeymoon suite was a crib in a large house of assignation. By dawn I was standing where I was told, circling off Manila Bay in a Martin Mariner flying boat, peering down through the open hatch at the ruined metropolis where my bride awaited her solitary honeymoon troop transport.

We floated over Taiwan, and the Navy doctor positioned next to me assured me that my acrophobia at the gaping hatch was nothing to worry about. "If you weren't anxious, you'd jump," he explained, not very convincingly. "Then you'd have reason to worry."

Like every other service man in the far Pacific who could manage it, he had trumped up some story to get him to Shanghai's fabled sinful opulence.

The fables were well founded. The doctor and I chose the Park Hote, which was running over with gold braid champagne parties and gorgeous White Russian copies of Marlene Dietrich.

"I veel cure your complexion," one said, running her fingers over my chin mole.

"I'm on my honeymoon," I had to respond

Shanghai Druggist
by Kevin Wallace
1939
Sketch for San Francisco Examiner 'Home From The Orient.'
Published newsprint on facing page

Signed by artist; Notated by artist
Unframed; Good Condition

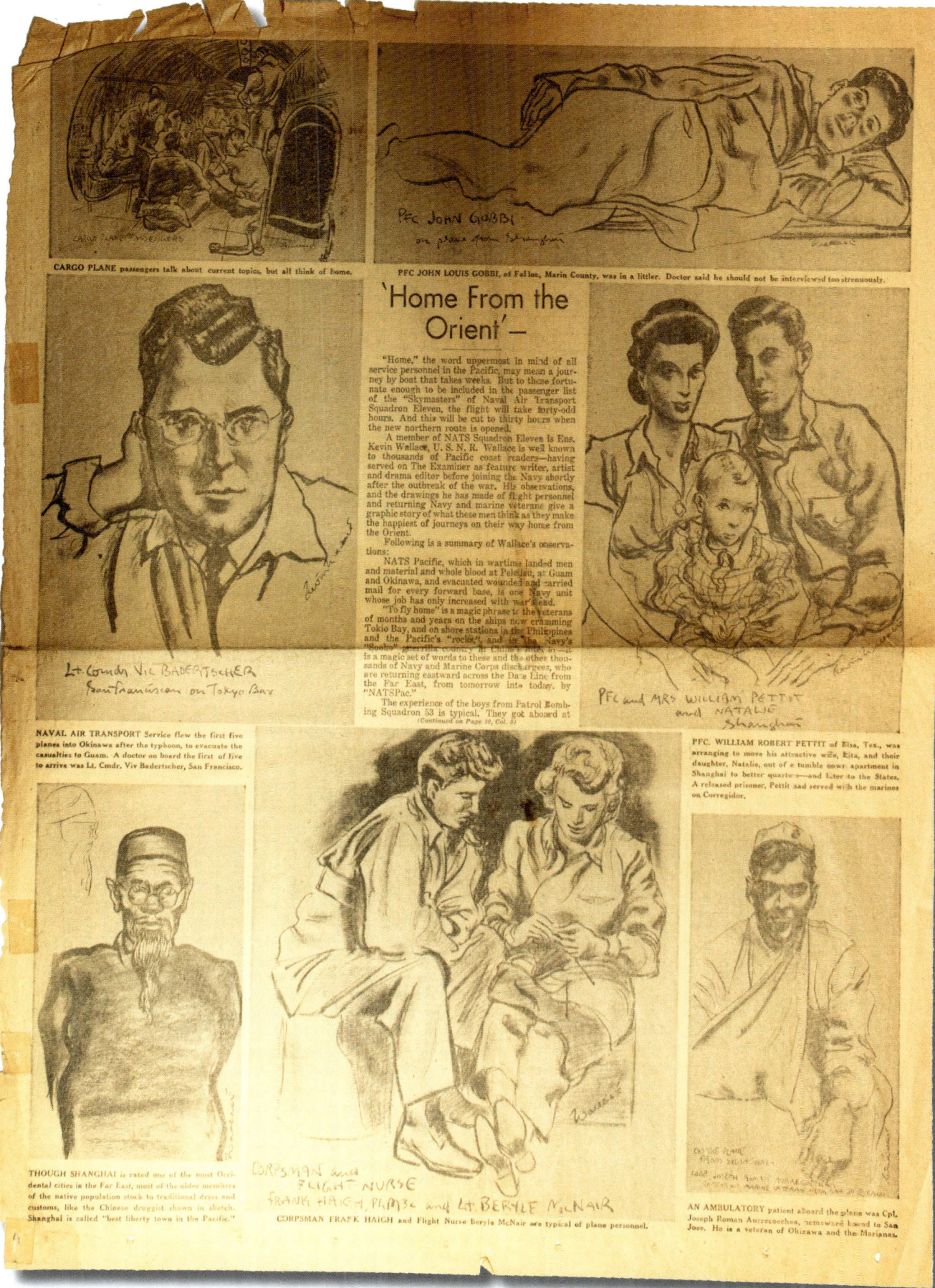

Couple Wed In Philippines

VIA CABLE, family members learned yesterday of the wedding of Lt. Helen Langworthy of the Army Nurse's Corps and Ens. Kevin Wallace, U. S. N. R., who were married October 11 in the Philippines.

Ensign Wallace, who was drama critic of the San Francisco Examiner editorial staff until he entered the Navy, is the son of the Grant Wallaces of Berkeley. Mrs. Guthrie Courvoisier (Moira Wallace) is his sister.

The justweds first met while attending the University of California. The bride, daughter of Mrs. Mitchell Langworthy of Berkeley and the late Doctor Langworthy of Spokane, Wash., is a member of Gamma Phi Beta sorority.

stiffly.

The doctor and I found a stateless French Quarter pharmacist eager to shut up shop and be our guide. We commandeered a Rolls Royce and an enlisted driver who called us "Sir" sarcastically. The surly shabby turned out to be on military leave from his job as chief editorial writer for the Nashville Tennessean, and also a Nieman fellow, an honorary title and distinction I recognized but couldn't define. His name was Nat Caldwell.

We drove past the Sikhs guarding the Lever Brothers' mansions into open country and paused to inspect a picturesque monastery on a tiny hill. Nast congratulated me drily on my poise in acknowledging the military guards through whom we clambered up the hill. I asked him why.

"Because they're unsurrendered Japanese," he said. "Sir."

Our guide, Abe Shmulevsky, got our names and addresses and endorsements of his character, and thus recommended he emigrated with his family to San Francisco before Mau's armies arrived to remove the fun from Shanghai.

I also interviewed and drew some prisoners of war, after I found them hiding out with Chinese brides in obscure sections of the gaudy, starving city. They didn't mind China except for the inflation, they said. A million of China's dollars wasn't enough to tip a beggar and ensured his lasting the night.

The evacuation people suggested I'd do better to go back to Guam where they were transhipping better specimens.

I hitched a plane ride to Buckner Bay in Okinawa, where a typhoon had just finished dumping great ships up on dry cliffs, and demolished all dwelling sturdier than the locals reed houses — and another through Sasebo to Tokyo, whose local beer combined with Canadian booze to make surreal the snowy night walk back from the Imperial Hotel, through flattened Yokohama to my plane ride at Yokosuka.

It was an exciting, unencumbered honeymoon.

Back in San Francisco, Helen's mother Madeline Thomas Langworthy ran into Moira at a museum cocktail party and told her the news from Manila. "He was the first drama critic Helen had seen in four years," Helen's mother theorized.

Helen steamed home, bought some new clothes, and arrived at Pearl Harbor open the first shipment of Navy wives on Christmas Eve.

We took Knauhale's guest house on Waikiki beach for a while, and then the gardener's cottage at Aunt Sarah's place on top of Mt. Tantalus, Mehemanuala, looking far down on everything from Diamond Head to Barber's Point.

My PIO career prospered. I distributed mimeographed stock stories for the Navy's Home Town News Service in Chicago, with blank spaces for all hands to fill in every time they arrived, departed, changed status, or went to the john, and soon was credited with getting more hometown stories printed every month than there were men in the squadron.

Meantime my time was at the enlisted men's beach and I with Helen at the officer's.

The Navy commended me and I became PIO NATSPac. One day I received orders to serve as officer-in-charge of a top secret flight taking a captain's wife's luggage to her parents' home atop lovely Waimea Canyon on Kauai.

"Why top secret and why me?" I asked my exec.

"Because as public information officer you're responsible for keeping word of this operation out of Drew Pearson's column," he said.

I escorted a newsreel cameraman by four-engine plane all over the Hawaiian Islands and Midway before he discovered his lens leaked and we did it again.

The public relations effort was worth it in preventing any admiral losing his empire. When Congress unified the services and expunged NATS, it was reborn under the name of Fleet Air Logistic Command.

The full jungle moon on the lawn atop Mt. Tantalus was romantic. So was the walk up the Pali through the tangled vines and flowers and palm fronds.

When I was discharged, it turned out the Navy wouldn't let wives ride on planes. For the first and last time in my Navy career, I got on a ship, the old President Wilson, and sailed home to San Francisco's earnest reality with Helen, who was pregnant.

The paper provided a temporary reprieve from getting at the Big Work by giving me its main city column in addition to my old critic's chores, for which I now had a matronly dapsone assistant who adored all movies indiscriminately. The column, whimsy with drawings, was a pleasure, it's only drawback being that it clearly wasn't what the Pleiades people had in mind for a bringer of light.

Conscience and a windfall accompanying compelled me to take a leave of absence from its delights when, after a year, I sold a fragment of The Ranch left by Hessie when she died in a hospital she checked into in her extreme eighties, giving her age irascible as "600-odd, and no one will ever know how old."

I assumed from Helen's expression she always knew I had it in me, though I hadn't actually broken it to her about my Big Work destiny. I just said I [planned to stay home six months and write a play, making me available as a sitter for our newborn daughter Deirdre.

This gave Helen a chance to catch up on string quartets, ballet and for-dancing, none of which I cared for, since they interrupted conversation. When I added to Helen that my play would have a pacifist message, she told me she admired General MacArthur, no matter what.

I gradually let on to the larger dimensions I had in mind for my Big Work — making it a transformative experience, rooting out war's causes by exposing the illogic of hostility in the individual human heart, and so on. Helen listened with eyes wide open, slightly glazed.

Towards the end of my six months I was lost in a sea of notes without a firm enough grasp of the underlying sociopsychology to suit me. I consulted the library for expertise. My eye was struck by a brand new volume called "The Writer and Psychoanalysis" by a Dr. Bergler.

Just what I needed, I thought — all the psychoanalytical insights into literary character that a psychoanalysis would give me, without the time and expense. But I was mistaken. Far from giving writers shortcuts at plumbing the depths of humanity, the book turned out to be an analysis of writers themselves, there extensive neurotic propensities, their fanciful claims to bearing a message for the ages, and their helpless dreaming up and spinning out the fantasies whose only function is to keep writers on a more or less even keel — which works only so long as they don't fall prey to writer's block.

The author airlily added that writers — and other creative artists and jokers — lack resources to avoid neurosis by such means as love and everyday sublimation, and are an unsteady bunch.

Shocked and betrayed, I looked further through the shelves, Unaware that the word "consciousness" was a that period a non-word in scholarly circles, owing to its non-specificity — the quality that years later brought it back to such prominence with the resurgence of mystical self-improvement movements — I looked for titles containing that particular word.

All I could find was "The Social Nature of Consciousness" by a Dr. Trigant Burroughs, whose other volumes had such names as "The Biology of Human Conflict" and "The Neurosis of Man." I rapidly became a disciple of this Dr. Burroughs.

I meantime filed my play and returned to the paper, which rebuked me for taking the leave by retaining its syndicated filler column in my old space, and grumbling they were overpaying me as drama critic. Stung, I rejoined the opposition in the Chronicle city room, and applied for a Nieman Fellowship to master Burrough's arcane technical phrases at Harvard.

These fellowships were founded as a means for Harvard to retain the million dollars that funded them without getting into the trade school in journalism the donor had in mind. They were awarded annually to the dozen journalists whose publishers didn't mind risking their finding better employment

Portrait of Madeline "Tommy" Thomas Langworthy c. 1929 by unknown artist "Doyle"

while off on what they mistakenly believed was going to be a freeload behind the ivy walls.

Our son Brian had arrived by the time we entrained for Cambridge, a destination Helen didn't really mind, since it offered access to ski runs and concerts and promised to get me home to diner a city room schedules didn't.

As to the Big Work on my mind, Helen's rapt big-eyed listening expression sometimes struck me as Mona Lisa-like, and my harangues about ending human conflict sometimes seemed to make her downright bad-tempered.

The Nieman stipend proved only just adequate for heating the Victorian house we rented but not for the rent or groceries or travel or winter clothes. This disenchanted fellows who had applied under the impression the honor brought a nine-month freeload, as they said endlessly over the beer at Houlihan's or Lovely Houlihans, as they called it.

Occasionally they dropped in on the more popular freshman lecture classes, a policy encouraged by Harvard to keep us out of professor's hair. But I stood on my rights and went rapidly out of my depth in special little classes on physiological psychology and cultural anthropology and, most rewardingly, a year-long interdisciplinary graduate seminar on the acculturation of the vomiting drive.

While this got into such specifics from Peabody Museum's Yale cross-cultural files as ritual vomiting Amon got Puka-Puka and Arizona Indians, it cas general light on the inventive human rationalization of biological function, as interpreted by Freudian, gestalt, field and old-fashioned stimulus-and-response behaviorist psychology.

Behaviorism was a dead duck except in the mind of Professor Skinner, who was busy matching monkey mastery of slot machines with that of the Harvard Nursery School's children, including our darling Deirdre's.

I brought word of this home from my vomiting seminar to Helen, who was on edge about anyone influencing the children. She marched over to the nursery school and raised the roof until they promised to let Deirdre cut slot machines.

For no apparent reason, I was an ex-officio officer of a dormitory called Winthrop House, my duties being to attend a banquet where I corrected the headmaster's impression that martinis were made of seven parts Vermont to one of gin rather than the other way around. He was a dotty old professor who, on sampling my martini recipe, began letting cats out of the bag, including the admission that Harvard limited its Jewish enrollment by quota.

Outraged, I asked him why scholastic standing wasn't the only criterion.

"Because that way we'd be exclusively Hebrew," he answered, rolling his eyes to heaven, " and it would be goodbye Harvard."

Nieman fellows couldn't afford their own martinis, except at the monthly dinners where we took care to make up for lost time before sitting down with some visiting editor of, like as not, The New York Times. The Times editors deplored the low estate of newspapers that functioned according to a budget, meaning all papers but their own, and departed on a note of cozy ill-will.

Selected professors were allowed into these routes to be fawned on by newspapermen who thought academia glamours, and to fawn on newspapermen who they thought glamorous, a satisfactory misunderstanding all around.

YOSEMITE'S SIGHTS INCLUDE TOURISTS

JOHN MUIR wrote that Yosemite's great mountain fastness heals the crowded city dweller's soul, and his message was heeded by the citizenry—in such force that the current summer vacationer's chief impression of Yosemite consists of other vacationers—unless he looks up. Luckily, that's where the scenery mainly is—up. Undoubtedly much of the world's real estate is as worthy to be looked at—but usually, there's something else to be done with it first: buy it, sell it, improve it, drive past it. But Yosemite is a National Park, so there's nothing to do with it except notice with your eyes (or with their modern substitute, the camera) that wonders never have ceased. That's what the vacationers on this page are noticing. But crowded Yosemite valley is only the least fraction of the entire National Park, whose relatively untouched "high country" is equally beautiful and not a great deal less accessible than the more publicized territory below. For a report on the high country, read L. Davis Bynum's account on this page.

Nearly everybody in Yosemite valley follows this line (for destination take a look at page 6)

BY ARRIVING at dawn, anyone can get this uncluttered view of Yosemite Falls from John Muir Rock. That is, if others haven't thought of it first.

WHEN LODGE'S tenants are looking at things, maid service is at peak.

HALF DOME'S other half is drowned, upside down, in Mirror lake, guaranteed against overcrowding by space limitations of the adjacent parking lot.

CHRONICLE 1949

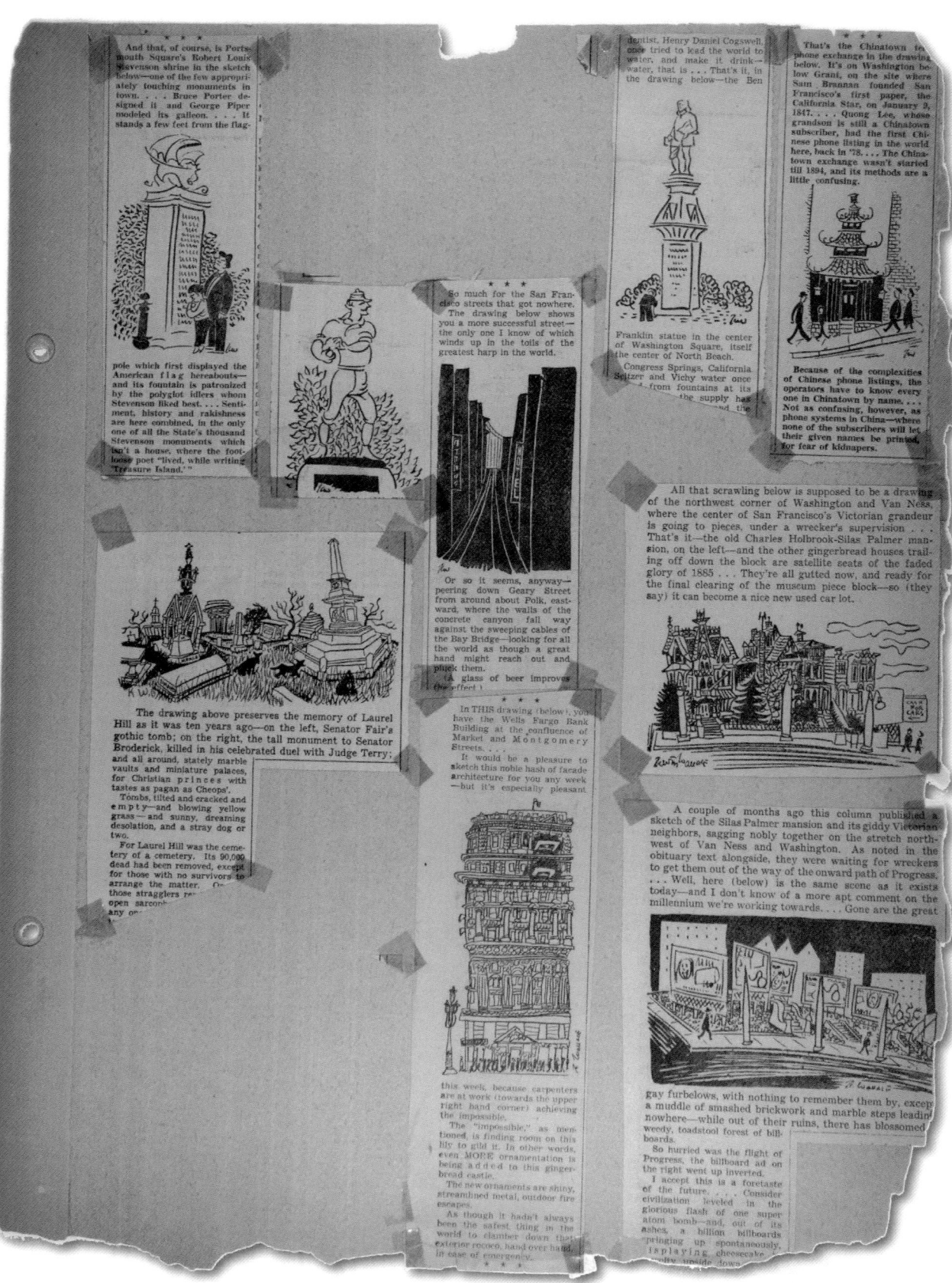

And that, of course, is Portsmouth Square's Robert Louis Stevenson shrine in the sketch below—one of the few appropriately touching monuments in town. . . . Bruce Porter designed it and George Piper modeled its galleon. . . . It stands a few feet from the flag-pole which first displayed the American flag hereabouts—and its fountain is patronized by the polyglot idlers whom Stevenson liked best. . . . Sentiment, history and rakishness are here combined, in the only one of all the State's thousand Stevenson monuments which isn't a house, where the foot-loose poet "lived, while writing 'Treasure Island.'"

* * *

So much for the San Francisco streets that got nowhere. The drawing below shows you a more successful street—the only one I know of which winds up in the toils of the greatest harp in the world.

Or so it seems, anyway—peering down Geary Street from around about Polk, eastward, where the walls of the concrete canyon fall way against the sweeping cables of the Bay Bridge—looking for all the world as though a great hand might reach out and pluck them.

(A glass of beer improves the effect.)

* * *

The drawing above preserves the memory of Laurel Hill as it was ten years ago—on the left, Senator Fair's gothic tomb; on the right, the tall monument to Senator Broderick, killed in his celebrated duel with Judge Terry; and all around, stately marble vaults and miniature palaces, for Christian princes with tastes as pagan as Cheops'.

Tombs, tilted and cracked and empty—and blowing yellow grass—and sunny, dreaming desolation, and a stray dog or two.

For Laurel Hill was the cemetery of a cemetery. Its 90,000 dead had been removed, except for those with no survivors to arrange the matter. O— those stragglers re— open sarcoph— any on—

In THIS drawing (below), you have the Wells Fargo Bank Building at the confluence of Market and Montgomery Streets. . . .

It would be a pleasure to sketch this noble hash of facade architecture for you any week —but it's especially pleasant this week, because carpenters are at work (towards the upper right hand corner) achieving the impossible.

The "impossible," as mentioned, is finding room on this lily to gild it. In other words, even MORE ornamentation is being added to this gingerbread castle.

The new ornaments are shiny, streamlined metal, outdoor fire escapes.

As though it hadn't always been the safest thing in the world to clamber down that exterior rococo, hand over hand, in case of emergency.

* * *

dentist, Henry Daniel Cogswell, once tried to lead the world to water, and make it drink—water, that is . . . That's it, in the drawing below—the Ben Franklin statue in the center of Washington Square, itself the center of North Beach.

Congress Springs, California Seltzer and Vichy water once — from fountains at its — the supply has —

* * *

That's the Chinatown telephone exchange in the drawing below. It's on Washington below Grant, on the site where Sam Brannan founded San Francisco's first paper, the California Star, on January 9, 1847. . . . Quong Lee, whose grandson is still a Chinatown subscriber, had the first Chinese phone listing in the world here, back in '78. . . . The Chinatown exchange wasn't started till 1894, and its methods are a little confusing.

Because of the complexities of Chinese phone listings, the operators have to know every one in Chinatown by name. . . . Not as confusing, however, as phone systems in China—where none of the subscribers will let their given names be printed, for fear of kidnapers.

All that scrawling below is supposed to be a drawing of the northwest corner of Washington and Van Ness, where the center of San Francisco's Victorian grandeur is going to pieces, under a wrecker's supervision . . . That's it—the old Charles Holbrook-Silas Palmer mansion, on the left—and the other gingerbread houses trailing off down the block are satellite seats of the faded glory of 1885 . . . They're all gutted now, and ready for the final clearing of the museum piece block—so (they say) it can become a nice new used car lot.

A couple of months ago this column published a sketch of the Silas Palmer mansion and its giddy Victorian neighbors, sagging nobly together on the stretch northwest of Van Ness and Washington. As noted in the obituary text alongside, they were waiting for wreckers to get them out of the way of the onward path of Progress. . . . Well, here (below) is the same scene as it exists today—and I don't know of a more apt comment on the millennium we're working towards. . . . Gone are the great gay furbelows, with nothing to remember them by, except a muddle of smashed brickwork and marble steps leading nowhere—while out of their ruins, there has blossomed a weedy, toadstool forest of billboards.

So hurried was the flight of Progress, the billboard ad on the right went up inverted.

I accept this is a foretaste of the future. . . . Consider civilization leveled in the glorious flash of one super atom bomb—and, out of its ashes, a billion billboards springing up spontaneously, displaying cheesecake — upside down —

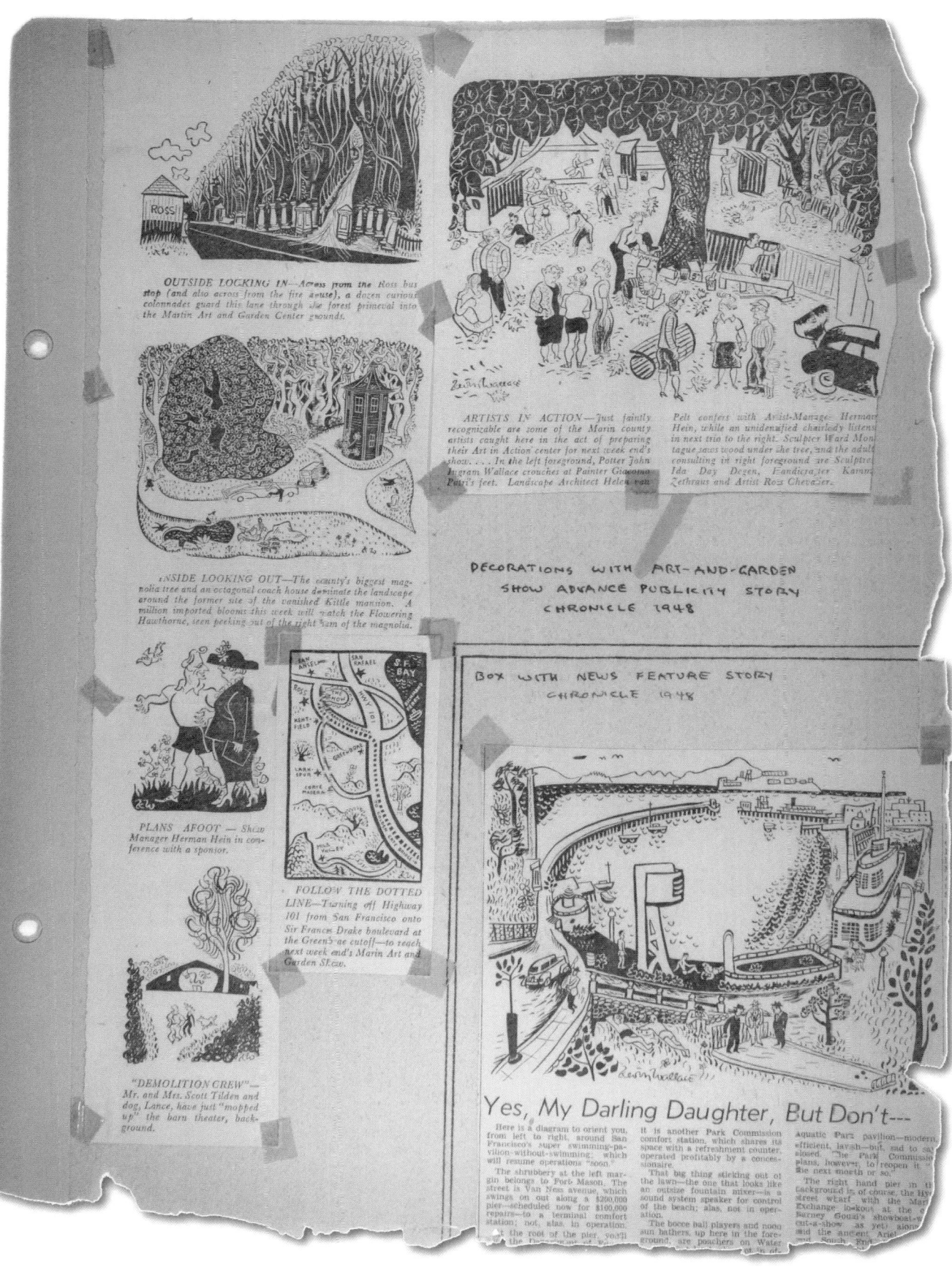

RENT-FREE COTTAGE IN CARMEL WOODS
The village atheist—up to date

'Stalinists... Are Capitalists'
Carmel's Communist Is Still Going Strong

By KEVIN WALLACE

CARMEL, Oct. 28—Norman Duxbury, California's o[nly] civil servant who is a registered Communist, is about as a[u]thentic a Red menace as Mickey Mouse is a mouse.

"Stalinists, Trotskyites—they're all capitalists like Re[pub]licans and Democrats," chortles the implacably cheerful and chatty old carpenter, ruddy of visage and white of mane. "I'm a Communist—a Marxist philosopher—and I haven't time to follow party lines."

Authentic or not, however, Carmel's homespun Commie emerges from his one-room caretaker's lodge at city-owned Forest Theater as a figure of bizarre significance in the world today. Loyalty oaths did it.

Violently anti-Communist professors have lost their jobs rather than sign special loyalty oaths, claiming grounds of democratic principle. But Duxbury—a government officer by virtue of his unpaid watchman's post at the pine-shadowed outdoor theater — signed promptly and without protest, garrulously claiming grounds of Communist principle.

'IT'S JUST SILLY'

"The loyalty oath is just silly, so why should I object?" he is glad to state. "Of course, I don't favor violent overthrow of the government. Its Squanderocracy is spending itself to bankruptcy as it is."

(He distinguishes his view from similar right-wing positions by objecting, besides, that the "squanderocracy" is losing its shirt in military instead of in public welfare projects.)

"Loyalty oath, indeed! Why, I signed the Freedom Scroll, too. Signed it 'Norman Duxbury, Communist.'"

The Carmel City Council regarded Duxbury's agreeable signing as unfair play, inasmuch as Communists are supposed to fly from loyalty oaths as bats from high noon. It wondered if Duxbury could be tried for perjury, or at least lose his free city housing, and it asked Police Commissioner Andy Martin.

THE ANSWER: NO

Martin asked City Attorney Thomas Perry (who shared the local Great Books discussion panel with Duxbury last month, on the topic, "Declaration of Independence vs. the Communist Manifesto").

Perry asked the District Attorney's office in Salinas, and the answer was "No — no prosecution."

Times have changed since the days when Carmel was founded as a woodsy seashore preserve for rugged individualists, and local officialdom has become worried about what people will say. "No" wasn't an entirely satisfactory answer, but the City Attorney is sitting on a strictly legal little notion he has that will fix everything:

"We don't know what tenure the Forest Theater caretaker's job carries, if any, because we haven't entirely figured out the filing system used by the late City Clerk, Sadie Van Brower, but it doesn't matter. "In a few weeks, after this Commie issue dies down, the City Council will decide that the Forest Theater doesn't need a caretaker—in view of the fact that three boys stole a cigar box full of greasepaint from the theater the other night, caretaker or no caretaker. "So Duxbury will go as a routine matter," Perry smiled.

HE WON'T STARVE

Duxbury, extremely spry for 67, says he doesn't care; he's an AFL carpenter in no danger of starving, and anyway "I'm having the time of my life... We Communists are finally breaking through the conspiracy of silence."

In evidence is an article labeled "Manners and Morals" in the current Time Magazine, giving the Nation a moderately garbled acquaintance with Duxbury's saga. Duxbury and J. P. Hudder, a local photographer, have offered pictures of [the] self-made cause celebre to T[ime] affiliate, Life, promising pr[ofits] to the Carmel Youth Assn., [and] other prominent financial ba[cking] include Bing Crosby of Pebble B[each] and ex-Mayor Fred Godwi[n of] Carmel.

Coverage of l'affaire Duxbur[y by] the Monterey Peninsula Daily Herald, a solidly respectable paper, was damned as "an advertisement for Communism and all its vicious[ness]" in a sample of letters fro[m] outraged subscribers—whom [the] Kennedy's editorial column calmly spanked for not believing "in free speech, Constitution or no Constitution . . ."

"The role of the village athiest [is] a traditional one in America. It [is] this role, with political emphasis—rather than the role of Russian saboteur — which Mr. Duxbury seems to be playing in Carmel."

MILES STANDISH'S WIFE

Duxbury, a Lancash[ireman re]lated to Miles Standish first [wife] Kate Duxbury," was a[ble to] talk it all over during dinne[r at] Carmel's Pine Inn dining ro[om, a] stylish layout boasting James R[ands]ball Mills' neo-Victorian decor [and] a maitre d'hotel who greets [Dux]bury by name, with a ceremo[nious] bow—decadent bourgeois livin[g if] you ever saw it.

Duxbury had worked all da[y at] carpentering, rested an hour in [his] whitewashed board-and-ba[ttage] tage and was hurrying through [din]ner now to escort a gray-he[aded] lady friend to the Carmel [Music] Society concert, Talley B[eatty] Tropicana ballet, at Sunset [School] Auditorium.

"We Communists," he sa[id] with cheerful smugness, "[are] last democrats. The Ir[ish] Progressive party is ter[rible;] just want to get elected [. So]cialist Labor party is[...] Karl Marx hoped the [...] would have sense en[ough to] over, but they haven[...] more sense than capita[lists...]

"Idealistic groups like [the] World Federalists are very g[ood-]hearted people, but they li[ve in] cloud-cuckoo land. Whereas [we] Communists..."

WE COMMUNISTS

He wasn't precise about just w[ho the] Communists, if any, answer to h[is] description of "we Communists. "I tried to join the Communist pa[r]ty in 1933, but I told them [I] wasn't willing to go to jail, [so] they wouldn't let me in," he [re]called wistfully.

"In 1932 I went to Russia [for a] $300 tour. It was a materia[l hell] but a spiritual heaven. A m[illion] people starved to death tha[t] w[inter...] [...] thrilled w[ith...]

Halloween Haven
Kids Find a Treat at One Saloon

By Kevin Wallace

Last night, Halloween, I had to miss my kids' costume spook party in the suburbs owing to the funny hours that reporters work. I began the dinner hour in the south-of-Market saloon where we spooks in related trades regularly convene at sundown.

We are rarely disturbed in our chattery evensong there; the neighborhood panhandlers know we're out of bounds. But at 6:15 last night, spooks intruded.

There were four of them, three girl spooks and one boy spook, all right out of the comic strip appearing on Page 23 of today's edition, Peanuts. The first was a boy smaller than Linus—about 2, I guess—and the fourth was bigger than Lucy, though resembling her—maybe 8.

All carried modest grocery bags, the size you use for one dozen oranges. Their mother waited outside with a shopping bag, the way mothers do in the suburbs.

Mother, who wore old flat shoes and no stockings and generally wasn't very well dressed, carried the Halloween equipment of any old posh suburban mother, the king-size brown paper bag that holds maybe 200 dozen oranges. This neighborhood is close to Skid Row and you rarely think of mothers and children living here, though they certainly do.

It was the next oldest girl, in disguise of a gypsy in some miscellaneous colored bits of clothes and a lot of rouge, who acted as spokesman, demanding heartily: "Trick or treat!"

The bartender couldn't hear her, behind the cocktail conversation. Some of the conversationalists heard. But nobody had any apples or cookies. And it would be discourteous to shell out the only goods on hand: dimes.

It was noisy in there, though. Few heard.

The gypsy-spook spokesman, or spooksman, looked firmly around, and then ordered a retreat. Outside, the threatened "trick" was direly executed: one small vertical mark on the barroom door's glass, with a bar of soap.

I found the group ten minutes later, six doors further south of Market . . . getting the deaf, glassy-eyed response at another gladsome harbor of us human vessels haltingly home-bound at vesper's hour.

To each of the fiercely-painted wishfully-fiendish little goblins, I conveyed the only goody I had in stock; a dime to drop into each dozen-orange-size paper sack.

In each sack, I found, the dime was the first and only contents.

I left the saloon when the spooks did. Outside, the smallest one — the Linus understudy — started to mark his soap on the door, in a kind of detached, routine, bureaucratic manner.

His horrified spooksman-gypsy sister stopped him.

"Don't," she said. "They didn't trick us in there. They treated us!"

NORMAN DUXBURY
"We Communists"

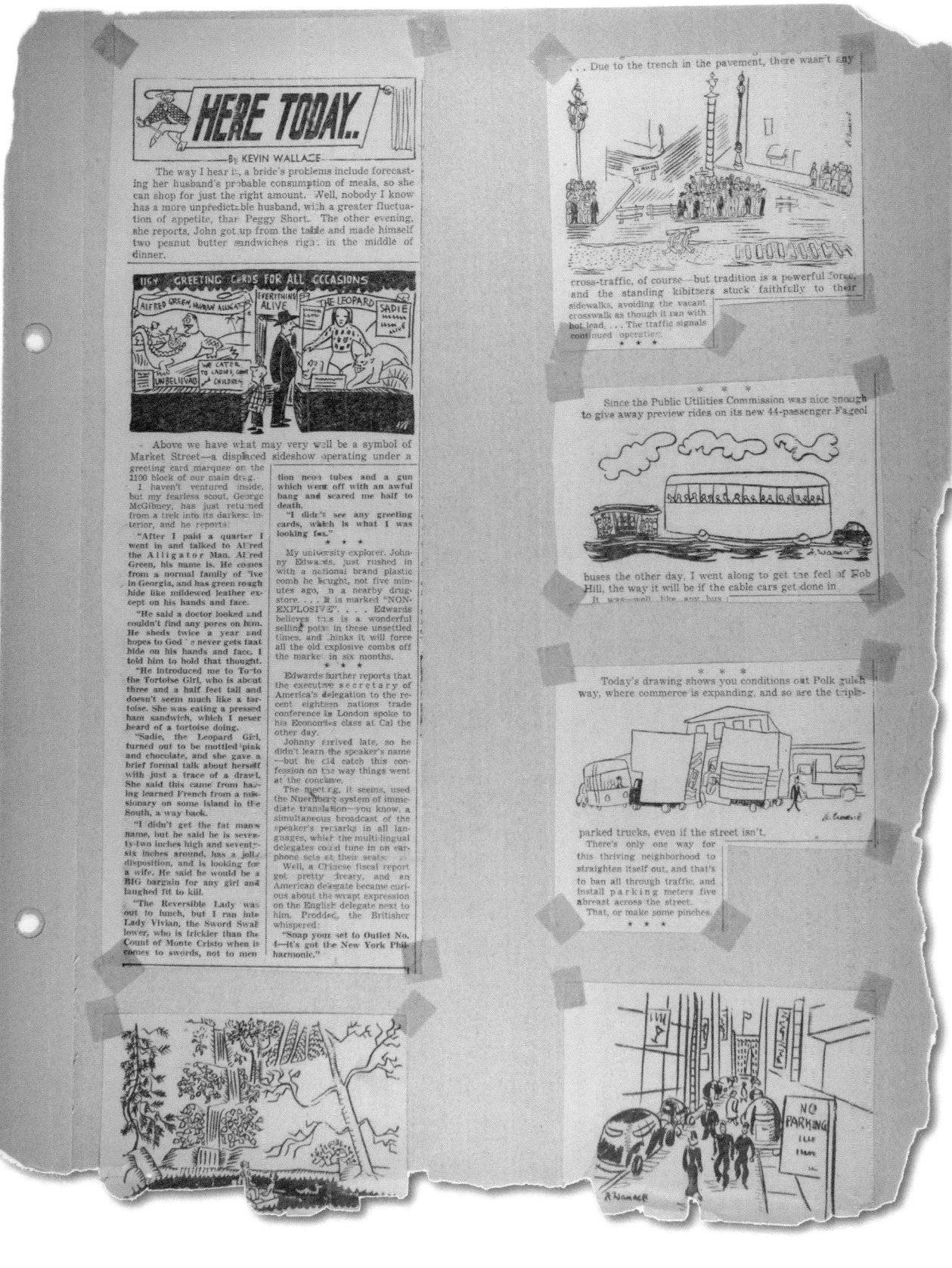

HERE TODAY..

By KEVIN WALLACE

"Classiest looking slum fronts in America," observed Author Nat Caldwell, casing the Fillmore area's Japtown gingerbread as background for a book on the Nation's tenements; "how come?" . . . The answer—provided along with today's guest art work by Architect Alec Yuill-Thornton—seems to show that pre-fab building and high pressure housing shortages are nothing new around here. . . . The facades Caldwell saw—idealized by Alec in the cartoon below—indicate that both conditions are a San Francisco habit. . . . So you'll recognize these open-air museum pieces when you meet them on the street.

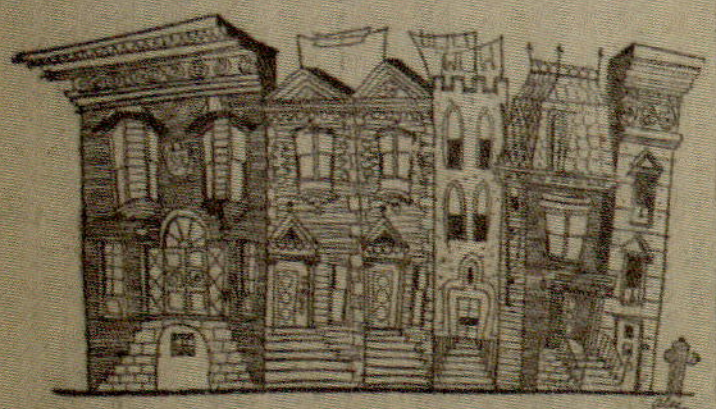

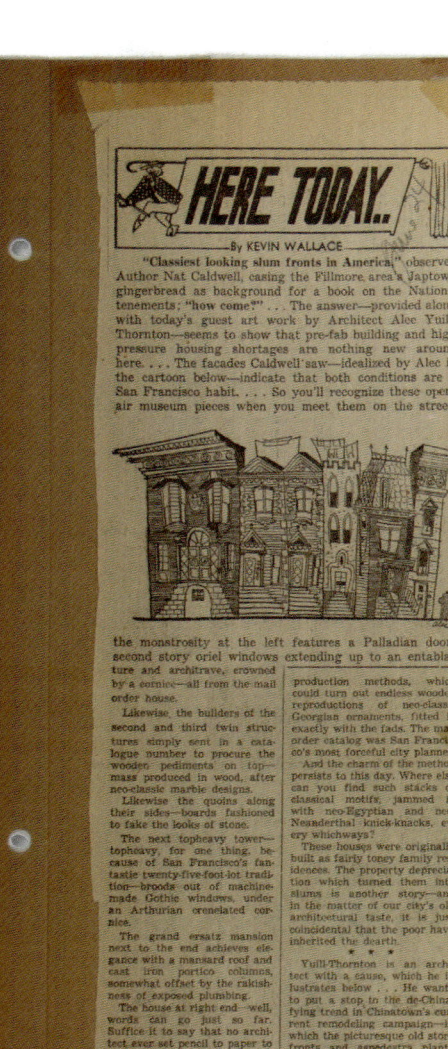

the monstrosity at the left features a Palladian door, second story oriel windows extending up to an entablature and architrave, crowned by a cornice—all from the mail order house.

Likewise, the builders of the second and third twin structures simply sent in a catalogue number to procure the wooden pediments on top—mass produced in wood, after neo-classic marble designs.

Likewise the quoins along their sides—boards fashioned to fake the looks of stone.

The next topheavy tower—topheavy, for one thing, because of San Francisco's fantastic twenty-five-foot-lot tradition—broods out of machine-made Gothic windows, under an Arthurian crenelated cornice.

The grand ersatz mansion next to the end achieves elegance with a mansard roof and cast iron portico columns, somewhat offset by the rakishness of exposed plumbing.

The house at right end—well, words can go just so far. Suffice it to say that no architect ever set pencil to paper to produce such plans.

These monuments are "unarchitected." . . . These, in particular, were also built in a great deal of a hurry, just after The Fire—when housing of any sort was wanted in a hurry.

Any sort was what they got, too—of sorts selected from fresh memories of the Bonanza boom, an era likewise featured by home-building frenzy.

Hurried housing has been the keynote, indeed, ever since a hundred years ago, when San Francisco was burning down and building up again with clock-like regularity.

The rush connected with Bonanza building, however, was a special feature of the flamboyant spirit of the nabobs. He who could get there the fustest with the mostest gingerbread was socially successful.

The home facade in those days was what milady's personal facade is today. As it now is in shop windows and fashion magazines, so it was then in housing—taste was confused with timeliness.

And the emergence of mass production methods, which could turn out endless wooden reproductions of neo-classic Georgian ornaments, fitted in exactly with the fads. The mail order catalog was San Francisco's most forceful city planner.

And the charm of the method persists to this day. Where else can you find such stacks of classical motifs, jammed in with neo-Egyptian and neo-Neanderthal knick-knacks, every whichways?

These houses were originally built as fairly toney family residences. The property depreciation which turned them into slums is another story—and in the matter of our city's old architectural taste, it is just coincidental that the poor have inherited the dearth.

* * *

Yuill-Thornton is an architect with a cause, which he illustrates below . . . He wants to put a stop to the de-Chinafying trend in Chinatown's current remodeling campaign—in which the picturesque old store fronts and aspedestra plants and elders with pipes are being replaced by black plate glass, purple tile, neon signs, and all things undistinctive.

Above eye-level, of course, the fine old gables and curly roof hips persist—but as his drawing suggests, they might

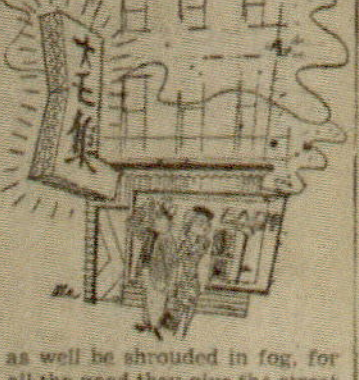

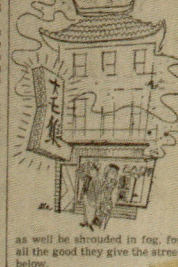

as well be shrouded in fog, for all the good they give the street below.

Tourists never look up.

HERE TODAY..

By KEVIN WALLACE

Remember the case of the limbo-lost theater building, which I couldn't get at behind the encircling store fronts on the Fillmore-Geary-Steiner-O'Farrell block? . . . Well, I never did penetrate to this haunted hall, with its secrets blocked behind a littered doorway—but one who signs himself **"Smiling Jack"** did, after reading my story about it.

"We went up through Victor Broo's rooming house," he writes tersely, "and saw the old building. Should have ropes for exploring."

Frank Grimm also writes to inform me that the mystery house (whose lonely existence came to light when Tom Stallard inherited it recently) was NOT Sid Grauman's National Theater, as I'd suspected.

The National's famous tent went up on the present site of Dreamland Auditorium, a block or so away, and Grimm recalls he **"had to get there real early, to get a front circus seat to hear Al Jolson whistle, and how he could whistle, and while the show went on they built a galvanized theater around it."**

But the real news comes from Mrs. Owen Cline, who

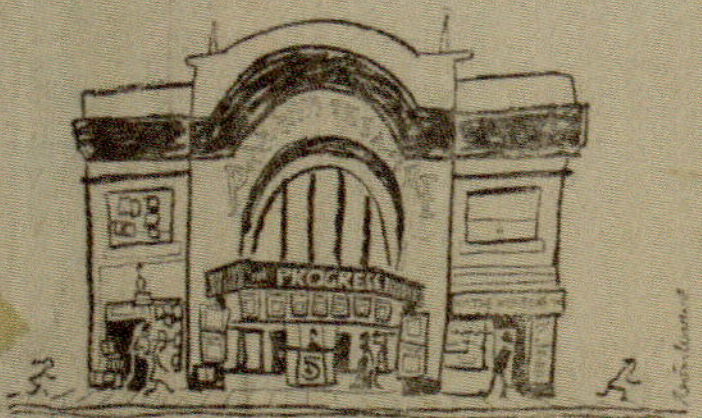

says the deserted edifice is the remains of the Progress (erstwhile Premium) Theater, whose once-proud facade I've revived in the drawing above.

"My dad," reports this lady, **"had one of the first garages in the Fillmore District, and our house backed on to the Jewish synagogue on Geary Street, while to our right was the back and side of the old Progress. . . .**

"By holding our breaths, we children could squeeze through a small alley behind the Progress and listen to its funny old pianist practicing. It was a very gay time."

The alley was also well situated for swiping grapes from the synagogue during Yom Kippur—an enterprise which employed the game of **"Sioux Indians"** for a marauding pretext.

The kids also played **"Coxy's Army,"** in which Mrs. Cline invariably was chosen to act as **"the enemy,"** due to the ease with which her long braids could be clutched during battle.

The neighborhood, in those days, was highly select, and the sign of local aristocracy was self-employment. Mrs. Cline's memories of the region scan the years from Jim Corbett to Paul Schultz and Harry Wolff and Yehudi Menuhin.

When she grew older and more dignified, she attended the Progress to admire Douglas Fairbanks, William Desmond, Mary Pickford and Marguerite Clark, as well as the funny piano player.

Her mother went in more for the heavy drama at Grauman's National, such as **"East Lynn"** and **"Topsy and Eva"**—while her father scorned such entertainments, in favor of training a pet lamb named **"Wooly"** to cadge pretzels at the old saloon on Ellis and Steiner.

"Wooly" finally got so sophisticated, he attended a St. Francis Hotel luncheon, all dolled up in a stiff collar and coonskin coat.

The traditions of Monday lunch at the St. Francis have come from all over.

* * *

I asked S. Lanz Lansburgh, president of the Light Opera Association, if he had any tender memories of the Progress Theater, but he said it was just a lousy nickelodeon, which got short shrift from him.

He had every reason to look down his nose at nickelodeons, for in those days he was one of the chiefs of the Old Orpheum, which compared favorably with St. Peter's job in heaven.

Many years after the Old Orpheum faded away, Lansburgh had reason to regret the prominence of his Orpheum connections, and the popularity of the place.

The reason came out after years of unsuccessful dickering with a property owner to buy a lot out on Eighth Street. The mysterious owner had staunchly refused to sell the real estate on the grounds that Lansburgh was an old so-and-so.

This character judgment, Lansburgh finally learned, was due to the fact that he had attended grammar school with the man—and fifty years later, the forgotten schoolmate had phoned him to ask for seats to the Orpheum's Sunday opening.

Naturally, he had been turned down—for the Orpheum's Sunday seats were more prized than health itself, and were passed on in wills—and he had never forgiven.

The greatest sign of civic prestige in those days was securing a free pass to the Orpheum. After years of maneuvering, Attorney Horace Platt finally wangled one—and he wrote the Orpheum a ten-page letter of thanks.

He said he would frame this token of honor, rather than trade it for anything so ephemeral as an evening's entertainment. And, to reciprocate in some small measure, he inclosed a pass to his own trolley line.

This pasteboard resembled the Orpheum pass—but in place of the theater's name, it read **"Geary Street Railroad."**

And in fine print, where the Orpheum ducat said **"Not good on Saturdays, Sundays or Holidays,"** his ticket read:

"Not good going east or west."

HERE TODAY..

By KEVIN WALLACE

Today is Memories Day, and we will pause now in a gesture of respect to the frugal servicemen who thronged our city through the war. . . . Uncomplainingly, they restricted themselves to the consumption of 52 per cent of one hot dog or hamburger apiece at the Pepsi-Cola Center, according to a recent backward glance on the situation in another morning paper—which relates with quiet respect: **"The Pepsi-Cola Center served 5,727,480 nickle hot dogs and hamburgers to over 11,000,000 servicemen and servicewomen."**

* * *

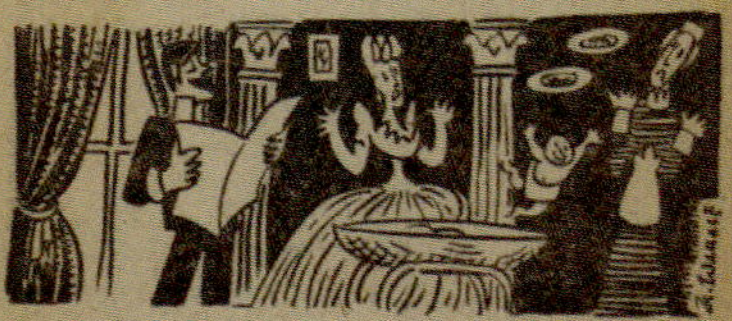

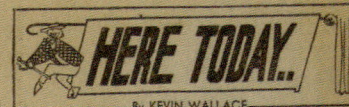

The Old Master above preserves a happy hour of yesteryear. It is titled **"Reading the Castoria Ad in the Sacramento Record Union of September 22, 1882,"** and the ad itself is reproduced below:

BABY'S PETITION

"Life is restless, days are fleeting,
Children bloom, but die in teething;
Warning take, all friends and mothers,
Watch the precious girls and brothers;
Read the home life of Victoria,
Children nine, all had Castoria;
No sleepless nights, by baby squalling,
Like larks they rise in early morning."

* * *

"Did Lizzie pan out?" I inquired last week, asking for information to augment my 1882 report on one Lizzie Strong's promising career as a painter.

"Yes, Lizzie did pan out!" reported a number of prompt letters—one from Vivian Breckenfeld of Berkeley, who knew the lady as "Aunt Elizabeth" in Carmel, where she finished her abundant and fruitful days of painting just five years ago.

"Apart from being related to **Robert Louis Stevenson,"** relates this scribe, **"her proudest claim was that she once fell into an open septic tank which some nonchalant plumber had under repair. Carmel being the quiet spot it is, nobody found her for about twelve hours. Nonole Locan, her sister, just thought she had stayed out pretty late sketching. Aunt Elizabeth was awfully mad."**

Another letter is signed by Louis Adolfo Sanchez of Oakland, whose mother performed a real labor of love by writing the beautiful but unremunerative "Spanish Arcadia," and whose clan was thick with Robert Louis Stevenson in his California days.

Sanchez reports that Lizzie not only panned out—she inherited Rosa Bonheur's mantle as America's leading animal painter, and was commissioned to paint the pups of Presidents.

She refused, however, to paint namby pamby dogs, and as the high spirited canines of her choice began to get on her nerves, she eventually switched to landscapes, which are more predictable.

Her brother, Joe Strong, married Robert Louis Stevenson's stepdaughter, Isabel Osbourn, thus bringing into one family circle three painters whose merit surpassed their recognition—Lizzie, Joe and Isabel's mother, Fanny Stevenson—the latter, according to Sanchez, **"one of the most loyal, self-sacrificing, courageous wives the world has ever known, yet it is only at this belated date that a somewhat lame recognition is being given to this magnificent woman."**

* * *

If you remember seeing the dream castle which is maligned in the sketch below, you qualify as an Old San Franciscan.

It is Cliff House III—an ornate, seven story chateau erected by Adolph Sutro in 1896, and burned in 1907. The story that it fell into the sea during the Difficulties of 1906 was exaggerated.

Cliff House I was built in 1858 by Sam Brannan, out of $1,500 worth of lumber salvaged from a schooner which foundered just out in front.

It was remodeled as Cliff House II in 1861, gaining a new wing—but this, unfortunately, was blown right off again in 1887, when a schooner loaded with dynamite hit the rocks below.

It seems like ships just can't stay away.

Cliff House IV, built in 1909, belongs to Whitney Brothers, and hasn't fallen into the sea, burned or exploded, so you can still get a good meal there, and exchange glances with the seals below.

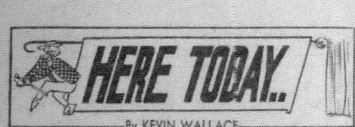

The Big Work

HERE TODAY..

By KEVIN WALLACE

HEDY THE HAIRDRESSER has come back, uninvited, from out of nowhere, to relay the following tale of the Eternal Woman's romantic imagination. . . . It was at a cocktail party attended by Lovey Fay Bush, a dazzling divorcee whose future marital possibilities are being closely watched by the F. Francisco set. . . . Mrs. Boris Kitchin saw Lovey across the room, talking to some man obscured by the haze . . . **"Look at Lovey's eyes,"** Mrs. Kitchin cried to Mrs. Drew Chidester. **"Whoever she's talking to is THE man! You can tell by her expression—she's MAD about him! They're planning the ELOPEMENT! Isn't it adorable? Isn't it di . . ."**

At that point the handsome stranger shifted his profile into view. Egad—MR. Boris Kitchin!

* * *

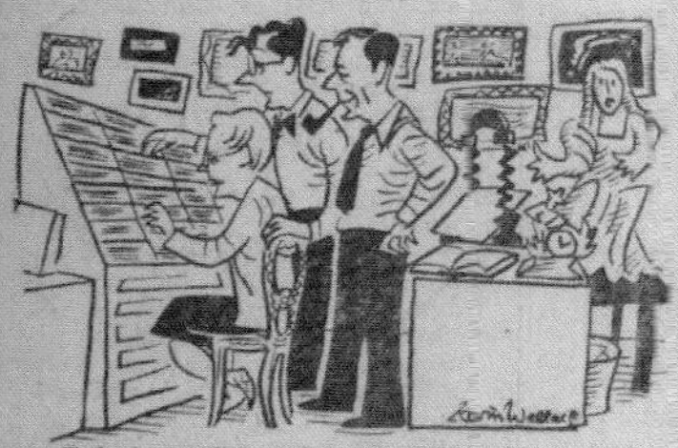

Today's expedition takes us to 1335 Sutter, in the former synagogue school whose present tenants are (left to right, above) Jane Grabhorn of the Colt Press; her husband, Bob; Bob's elder brother, Ed, of the Grabhorn Press; and a wistful lady of polychrome plaster, name unknown.

The Colt Press and the Grabhorn Press are the main reason for San Francisco's reputation as a world center of fine printing—limited editions, private printings, collectors' items, all printed and bound by loving hands in this mussy museum of primitive California paintings, pistols, documents and dofunnies.

"You'd better not write about us," said Bob Grabhorn, with the sort of preoccupied sincerity that musicians must show when doping out a sonata. **"It's hard to explain anything here and you'll probably get it wrong. Just mention it as a weird San Francisco spot."**

"Isn't it true," I pried, **"that yours is the best printing anywhere, and all like that?"**

"No," he responded, thoughtfully. **"But we DID help out the 'I AM' congregation next door, by piping heat in when their furnace went out. They tune in on vibrations all the time, but I guess they couldn't get the wavelength to keep 'em warm."**

Ed Grabhorn absented himself from the felicity of the type-tray long enough to show us some recent acquisitions on the wall—contemporary paintings of Vasquez being captured in Los Angeles; of Three-finger Jack persecuting a Chinee; and of Old Man Studebaker in his Placerville tire shop, before he steered his whiskers down to the lowlands to start his vehicle empire.

Time has put a price on these specimens, but its inflationary touch has worked faster on Grabhorn books—such as the "Joaquin Murietta" volumes which retailed a few years ago at $2.60, and now take a cool $75.

The Grabhorns were able to keep working through the war's paper shortage, due to their luck in buying nine tons of the bankrupt French Paper Company's stock in 1939. They don't know HOW many titles they've published since Ed started in 1915 at Indianapolis.

"I think it says in a book," Ed said, looking around unhappily, **"somewhere."**

* * *

A mechanical delay prevents our giving you the details—yet—on last night's wedding of Sunny Taylor and Jerry Clrincione, attended by midget flower girls and a bridesmaid whose steady work is in a carnival as a fat lady. . . . However, we are prepared to tell you that somebody named Elinor Arnold, who runs an "Introduction Service," whatever that may be, has caught a fish with a gumdrop and a safety pin. . . . Also, Hal Burroughs has conducted a survey of egotism in business, and discovers that "MY" is a three-to-two favorite in shop names over the more altruistic "OUR" or generous "YOUR." To wit: San Francisco has My Cleaner, My Florist and My Rendezvous—Our Beauty Shop and Our Own Rug Cleaning Company—Your Beauty Salon and Your Neighborhood Cleaner.

Target for Today

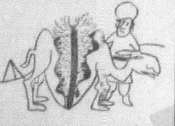

Here is the straw that broke the camel's back. . . . If you can't pick out from the drawing exactly which straw I mean, you'd better vote today and see how the parable works out in action. . . . With this I conclude my political activity for the season.

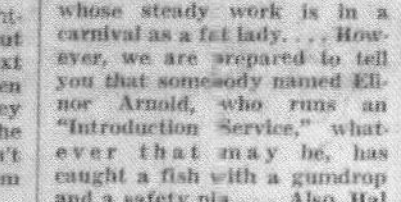

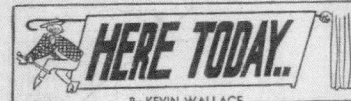

HERE TODAY..

By KEVIN WALLACE

Many, many, many letters have come asking, **"Whatever do you suppose the OPA can be thinking of?"** The answer is—Mrs. Gladys L. Sanderson.

Mrs. Sanderson—the OPA's chief clerk for the local ration board's volunteer exec board—got into a row with District Director E. J. Bennett last May and was bounced, over her co-workers' objection.

This irked Mrs. S. So she appealed for a hearing—to (1) Mrs. Auzzie Ireland, OPA district head of civil service, (2) Bennett, (3) Samuel Kaplan, regional OPA office head of personnel and civil service, (4) Ben C. Duniway, regional director of OPA, and finally (5), Paul Porter, national administrator of OPA.

No. 5 was the only one that took—and by that time it was August 6.

On August 21, Mr. Porter referred the appeal to Wallace S. Sayre, national head of OPA personnel and civil service . . . Some time later, Sayre referred it back here to Kaplan . . . KAPLAN thought about it a long time, and referred it to BENNETT.

Bennett was last reported still thinking about it . . . Since the organization seems to have been pretty well canvassed without an **"aye"** or **"nay"** being sounded, my bureau here offers this counsel—reinstate Mrs. Bennett and give HER the appeal to worry about!

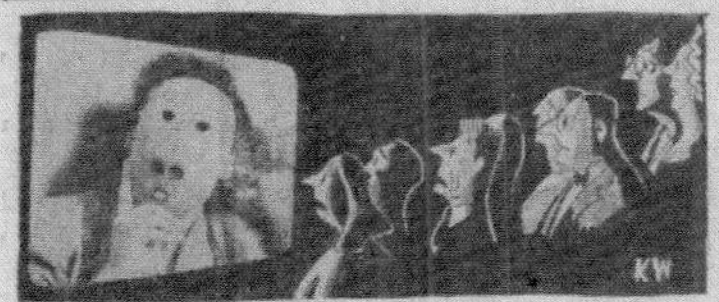

No less a personage than Anna Louise Breakdown has put in a call from Telegraph Hill, to excoriate this column for **"wilfully distorting"** modern art by cartooning it. . . . Hence, we make amends by printing (above) an actual scene, right out of the camera, from Phelan Award Winner Jim Broughton's locally made modern movie, "The Potted Psalm"—with, of course, our own conception of next Friday night's premiere audience for the film, at the Museum of Art.

Truth is our aim. We make no comment.

* * *

One who signs himself "Serious Thinker" writes in to ask why certain ladies prefer dogs and cats to kiddies about the house. The answer is that you can brag about dogs and cats without either (a) sending them out of the room or (b) having them glare at you and snarl **"Oh, MOTHER!"** . . . Lloyd Campbell, who employs Anson Weeks at the Music Box, suavely accepted a patron's settlement for his check in Canadian coin—calling a banker friend, while making change, to learn the current rate of exchange . . .

Real Estater W. N. Dirks of Oakland is depressed about my suggesting the sidewalk flower stands are only thirty years old. (I meant the stand I drew was that age—that's all.) Dirks recalls inhaling the stands' fragrance when he was cash boy at the Golden Rule Bazaar, 718 Market Street, back in '91.

If you don't know how penicillin is administered, consult your family doctor. All I'll say is that it is no fun—and Nurse Jerry Englund was right in trying to soften the blow for a Mexican at San Jose Hospital by murmuring **"Dolor poquito"—"It'll hurt JUST AN EENSY-WEENSY BIT!"** Penicillin must be pretty good, because the jab taught the patient English. **"Poquito not so damn!"** cried he.

Totally undecipherable excerpt from the conversation I just heard at dinner: **"You mean to say I can't genuflect OR desqua mate?"**

And our San Jose correspondent wishes to add—not only that the basement was recently stolen from a Mountain View Church—but the San Jose City Building Inspector's name is Lotz!

* * *

Our recent mention of the Randolph Hale's daughter, who thought our Mr. Fried's first name should be Sieg, has reminded Mrs. A. L. James of the time she told a young friend of the passing of the brewery king, Adolph Busch.

"Dear me," she had said, **"Busch is dead."**

"You mean," queried the other, **"Tannhauser?"**

* * *

Target for Today

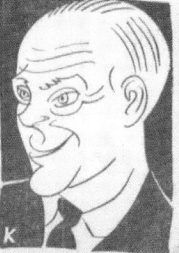

Here is the least photographed city official in captivity, JERD SULLIVAN, president of the Police Commission, vice president of the Crocker First National Bank, former head of the California Bankers' Association, foreman of one of the city's most famous and efficient grand juries, and husband of one of the prettiest (and most photographed) wives in town . . . Mr. Sullivan was first known as Jeremiah Jr., son of the judge who headed the local Bar Association. He quit Cal to enlist in the Navy in 1918, and came out as an ensign under the name of Jerry. He got into the banking business and changed his name to Jerd, which seems awfully short for a man who stands six-feet-four in his stocking feet.

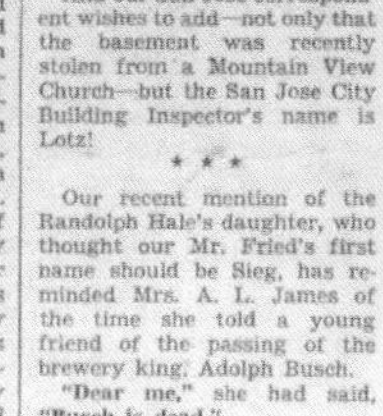

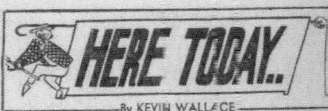

HERE TODAY..

By KEVIN WALLACE

Ominous note of preparedness: The Bomb Junk Company, 778 McAllister, promises to **"buy and sell everything"**—and if they can stick around long enough, I wouldn't be at all surprised if they did.

* * *

Jack Benny has called up my fraternity—the local Newspaper Guild—to tell them never mind about finding transportation and housing for his forty-five man show, which he's donating to their big Civic Auditorium Frolic on March 29. . . . He says he'll attend to it all himself, and pay all the expenses, on condition that the gesture isn't capitalized on to look like favorable publicity for him. . . . I am glad to co-operate in this matter, rendering only unfavorable publicity—for obviously this item undermines public confidence in the comedian's much advertised stinginess, so well known to those who experiment with listening to Marconi wireless sets.

* * *

The drawing below shows you David George Davis in a brown study—or, to be exact, in an Old Rose wall-

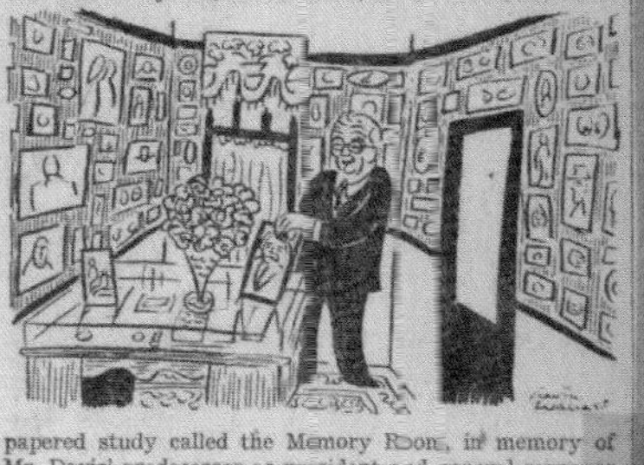

papered study called the Memory Room, in memory of Mr. Davis' predecessor as president and general manager of the store around it.

You may have noticed it as you passed through the book department of the store, which was called Davidson & Lane when it opened in 1854, approximately where Jack's Restaurant sits today, on Sacramento off Montgomery.

At present it's called the White House, or Raphael Weill and Company—and the Memory Room is the late Mr. Weill's old office.

Its tenants include endless photographs of vanished San Franciscans, transplanted from Raphael Weill's St. Francis Hotel apartment; a showcase of medals and plaques, and a bowl of fresh posies, renewed daily.

Some days they're roses, and sometimes not. Every December 9, however, they're orchids, increasing by one each year. There were twenty-six orchids last December 9, which indicated it was the twenty-sixth anniversary of Mr. Weill's death.

(His birthday is marked out in the aisle, where 110 roses counted the years last February 24.)

Mr. Davis—who joined the shop sixty-two years ago as a $25-a-month stockboy—drops in here every so often to look over such old acquaintances as Mayor Taylor, Reuben Lloyd, Judge Coffey, Colonel Hawes, General Funston, John Landers, Judge Campbell, Police Chief White, Senator Phelan, Judge Harrison, David Warfield, Frank Unger and Uncle George Bromley.

It's an odd office, a dead center in the tumult of the area bounded by Sutter, Kearny, Market and Powell, which is the largest concentration of retail merchandise traffic in the entire world.

* * *

Yes, apparently that superlative is true about the downtown swank shopping sector — and probably it'll stay true, even after Van Ness boots its auto

dealers out and becomes the city's Champs Elysees.

And in the sketch below, you see the gent who knows more of its wealthy shoppers, by sight and by name, than anybody else in the world.

He's a Kentucky boy named Joe Foreman, who started out to see the world a long time ago. After glimpsing the Philippines, he visited the corner of Post and Grant, and he's been standing there ever since—ever since 1909.

"Joe Shreve" is the name most people call him, giving

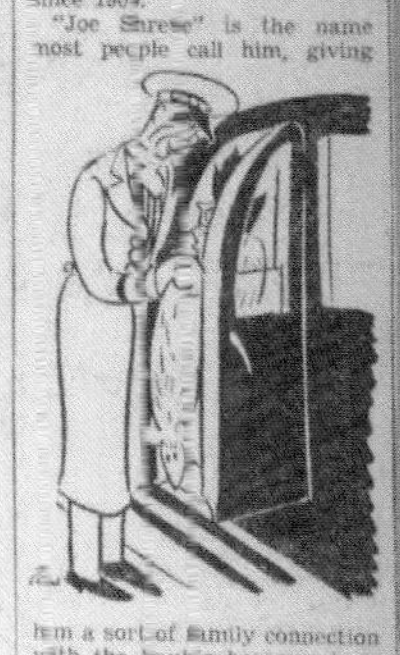

him a sort of family connection with the haute bazaar whose door he guards.

As a matter of fact, he really does guard the door—with a concealed gat—but his principal function is that of footman, and a more courtly functionary will not be found this side of Charles Dickens.

Every so often, Shreve's lends Joe to the opera or some similar super-dowager, with all the fanfare used by M.-G.-M. in lending Clark Gable to Warner Brothers. Lent or not, the past thirty-eight years have been mostly a round of social how-d'y-dos to Joe, who never gets a day older.

Sociability suits him.

HERE TODAY..

By KEVIN WALLACE

When the Ferry Building surrendered its actual and symbolic chores to the two bridges, it dissolved in the local public mind as though the Bay had absorbed it. So I guess you'll be as surprised as I was to learn that it's still something of a tourist mecca, by virtue of an attraction called **"California, Paradise in Panorama."** Never heard of such a thing? Well, that was the prize-winning title dreamed up on November 19, 1924, by Annie Odile Porter, daughter of the Langley Porters, for the Ferry Building's second story bas relief map of California, unveiled that evening. . . . The next day, thousands of commuters were late to

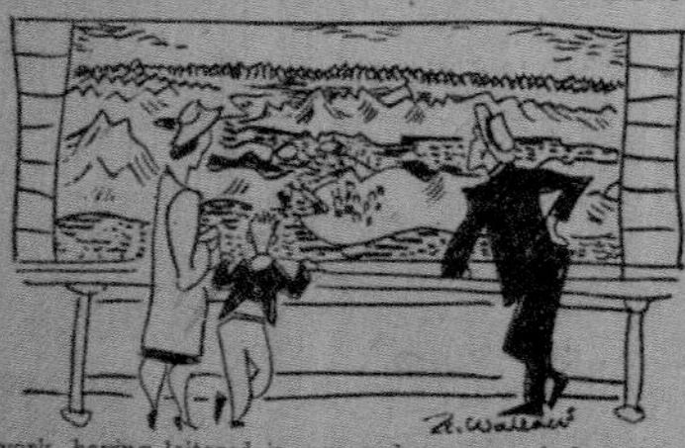

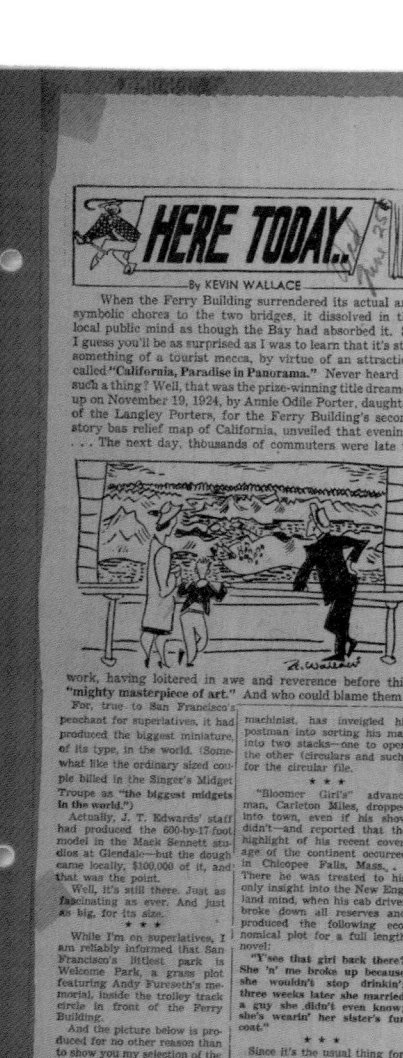

work, having loitered in awe and reverence before this **"mighty masterpiece of art."** And who could blame them?

For, true to San Francisco's penchant for superlatives, it had produced the biggest miniature, of its type, in the world. (Somewhat like the ordinary sized couple billed in the Singer's Midget Troupe as **"the biggest midgets in the world."**)

Actually, J. T. Edwards' staff had produced the 600-by-17-foot model in the Mack Sennett studios at Glendale—but the dough came locally, $100,000 of it, and that was the point.

Well, it's still there. Just as fascinating as ever. And just as big, for its size.

* * *

While I'm on superlatives, I am reliably informed that San Francisco's littlest park is Welcome Park, a grass plot featuring Andy Fureseth's memorial, inside the trolley track circle in front of the Ferry Building.

And the picture below is produced for no other reason than to show you my selection of the

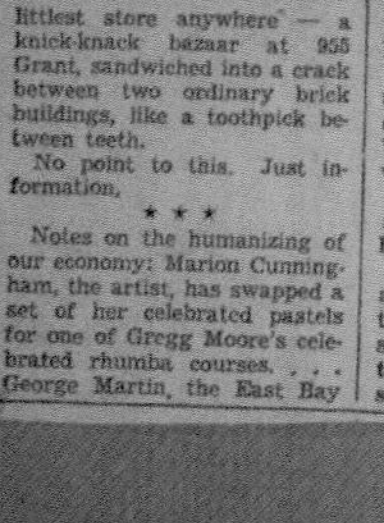

littlest store anywhere — a knick-knack bazaar at 955 Grant, sandwiched into a crack between two ordinary brick buildings, like a toothpick between teeth.

No point to this. Just information.

* * *

Notes on the humanizing of our economy: Marion Cunningham, the artist, has swapped a set of her celebrated pastels for one of Gregg Moore's celebrated rhumba courses. . . . George Martin, the East Bay machinist, has inveigled his postman into sorting his mail into two stacks—one to open, the other (circulars and such) for the circular file.

* * *

"Bloomer Girl's" advance man, Carleton Miles, dropped into town, even if his show didn't—and reported that the highlight of his recent coverage of the continent occurred in Chicopee Falls, Mass. . . There he was treated to his only insight into the New England mind, when his cab driver broke down all reserves and produced the following economical plot for a full length novel:

"Y'see that girl back there? She 'n' me broke up because she wouldn't stop drinkin'; three weeks later she married a guy she didn't even know; she's wearin' her sister's fur coat."

* * *

Since it's the usual thing for publicity men to speak more tactfully than truthfully of their clients, it's refreshing to get Stanford University's press blurb for Prof. Ronald Hilton's recent compilation of a definitive "Who's Who in Latin America."

This man of learning, says the release, is **"a man with a harrassed expression"** and **"his hands shake when he opens letters . . . from Bolivia, Chile and Peru."**

The reason is that **"a few, a very few"** of South America's leading professional personalities are inclined to respond with Latin hot-bloodedness to his requests for information. **"United States propaganda,"** they charge.

Others, meeker, reply with full books on themselves—heavy going to eke out five essential lines.

Still others, who seem to think of themselves more as candidates for **"Who WAS Who,"** just write about their worries.

And those who don't respond at all, later file the most **"voluble protests at omission."**

Don't let anyone kid you that all runs smoothly in the production of our books, the release seems to say. **"Professor Hilton . . . jumps at sudden sounds."**

HERE TODAY..

By KEVIN WALLACE

Well, the Old Year will die tonight—along with the usual hordes of jolly folks, and hapless passersby at intersections, as they drive home from tilting a horn and quaffing a goblet and bidding care begone. . . . Tiresome old newspapers and posters have come out against drunken driving for years—but the happy crowd is determined to die for its rights, so let's cheer them up today, while there's time.

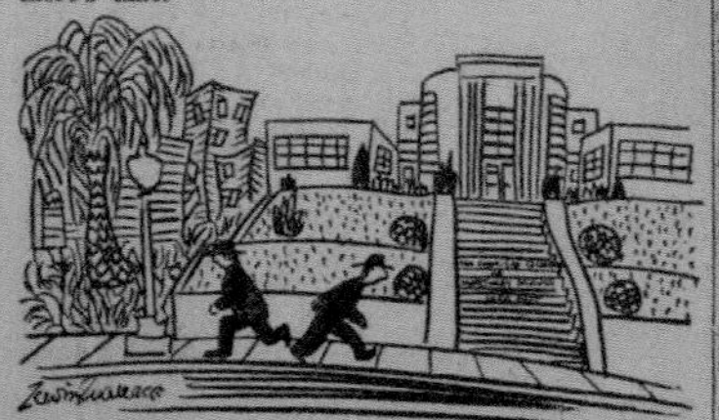

As a bracer to those who plan to drink and drive tonight, we print (above) a picture of the temple dedicated to their case. It rises out of the squalid neighborhood at 1450 Post like the pyramid of Cheops staring out of Egypt—high and noble, terraced and serene, orderly and encouraging, untouched by the surrounding ravages of life.

It is the San Francisco College of Mortuary Science.

Be carefree, kids! Tootle off on your merry chase. Beat the others away from the stop sign . . . Trained specialists, artists at their work, are waiting to take care of you. If you don't overdo it, they can glue you up to look natural as anything.

* * *

Have you seen the distinguished looking gent in the camel's hair coat, wandering around Union Square with a sort of sandwich board slung over his shoulder, saying:

"WANTED TO RENT — ANY APARTMENT UP TO $125"?

No, the shortage isn't over, and an ex-Army captain named Bill Rafter—whom I met on a house-hunting expedition last summer—still hasn't lined up a hut, to judge by today's mail from Telegraph Hill.

Every house on the hill, evidently, has received a mimeographed letter from the Rafters, who seem to be getting a little delirious. At least, the circular ends up:

"Owing to the excessive demand for tenants of our caliber, we advise you to avoid the rush by submitting your bid immediately. All offers will receive individual attention and UTMOST consideration . . . proposals of marriage will be accepted sight unseen, provided suitor has an apartment or flat."

* * *

Probably you noticed the ads of that lower Post Street haberdasher, who offered to accept all the loud Christmas ties brought in by malcontent husbands as down payment on a conservative tie.

The turn-in value was one dollar.

Well, a check on the management reveals that the plan has worked out very well. In the first three business days after Christmas, about three hundred wild cravats turned up.

A lot of them were expensive types—hand-painted, especially.

The prize is a custom job which still smells of paint, and has sequins ornamenting gruesome likenesses of dismembered hands and feet. A runner up is an electric blue knit tie with funeral flowers painted all over it.

The shop is amassing its turn-ins on a rack, and eventually will exhibit them in a window display as horrible examples of what wives will do to their husbands.

After that, they'll be turned over to a charity for bazaar purposes. Or bizarre purposes, if the charity people want to wear them instead of sell them.

Not all of the shop's customers have caught on, however. Fifty of the terrible ties have been bought from the horrible example rack. Price—one buck.

Target for Today

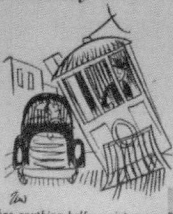

I think the critics of the Municipal Railway are off on the wrong foot. San Francisco's street cars aren't broken down — they're QUAINT! Take this one—a tilted job I saw south of Market the other day . . . I think it was a 20 car on Fourth Street, and I think it had just sprung a spring—but I decided to clear the street without investigating further, on grounds of self-preservation . . . I don't know what kept it on its wheels. Suspension from the overhead trolley, perhaps . . . What other town has anything half so picturesque? Aren't you proud?

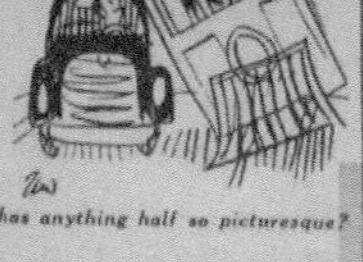

HERE TODAY..

By KEVIN WALLACE

As Prehistoric Man hovered anxiously over the dying embers of his lightning-kindled bonfire, so the Black Cat of Upper Montgomery has conscientiously fanned the fainting brow of ragged old, talented old, thirsty old Bohemia—unwilling to let it expire, though uncertain, perhaps, as to why. . . . Sunday night, for a change, the drinks were on Bohemia itself, when the Black Cat's staff and clientele were transported up to the artistic Farwell Taylors' svelte Washington Street penthouse.

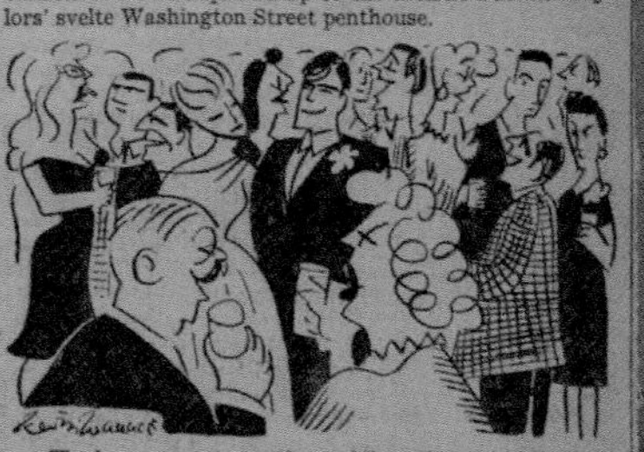

The happy event was the wedding of the bistro's chief barkeep, Frederico Guillermo Jorges Clark, who bestowed the last and least of his names on a beauty by the name of Dorothy Hawks.

For a little while, the denizens of the Montgomery Block's canyon shadows wandered around blinking at the light. But very shortly, the gathering took on the look of any other gala festivity on the art museum level.

Henri Lenoir, a sturdy survivor from the dear dead days of the avant garde, was busily showing off his sartorial elegance.

"I wore my new coat," he confessed with pride. **"I like it. I think I'll buy it."**

Myrio Dundas, the detective novelist, was self-assertedly in search of material for a new murder mystery, but nobody so much as flinched.

Gene Smith, another representative from the bar, nervously fingered his curled mustachios—which were once stolen by a razor fiend, to the detriment of his credit with Lloyds of London. Lloyds had insured them for $530.

Then there was a dark, brooding young lady who walked up to me and asked if I was stuck up or something . . . Altogether, there was a lot of champagne, and everybody had a good time except the Taylors' small daughter, who asked her ma who all those people were and what they were hollering about.

She had her ma there.

* * *

Yes, San Francisco is a great place for the arts, and it has a rather smug idea of itself as second only to New York in its patronage of them . . . The impression—though possibly true—doesn't mean much, however. . . . Here is Maxim Schapiro's report on his recent Alaskan concert tour:

"In Juneau, 1,000 people heard me out of a population of 6,000. Suppose the same thing were to happen in New York: population, 7,000,000; audience—1,150,000! My goodness!"

YOUR goodness, Maxim! Why, last week in Laramie, Wyo., (population: 10,380), 2,200 people went to see the Geary's new "Anna Lucasta." On the same ratio, that would make a New York audience of 1,540,000.

* * *

Anyhow, a Happy Chinese New Year to you today.

The phrase is one that will be worked to death down in Palo Alto today, where Donaldina Cameron will hear it from many of the thousands of former slave girls whose emancipation she arranged.

The drawing below shows you Miss Cameron, whose forty years at the old Chinese Presbyterian Mission at 920 Sacramento Street were covered in Carol Green Wilson's "Chinatown Quest."

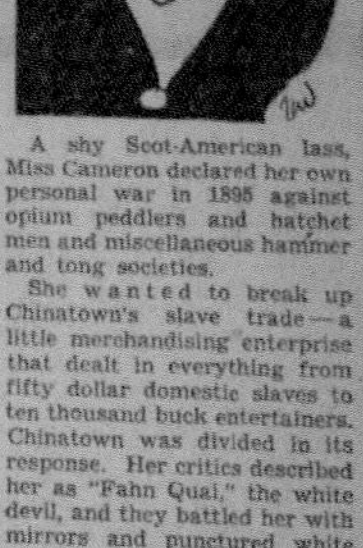

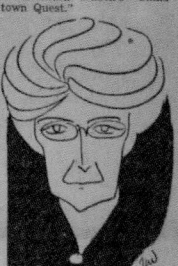

A shy Scot-American lass, Miss Cameron declared her own personal war in 1895 against opium peddlers and hatchet men and miscellaneous hammer and tong societies.

She wanted to break up Chinatown's slave trade — a little merchandising enterprise that dealt in everything from fifty dollar domestic slaves to ten thousand buck entertainers. Chinatown was divided in its response. Her critics described her as "Fahn Quai," the white devil, and they battled her with mirrors and punctured white paper, which are death on devils, ordinarily.

Miss Cameron fought right back, armed with an umbrella and a police whistle, and she was cheered on by the approving factions. They called her "Lo Mo," meaning mother.

She won.

HERE TODAY..

By KEVIN WALLACE

One of our senior operatives, Bobs Purcell, was haled into court the other day by Judge Theresa Meikle—not because he'd done anything wrong, but just to act as a witness for a marriage the judge was formalizing. It was all routine, except afterwards, when Judge Meikle fixed the unsteady groom with a firm eye and ordered:

"Now comes the fee—and make it as large as possible, please."

The victim, a Navy warrant officer, nervously peeled off a ten spot—and the judge (who is possibly fed up with the domestic turmoil of the uncontested divorce court she runs) passed it right over to the bride, remarking just as firmly:

"Now here's your first wedding present—and I hope you get a lot more just like it, from now on."

* * *

Today's excursion (see drawing) takes you up the ramshackly steps at the right of Golden Gate Park's con-

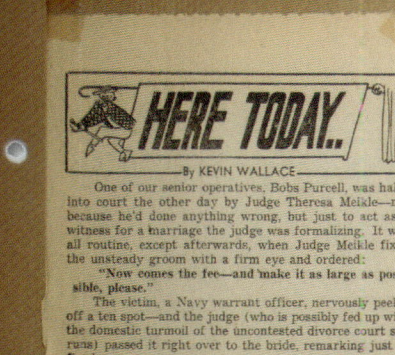

servatory, to an enchanted amphitheater which might have modeled for the forest sequences in Disney's "Snow White."

Soaked in the perfumes of spring, and appropriately garlanded, it is the rendezvous of old San Franciscans, laden with ancient yarns and bags of goodies. The former are for each other, and the latter are for their regular clients, whose celebrities have been catalogued for this office by our Mr. Hinman:

Muggins is the name of the senior squirrel. He is a tough old case, who lords it over the other animals—but they all get fed. With a flirt of the tail, the squirrels are climbing all over you, looking for peanuts, the minute you sit down.

The quail contingency is led by one with a crooked tail, who is the mother, and one with a gimp, the father.

There is one rabbit, and he scorns carrots and lettuce, preferring to concentrate his attention on soda crackers.

Salted soda crackers, that is. None of your dull, unseasoned, rabbit food for him.

There is also a brown rat who drops past daily to meet an elderly lady friend. She always brings him a vanilla ice cream cone, which he eats thoughtfully, and departs.

Once they get outside the amphitheater, they're wild animals again.

* * *

Across the park's main drive from the scene above, you'll see the alert looking sportsman drawn below. In spite of the obvious fact that he is pitching, he has become known to passersby as **"Casey at the Bat"**—an error which isn't corrected by the plaque on his pedestal, saying only:

"Presented to the Golden Gate Park by a Friend of the Sculptor, as a tribute to his Energy, Industry and Ability."

In small print, around on the side, the sculptor is identified—Douglas Tilden.

And that's the only memorial we have of the deaf mute genius whose struggles gave many others a permanent niche in memory. For instance, his marvelous Donahue Memorial, **"The Mechanics,"** on lower Market Street, and his **"Junipero Serra"** in the park.

Born in Chico in 1860, Tilden got the idea that California was meant to be a reincarnation of ancient Greece. Sculpture was his contribution to the revival that never came.

The late Senator Phelan staked him to a lot of the bronze he brought to life—but not everyone was so kind, and much of his life had to be spent as a mechanic, and a teacher of the deaf.

His Spanish-American War Memorial at Van Ness and Market was the first new structure to rise out of the ashes of San Francisco in 1906. . . . He was the first artist to establish a studio in Berkeley—in '83.

That was where he died, too, twelve years back—alone, and broke.

HERE TODAY..

By KEVIN WALLACE

That cartoon below (to get it over with) shows you the view from Coit Tower on Telegraph Hill. Or, rather, it shows you people looking at the view, which is something which Man finds it hard to do, and just let it go at that. Either he has to take a snapshot of it, or distort it through binoculars, or explain it all to the poor soul alongside him, who keeps saying **"Mmmm"** and **"Well, I'll be!"** Ten minutes of eavesdropping at Coit Tower will supply you with more misinformation about local landmarks than ten years of reading this column. . . . Those slot machine binoculars—there's one in use on the left and a free one on the right—are employed a good deal at night by Peep-

ing Toms, who train them on the wide windows of the hotels and apartment houses crowning the hills of the city. There's a safe and sane way to do anything.

* * *

Around Christmastime, I referred perplexed husbands to an Examiner classified ad which offered a $200,000 real estate property as a trifling gift suggestion for the wife and kiddies.

The broker involved, Elias Rhine, now informs me that one of my highly impressionable readers has bought it, and today I am going about my work with a new serenity and sense of accomplishment.

I had no idea any of you people were so rich.

* * *

The Society Page is pressed for space today, so I have taken over its news release on the hub-bub of social activity set off by the happy expectancy of the J. Waldo Rittlers of San Leandro.

The list of stork showers given recently for Mrs. Rittler is too copiousto report, aside from notnig thatMrs. Charles Schlegel hostessed one with **"pink diaper nut cups and napkins in the form of small saques"**—a touch of surrealism which Mrs. Adam Peterson and Mrs. C. B. Fisher bettered with a really extraordinary job of cooking.

"The supper," says the report, **"was elaborately carried out in pink and blue."**

Well, the female mind is ever elusive, and I hope you don't think I'm saying that critically. Mr. Rittler, however, somehow got rung in on these rites, and was given a shower by Mr. and Mrs. Howard Wilken.

"A beautifully planned buffet supper preceded the 'poppa' shower," I quote, **"at which Mr. Rittler received such appropriate gifts as ear stops, smelling salts, chewing gum, rubber heels, baby food, records, cigars, matches, cigarettes, and an amusing assortment of bottles containing varied and assorted sundries."**

This cryptic allusion to bottled sundries disturbs me. A man in a delicate state, thus exposed, is liable to snatch up and drink the first bottled sundry that comes his way, and I hope it wasn't poison.

* * *

Speaking of the female mind, here is a thought for today excerpted from the San Francisco College of Women's Tower magazine, announcing next weekend's school play:

"'Romeo and Juliet' is a most apt play for a group of young women to give because the male parts are all young men."

* * *

The telephone strike has interrupted the habit patterns of several dogs, judging from the response to my story on George McCabe's dog answering the phone.

Beth Beri Carruthers reports that her Kerry Blue terrier **"not only answers the phone but hands me the receiver"**—a fine thing for a healthy, grown dog to be doing, when he should be outside in the fresh air!

George M. Hearst, who helps to give The Examiner composing room its composure, has a convivial dog who won't come home until George phones for him.

"Put Rowdy on the line," he tells the dog's host. **"Come on home,"** he tells the critter, and home he comes.

The people at Paul's Horse Ranch in San Bruno have attracted my attention to a goat named Horace, who hangs around the Millbrae Riding Club, cadging beer and operating the candy vending machines.

They compare him favorably to dogs who answer telephones, but I don't see any grounds for comparison. Goats are different. Let's keep on the subject.

HERE TODAY..

By KEVIN WALLACE

Dentist-bound on a Sutter Street car, Frances Forcade forgot all about her toothache by trying to place the familiar look of a hat adorning a lady in front of her. . . . Just before the lady got off at Powell and headed smartly towards the St. Francis, Miss Forcade identified it—a child's miniature wicker chair, upside down with the back over the forehead, the feet in the air, and sweetpeas tucked into it.

* * *

On Tuesday in The Examiner's comic page, Rip Kirby was telephoning the city desk over a mobile unit identified as Radiophone Press Car WJ-62320. Allan Jackson, INS war correspondent and Oakland Post-Enquirer reporter, also has a press car radiotelephone licensed as WJ-62320. Kirby has the wrong number, like everybody these days. . . . (My sister phoned twice from Carmel to Berkeley and got New York City first and Sioux City next. So she drove up to Berkeley, phoned to Orinda, and got Denver. She feels the emergency operators are just trying too hard.)

* * *

In the drawing below you have "daliel's," a new Berkeley booke shoppe and arty gallery, appearing superficially to be just another of the exotic blooms which occa-

sionally make an expensive appearance on a prosaic block, vending pamphlets which are understandably rare, the way purple cows are rare.

But the April Harper's, mentioned last week by Freddie Francisco, has changed all that. In her account of northern California's **"New Cult of Sex and Anarchy,"** Mildred Edie Brady of Berkeley names **"daliel's"** as one of the fountainheads of a rare new hobohemianism, a rather cozy heresy with an unusually intense attitude towards domestic bliss.

From what Mrs. Brady says, the cult sounds like just another variation on the sort of thing that has been bouncing around the coast's shabby esthetic circles for generations. Not much for anybody to get excited about, except the targets, who ought to be raging mad.

Not at all, though. In "daliel's" window display, four copies of the nefarious magazine issue are exhibited. They're just for show, however. If you go inside and ask for one, you go on a waiting list.

The rare book business is rare indeed.

* * *

While the rest of the world goes to hell, the Steinhart Acquarium people stick with the eternal verities, and it's nice to have them around.

This week their news release concerns a fish in Tank 177 with a swelling under her jaw. The swelling indicates that she has just become a mother, and she is keeping the eggs in her teeth like spitballs, waiting for them to hatch.

She is an Egyptian Mouthbreeding Fish, so there's nothing unusual in her behavior as far as she's concerned.

Over in another part of the California Academy of Sciences at Golden Gate Park, Velma Harris announced matter-of-factly:

"I am now working on sky blue mushrooms. I have just finished a chocolate colored group and a brilliant orange and magenta mushroom is ready to install."

What the lady is up to is merely making wax reproductions of Tiburon mushrooms which really grow in those interesting tints.

Back in the acquarium branch of the organization two oysters, complete with pearls, have been received, along with five barrels of fish, from a Mr. Mikimito in Japan.

Everyone is busy and happy and going about his work.

* * *

Having talked so much about the handcrafting (not to mention ghosting, laundering and mining) on Grant Avenue's fabulous 1400-block, I am obliged to invite you at this point to an exhibit of the block's efforts, Sunday afternoon 1 to 8, 1415 Grant.

It is my less happy privilege to announce that Paramount's **"Calcutta,"** which opened very quietly here a week ago, was actually having its world premiere in our blessed city.

Nobody realized it, though, until several days later, when word got out that the glamorous premiere for the affair is scheduled for New York City, next week.

Lenny Bernstein, the musician with the polka-dot bow tie, surfaced. He was in town to show the score of a little opera he was writing, "Trouble in Tahiti," to Aaron Copeland, who was giving a music appreciation course that year. He brought Copeland around and tingled his opera's Tahitian dance motif on our piano.

"That's not Tahitian, it's Portuguese," I cried. "Listen to the real stuff."

I put Angie Goupil's Tahitian dance record on the phonograph. Bernstein cocked his noble head in an attitude of disinterested learning. But he said, "I like the drum work, but it doesn't sound right."

"Trouble in Tahiti" came out with its Portuguese dance music intact.

Copeland invited us to his birthday party in a queer old riverside mansion where he seemed to be rooming. Helen and I fell into conversation with the landlord whom I'd seen around the Yard and thought the image of Ralph Waldo Emerson. He confessed he was Emerson's grandson, name of Forbes, and emeritus professor. I asked what school he was associated with.

"Finnatz," said the Brahmin.

"Finance? The Grad School of Business Administration?" I asked.

"No, no," he said, enunciating with greater care, "Fin Aatz — Fogg Museum."

***

Grant was getting well into his eighties, and his relationships with the Pleiades people had taken a on a causal and sporadic character, as between any old colleagues of not always trustworthy aspiration.

The math projectors simmered down to jiggering with the intransigent Truthmeter, Oren getting sidetracked by inventing word games and mathematical puzzles just for the hell of it. One of these developments Grant tried to market under the name of Quizzems, though not with undue effort.

Still a handsome and august old gent, Grant liked to spellbind my friends, not with metaphysical stuff he knew they couldn't handle, but with Grand Canyon and Manchuria war and turn-of-the-century Greenwich Village anecdotes, and philosophical speculations drawn from them.

He also enjoyed swiping cuttings from neighbors' gardens up and down Tamalpais Road in Berkeley, and in Carmel, too, for Peggy's machinations with developers at The Ranch eventually were rewarding enough to pay for a second home back in Carmel again.

It was their early-Carmel neighbored John Kenneth Turner's shabby little board-and-bat cottage, sitting without foundation in the middle of the last five otherwise undeveloped building lots in the city limits, inside a table of oaks and nasturtiums and yucca in the draw above the Mission.

With the house came the last in the series of "hired men," a natural-born alcoholic Arkansas genius named Oddie, left on the premises by his uncle, who had been summoned to fix a leak in the room. Oddie's resourcefulness was unbounded and original. When the starter went out on Peggy's care, Oddie retired things so that the car started by touching the ignition with a teaspoon.

Peggy's aura distracted Oddie from boozing, but only so long as she kept him busy and didn't pay him. She started out paying him, but found this led directly back to the drunk tank. She tried storing his pay in a savings and loan account, which contained a good sum when he heard about it, and transferred it to the a marvelous binge.

To keep Oddie busy, Peggy had him add rooms and decks and picture windows onto the fragile old cottage until it become an extensive structure, charming and cockeyed, since Oddie had no use for a T-square and improvised angles as the mood hit him. In Berkeley, Oddie was given my old garden shack. Grant got along famously with Oddie, who reminded him of a coon dog he'd owned and favored as a boy.

Grant died in his eight-seventh year in the house in Berkeley, not of anything in particular, just use. He was haughty as usual about the tiresome procedure, which he regarded as typical of the whole badly arranged business of dredging karmic incarnations.

"I'll be glad to get rid of this pesky clay cage and out of this kindergarten," he remarked airily.

Whether the Pleiades people had been on the level or not didn't trouble him, nor was he bothered that their collaboration hadn't been finished, since truth will out one way or another, and his responsibility had been discharged so far as practicable.

What did annoy him was his Fairoaks relatives' offer of a headstone if he'd consent to enter the family plot.

It had been a good many years since I'd sought his option on on my assignment to carry on his Big Work. I had a vague idea that I was probably somehow involved in doing just that, though on a course that its clear perception.

After he died I sat by his body a while before calling the crematory people to make their pickup. I tried to decide if his life added up

Moira and her third husband Guthrie Corvoisier launched the Courac of Monterey company, producing decorative plateware featuring Guthrie's one-of-a-kind black plastic and Moira's inlaied artwork.

O Well
by Kevin Wallace
1961
Copyrighted Reproduction
Produced by Museum Pieces, Inc.

Manufacturer's stamp
Minor damage

satisfactorily against his aspirations, but it didn't seem to be a matter of sums — as one of his old editorials said, " a question not of destination but of adventures along the way."

To outwit the Fairoaks contingent's lobbying to get Grant buried beside his first wife, Peggy ordered a little inurnment ceremony, where I met my half-brother Grant Junior for the second time in my life. A printer about to retire, he lived a few blocks from us in Berkeley, and amiable fellow.

I flew the next day to represent the Chronicle on a junket arranged by the United Fruit Company to show the press that it and the CIA hadn't engineered the rightest coup they had just pulled off in Guatemala City. Their nervous new Guatemalan president showed us a room full of allegedly confiscated Soviet tracts — prompting a New Orleans journalist to ask who besides United Fruit had cargo space to import it all — but otherwise no proof of the previous regine's subversive nature spoiled the tourist agenda.

My limousine driver to and from Chichicastenango's market day was fatalistic about being shot in the near future as an intellectual revolutionary aristocrat.

In Chichicastenango cathedral the Mayans were burning bird at candles in masses of flower petals and a fog of incense, it being one of the six pagan days celebrated to balance the Catholicism every seventh day there.

The night before we took the toner I'll down the slope to board a company ship for New Orleans and home, our United Fruit Company host took me along to visit a local manager, shuddering in the watch tower of his electrically-fenced, heavily gated and grated suburban mansion.

"The Communists are going to get booze to those Mayans, who'll get in and murder me," our host declared. "Just take it easy, "my companion soothed him.

The toner I'll paused on its downward flight next day, past aimless little bands of soldiers toting guns, for us to prowl around the marvelous carved stone images at Quiriqua, where Grant had been a Mayan priest, 873 A.D. to 963 A.D. The knowledge made me right at home.

***

Before Peggy died, ten years later, suburban development caught up with The Ranch, and she had become a mistress of the fine arts of pulling the wool over the eyes of wily developers.

The courtier they became in anticipation of fleecing this unworldly lady with the flowing auburn hair, and palming off inferior construction and design on the witless public, the more other-worldly her vagueness became, until they found themselves doing things precisely as she decided they must be done.

I moved meantime with Helen and the children to New York, on another expedition intended to quell Divine discontent with such Big Work as was available in the magazines world with the New Yorker Magazine.

Peggy, whose old Carmel tastes had little use for cash and less for paying capital gains tax, deferred the latter by trading The Ranch property for lovely building sites around Carmel, down the coast and up the valley, as offerings to lure us back from the east.

As we scorned each in turn, she would trade it for another ideal site, a game she enjoyed for its own sake, partly because her ancestral image was so involved with Antrim's similar terrain, and partly because of the battle of wits she enjoyed with a fiendish real estate woman named Virginia who arranged most of the trades.

Virginia became notorious for her crooked dealings and was involved in scores of simultaneious lawsuits with dissatisfied clients. But her machinations in trying to manipulate Peggy's ebullient sentiment over lovely vistas and enchanted trees were good enough for Peggy to relish even as she saw through them. And she was confident she could prevail.

One trade Virginia arranged provided Peggy with quite a large and precipitous redwood forest around the headwaters of Garrapata Creek. The idea being to give Oddie a calling, making roof shakes on a mill he improvised from old auto parts in the deep shade of a creekside grove.

The trouble was that he also sold the shakes for money and money was his instant ticket back to the county farm.

Virginia tried to fleece Peggy out of a lot she wanted back, claiming Peggy had forgotten her oral contract approving the transfer. Challenged, Virginia produced he carbon copy of a fictitious letter of acknowledgement of the agreement, citing her visit to Peggy at her cottage that same day.

The letter happened to be dated during a period documented by bills as that of Peggy's hospitalization for pneumonia — a finding I made and pointed out when I visited from New York, first to Peggy and then by phone to Virginia, who answered that Peggy had lost her wits and concluded "Sue me!"

Peggy still was inclined to charity towards Virginia, until Virginia went too far. She wrote to Peggy's lawyer that Peggy had grown unsound of mind, which was too silly to offend Peggy, and that this was due to a particularly poisonous hair dye seeping through Peggy's scalp, which was Virginia's error.

"I've never used anything but Miss Clairol in my life," Peggy exploded, and got into the fray. Virginia surrendered the lot.

(above) Merry Christmas from the Wallaces: Helen, Deirdre, Brian, and dog Mee-Too. (right) Brian and Deirdre practice instruments while home for the holidays.

Peggy died in her eightieth year, by no means eagerly, though her blithe frame had been used up. Besides Miss Clairol, she had used cold cream every night, and a young heroine's overoptimistic outlook, and there wasn't a wrinkle on her face.

Moira and I came by her hospital room one night during Peggy's last illness and were told, erroneously, she had a few minutes to live. Some discussion ensued as to whether we should disturb her "to reassure her." The pros and cons of waking anyone bound to die in a few minutes in order to reassure her was and is too much for me to untangle. Peggy sometimes said she though "Laughter is at the heart of the universe," which may have applied.

Her superannuated and flimsy little Carmel cottage, with its cockeyed additions by Oddie, was sold afterwards for. A good price because of the five building lots it sat athwart. So I was astonished on my next visit to Carmel to see it look n the same as ever, and to find that its reverent buyers had paid a fortune to take it apart, install a firm foundation, and reassemble its every skewed corner and joint in place, as an enduring monument to "early Carmel architectural history."

We settled in New York first in a Riverside Drive apartment house that had gone downhill since John Barrymore kept a mistress there.

Winter gales drove across the Hudson River's ice flowed through our window frames to blow our weighted drapes horizontally across the ceiling and route us for shelter to the kitchen. There the garbage chute emitted cinders and sparks from the basement, and the boom of the super's rifle blasting rats.

In the sultrier seasons the front windows gave a good view of roving bands of hoods mugging Brian, and the foot patrolman hastening the other way.

The city seemed definitely inconvenient. We moved fifty miles north on the Harlem Division commute train, and ten miles east of the depot, where we bought a cottage on a lake amid wooded hills.

Deirdre joined the Presbyterian youth trough without any questioning about her religious training, and went on outings to West Virginia to dismantle Baptist churches for firewood for Appalachia's poor.

Brian joined the Boy Scouts and was threatened with expulsion when he said he didn't know if he believed in God. I told him we believed in God as some sort of immanent rationality that we try to recognize and pin down, unsuccessfully. The scoutmaster let it go, but Helen claimed I was espousing bigotry and superstition.

The geographical cure for domesticity was going not too well.

Helen finally settled her original question as to our being matched, in the negative, and this revived romantic enterprises to a fair pitch for year. But she was determined to reinstate me wholly to my original splendor as unattainable ideal. I still refused to abandon her. She grew more distressed. I yielded and moved out.

"You haven't lost a father, you've gained a weekend townhouse," I told the children, introducing them on alternate weekends to my dark new apartment on the fourth floor rear of a converted brownstone in the East Seventies. My terrace adjoined that of the resident burglar in the abandoned brownstone next door, with whole I had a nodding aquaintance.

Helen flew to Juarez and back with a divorce. Pining, I filed a night letter asking her to marry me, realized it would simply drive her to fury, and cancelled it, and next morning drove out to pick up the kids for a visitation drive. As I came down the path Helen's phone rang. It was Mrs. Henry Wallace down the lake. During the night her husband, the former Vice President of the United States, had passed away.

"I have a night letter here that seems to be for you," Mrs. Wallace told Mrs. Wallace.

Helen was amused after all.

I was seeing a Park Avenue psychoanalyst but couldn't make out what he wanted me to do. He was non-directive. I decided to embrace the opportunities of bachelorhood. I went to a large party Joan Fontaine gave for Adlai Stevenson. She was expansive, he dapper, and the crowd scintillating.

A classy blond said "you look so disapproving" and led me out.

She was Dotty, a skilled houseguest all over Europe with a tiny apartment near me overlooking the Park, the scene of in time gatherings where Marcel Duchamp was lionized and NOrman Mailer was quarrelsome. The icebox contained champagne, syringes, and prescriptions from seven doctors unknown to one another.

Dotty was so buoyed by my disapproval that she bought herself a new white mink coat and dragged me to the Apollo Theatre and Sweet's Ballroom in Harlem, which was at the time out of bounds to whiteys.

We did New Year's at Al and Dolly Hirschfeld's, skipped the Strasbergs' and afterwards Dotty persisted in unleashing her demented Afghan for me to pursue through Central Park's snowdrifts and shivering degenerates. The dog went everywhere with her, ruining rugs and eating fine wallpaper while Dotty exuded charm.

She had a gangling thirtyish son who wandered in from Dublin occasionally with news of peyote and mushroom cults.

She was widely acquainted, and was able to identify the loud grating sounds that erupted in the middle of the night from the apartment above mine.

"Prince Georgi lives up there," she said. "To get settled for sleep, he likes to shove his steamer trunks around."

She added that Georgi, an UN translator, was the brother of a princess named Missie, who lived in Barcelona as the current wife of my original brother-in-law, Peter Harnden, who commuted to New York on gallery business.

So it was not surprising when, one midnight, I answered Dotty's anguished call for a hot water-bottle and descended her elevator, only to find Harnden himself waiting in the lobby, clutching another hot water-bottle.

"Peter!" I cried.

"Kevie!" Said he, and ascended.

***

Deirdre grew in beauty, finished college and married. Brian started playing rural nightclubs at 15, and was a cabaret star after classes at Harvard where he pioneered integrating Radcliffe dorms. His conscientious objector petitions foiled his drafting into the Vietnam war.

The kids went with me on summer holidays to Europe and California and Puerto Rico and Mexico, where I picked up a severe case of hepatitis, putting a crimp in my patronage of the Harvard Club bar.

The bar, a Brooks Brothers version of O'Neill's "The Ice Man Cometh," was a refuge for reluctant commuters. Hepatitis gave the bar routine a new unhinge game effect, landing me in a hospital with what was called extreme exhaustion.

An Alcoholics Anonymous crew visited me in my pain, and I accepted their invitation to a meeting, where I found half the actresses I'd met with Dotty around town. One in particular, reduced to daytime soap opera work, was every night a star again in the redemptive AA confessionals all over town, where for a week I accompanied here.

But I hadn't sins enough for confessing, and was not yet content that my foot was on the path, nor my eyes on the Big Work. I attributed this to my office.

Though in its youth it had been frivolous, my magazine had grown mature, and in the nature of earnestness, inclined to accept any bill of goods with reverence. My editors saved me from awkwardness by excising little flippancies I introduced by way of distancing. For a time I tried to be as important in outlook as it was, temperate, measured.

I had intemperately told Lenny Bernstein, the talented young musician, that his music for "West Side Story" was fine, but the book and lyrics awful, only to hear him say, "But I wrote some fo the lyrics myself."

Subsequently, on the say-so of a producer who said Bernstein would compose a score for Huxley's "Brave New World," if I would write a presentable adaptation, I sketched one, and was informed by the composer, "Never write a free book for the theater."

I saw the folly of intemperate speech, but chafed to use it.

The magazine had me do the definitive status report on psychical research, at the time geared to the statistical card tricks of the moving disappointed but hopeful divinity student, Dr. Rhine. Even Eileen Garrett's holy Institute for Parapsychology, while livelier than Grant's old American Society for Psy-

chical Research, wasn't a patch on Grant's old Carmel studio.

I painted, sculpted and looked on at an acquaintance, one of the prime movers of Madison Avenue's gallery industries, discovering and anointing a new genius in a two-minute call on a loft containing a vast canvas with a shoe embedded in featureless impasto.

"I could be wrong," he said as he trotted ahead of me down seven flights of stairs afterwards, "but it was too cold to take more time."

I undertook to write a major opus on my childhood acquaintance from Edward Weston's salon, Ansel Adams, and wrote it five times without getting it to suit me. I studied Ansel's methods and became a not bad photographer, cutting into my sculpting and painting sidelines. The trouble was artistic status. How great was he, or how overrated?

As a boy in San Francisco, Ansel had dedicated himself to art, studied for the concert piano stage, and supported himself with photography, not then regarded as art. He decided to drop the piano in favor of photography, on the condition that the latter be elevated to the status he had dedicated himself to, and set about contriving the elevation.

He published photo art criticism and how-to books of photo art standards, and he master-minded the introduction of a photo department into the Museum of Modern Art. The department's existence certified photography as art, inviting contrary critics and photographers and dealers to controversy. The positive result was the opportunity for photographers' prices to rise — thou never to the realm of one-of-a-kind hand-drawn articles — but the accompanying crucial murk led photographers to join painters and sculptors as illustrators of silly philosophical dicta.

I saw I must again evaluate my destined Big Work in the light of the contingent nature of metaphysical knowledge and artist merit. My interior voice club as ever to the interlocking cheerfulness of all being vanity, and home springing eternal, in this best of all possible worlds.

After Peggy's death, the land sale netted a fortune which, invested under prudent management, rapidly vanished

My children were now full grown and I was free to abandon New York, the eyes and ears and mind of the Midwest consumer, with its weather unsuitable for human habitation, and returned to San Francisco, where my lungs felt at home.

Deluded that New York surgeons were best, I tried to have a cataract lopped from one eye, precipitating a string of four retinal detachments, spurring the surgeon to more desperate trial-and-error strategies with knives and sewing needles each time. He claimed my case was unsuitable to laser, which he didn't have.
The last time he ordered me back to surgery, I took the next plane from San Francisco where a laser surgeon repaired as much damage as possible, and the Bay commerce under Telegraph Hill gradually was reborn to my grateful apprehension.

I'm back in the old city room, where unlike The New Yorker, they don't mind my doing freak stuff, great work, big work, and art if you ever saw art, and felt its megalomaniacal rewards, as I reduced environmental menace to drollery, and destiny to a snappy comeback.

There is an embarrassing resurgence of interest in the occult of all sorts around the Bay Area these days, and I frequently am called on to interview its leaders, who in the radiance of discovered would not likely credit any tale I might tell about all this having happened before.

I encouraged Moira in Monterey to rise above the fiats exhorting her to throw down her paints and brushes in favor of art concocted of videotapes and destruction of random objects, for I claim art is what she prefers it to be, even if her preference is for good look paintings.

Art is occupational therapy to please the ego, a sociable fantasy in a frame that prevents it spilling over into hallucination and mad action.

One calls it Big Work and claims for it the power of prophecy, but that is just salesmanship, a necessary hype to mislead the critical faculties that would spoil its fun. It hasn't really magical powers because there aren't any, and the views we get are the glimpses we are equipped to get.

It's 1979, and here at my desk I counsel my younger colleagues that we are all cartoonists doting the Big Work of starving off our propensities for depression by selecting and distorting the world's neutral materials pleasingly rather than distressingly, to ourselves and to whoever responds similarly.

Some of my communicants are advocacy journalists who believe Big Work must shove institutions around with the bringing of light to the darkened mind. I tell them they're talking about advertising. At the heart of advertising is the seed of depression, the assumption that fate has unjustly put one in a state of deprivation that must be ameliorated by acquiring a better car or brighter toothpaste or more righteous cause. It creates interest and excitement but not innocent pleasure.

Art does not browbeat. With it, one is already there, absorbed and invulnerable, for the moment.

- 30 -

The author, Kevin Wallace, photographed in the *San Francisco Chronicle* newsroom before his death in 1979.

Art Order: *SF Chronicle*

Original Illustrations for newsprint by Kevin Wallace

Kevin Wallace sketched as quick as his wit, enabling him to draw up a masterful illustration of a feature story, daily news item, or current event, and still meet the evening deadline for his written column to go with it. In this collection of "Art Orders' submitted to the prepress operators of the *San Francisco Chronicle*, capture the magnificent vistas of San Francisco and the Bay Area. The illustrator's hand-written notes also add surprise and delight, like the personal message to the press operators: "fragile—do not drool on the ink, because it runs. Return to K. Wallace."

Old Farms
by Kevin Wallace
9-16-1974
Bay Area Farmland

Signed by artist
Original art order card
Unframed; Good Condition

Bunkers No. 1
by Kevin Wallace
10-15-1974
Fort Bragg

Signed by artist, Original art order
Unframed; Fair condition

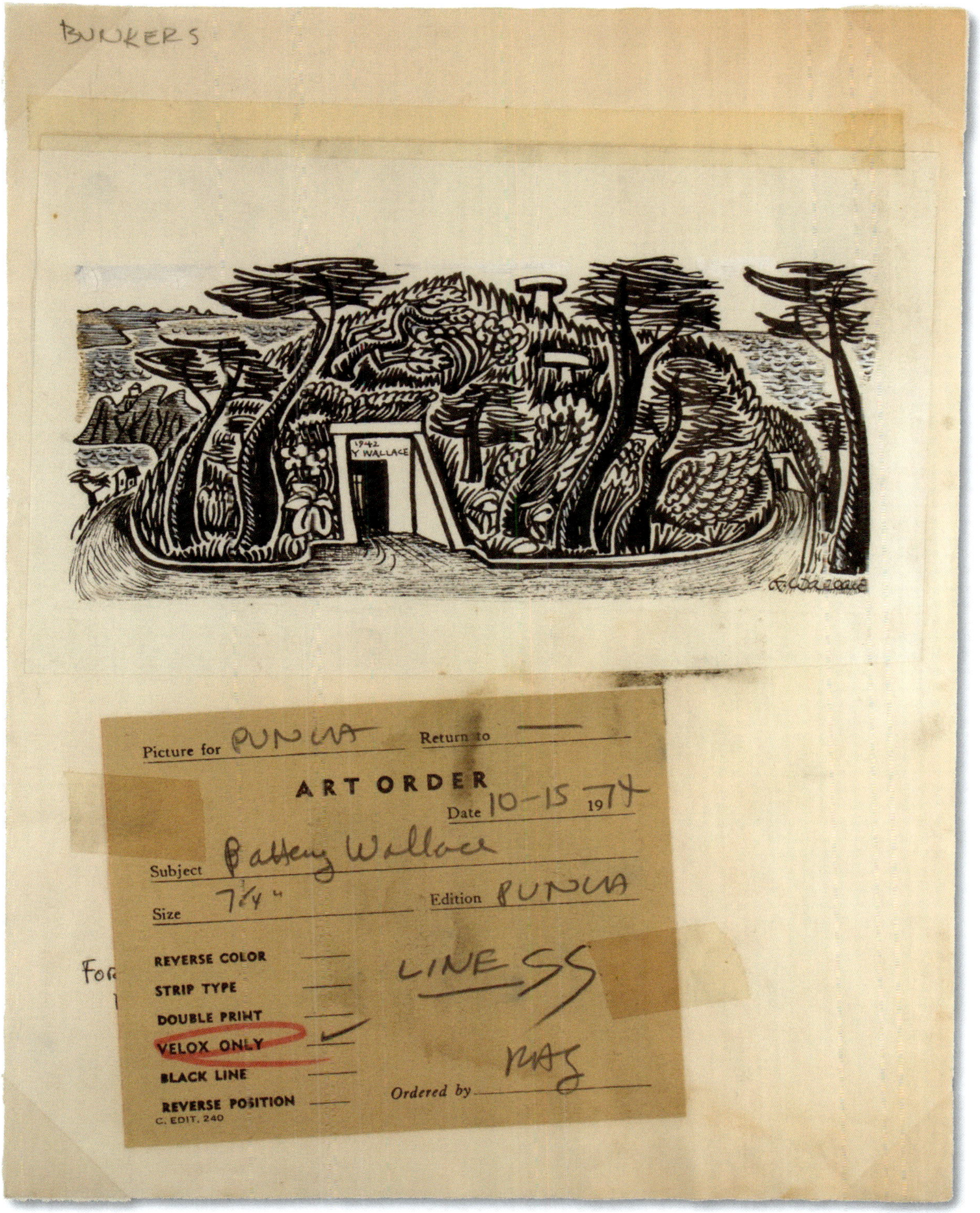

kw0016

Bunkers No. 2
by Kevin Wallace
10-15-1974
Battery Wallace

Signed by artist; Original art order
Unframed; Good Condition

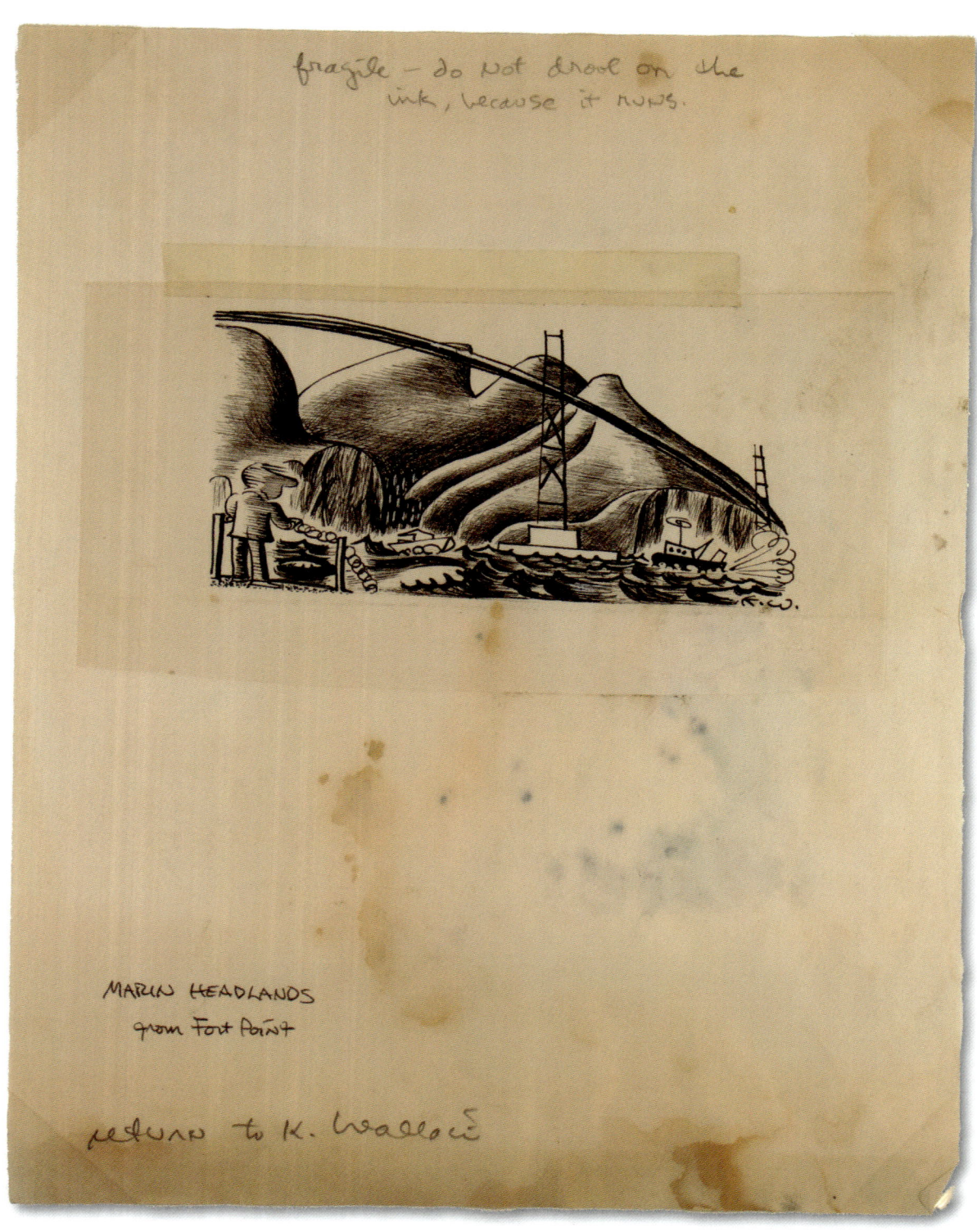

Marin Headlands from Fort Point
by Kevin Wallace
c. 1974
Fragile—do not drool on the ink, because it runs.
Return to K. Wallace

Signed by artist; Original artist notation
Unframed; Fair condition

Fishing Fort Point
by Kevin Wallace
c. 1974
78

Signed by artist; Original artist notation
Unframed; Some water damage

Fort Point Coast Guard Station
Alcatraz and Fort Mason in the background
by Kevin Wallace
c. 1974
Return to K. Wallace

Signed by artist; Original artist notation
Unframed; Some water damage

Fort Mason from Acquatic Park
by Kevin Wallace
c. 1974
Please return to Kevin Wallace

Signed by artist; Original artist notation
Unframed; Some water damage

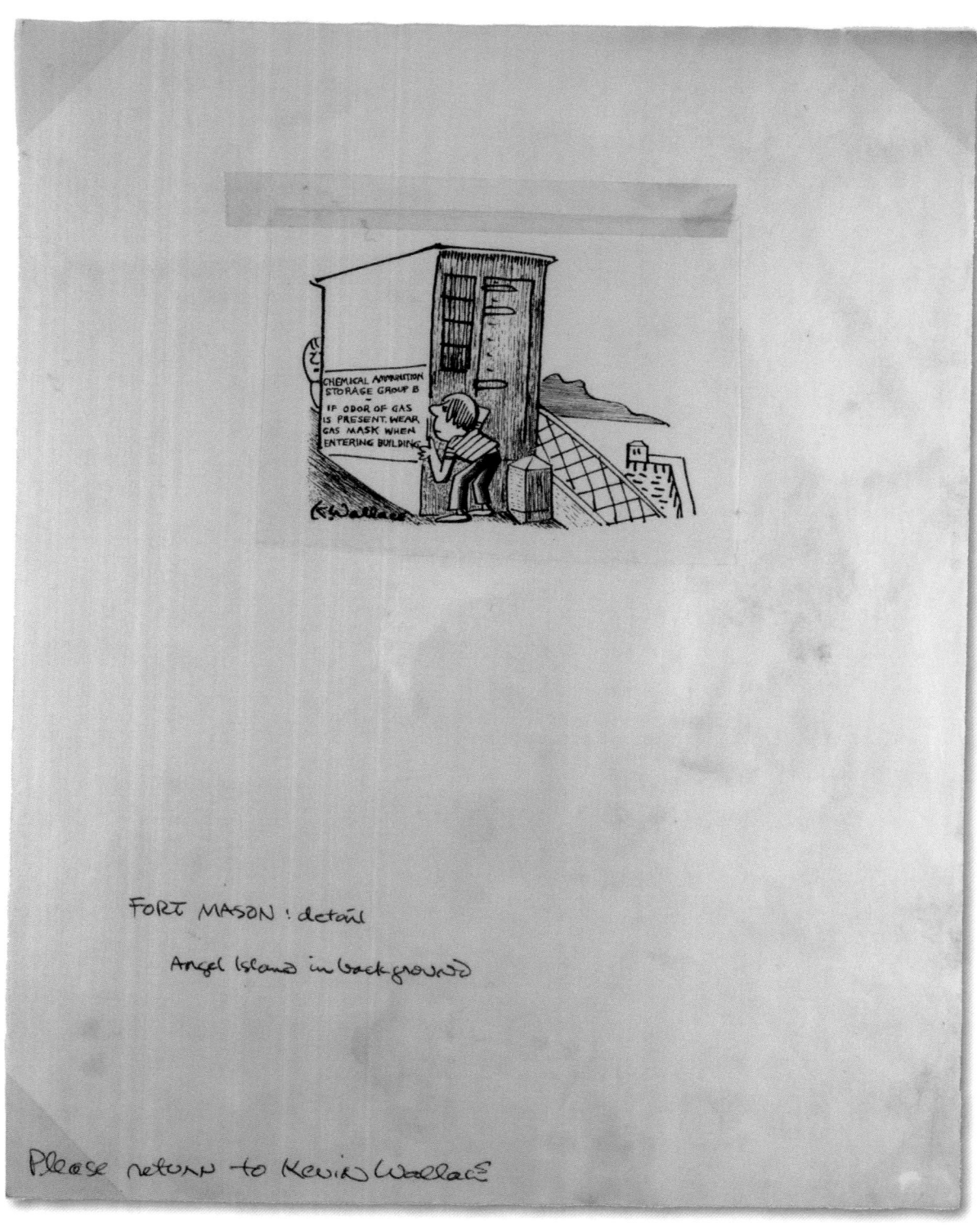

Fort Mason detail Angel Island in background
by Kevin Wallace
c. 1974
Please return to Kevin Wallace

Signed by artist; Original artist notation
Unframed; Fair condition

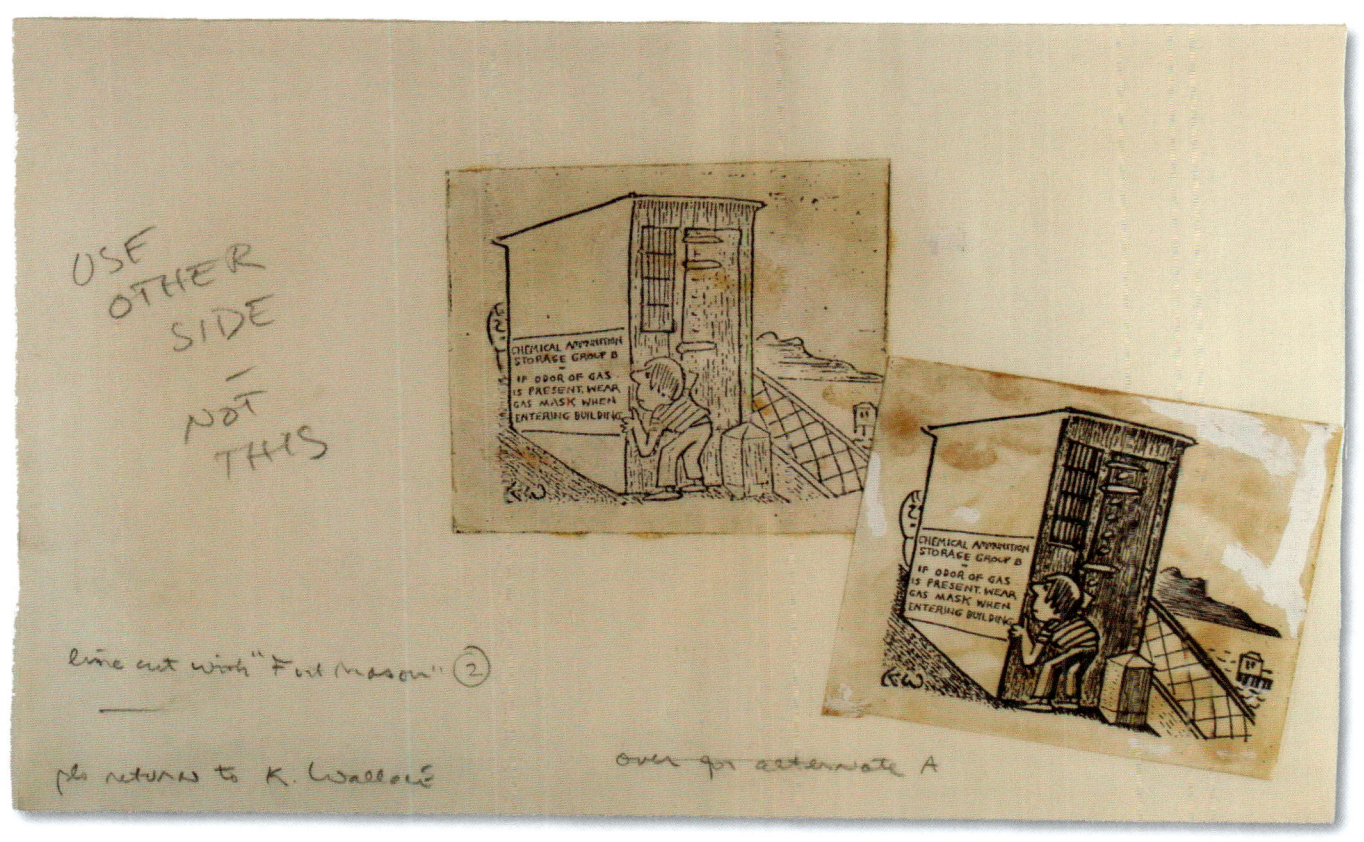

Fort Mason detail
Angel Island in background
by Kevin Wallace
c. 1974
Use Other Side—Not This
Line cut with "Fort Mason" 2
Please return to Kevin Wallace

Signed by artist; Original artist notation
Unframed; Fair condition

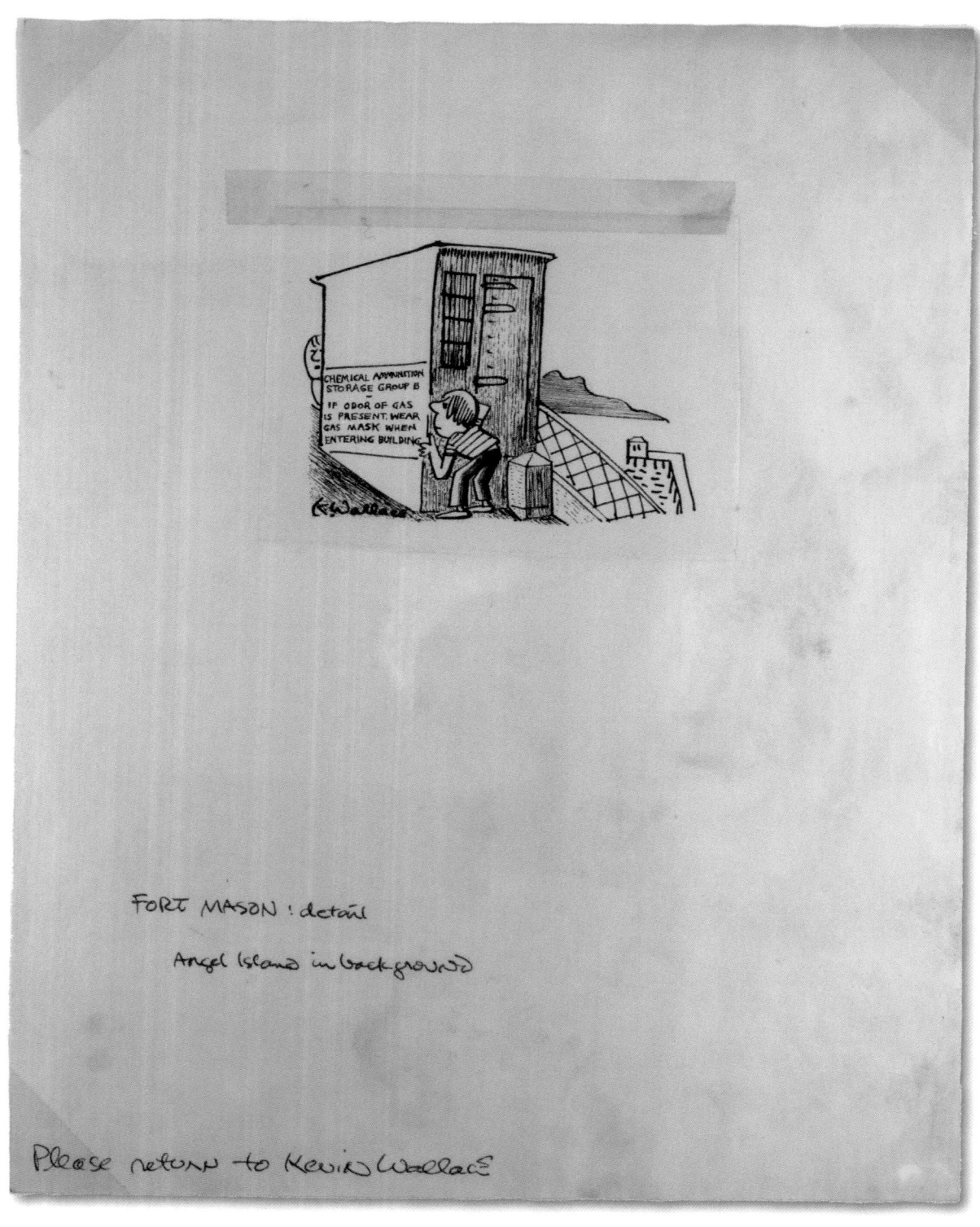

Fort Mason detail Angel Island in background
by Kevin Wallace
c. 1974
Please return to Kevin Wallace

Signed by artist; Original artist notation
Unframed; Fair condition

kw-0024–kw-0026

The Pacific West Coast
by Kevin Wallace
c. 1974
Pen and paper sketches

No artist signatures,
Unframed; Good condition

The San Francisco Bay
by Kevin Wallace
c. 1974
Pen and paper sketches

No artist signatures,
Unframed; Good condition

Point Richmond
by Kevin Wallace
c. 1974
Pen and paper sketches

No artist signatures,
Unframed; Good condition

Postscript:
The Ordinary World

Every year around winter time here on the Pacific Coast of California, if you look up into the clear night's sky, you'll see a faint cluster of stars glimmering in the shape of a tiny dipper. It's a little hard to find if you don't know what to look for. First locate Orien's belt, then follow that an arrow's shot to the West. There's where you'll see a shining faint cluster of glitter. You might need to squint to make it out.

The tiny constellation is called the Pleiades. It's nicknamed "The Seven Sisters" because there are that many of them. And it's been observed for thousands of years by people of different cultures and religions around the world. Ancient civilizations in China, South America, Australia, Europe, the Middle East have all documented the star cluster — and named it — contributing to its existential story through space and time.

Since discovering the Pleiades myself more than 30 years ago, the constellation has become a guidepost for me, influencing the many phases in my life — like a nightly Horoscopes in the sky.

Now a father, husband and professional here in the Valley of the Silicon, flat as can be in all directions for miles, the Pleiades appear center screen in the sky each winter through spring dancing like ballerinas across the universe each night around 8 p.m.

Five years ago — star-gazing from my backyard patio on the edge of Los Angeles — the Pleiades appeared in the center of my picture-window universe in my backyard. Palm trees bordering both sides; power lines framing the top and bottom. And between it all the Los Angeles purple-blue-black skyline filled with stars and planets and air planes lining up for arrival at LAX.

Five years before that — I watched them glimmer from the stilted porch of my

Deirdre Wallace marries Edward Berger, a Jewish biologist from The Bronx, New York, creating a family of four: Alexander, Nicholas, Tanya, and Matt.

new family's cabin in the "woods" of rural Western Connecticut. Cold clear nights offered the best views. So I shoveled a path from the back door to the edge of the deck, braving the frigid night-time air and I'd gaze upon the Pleiades against the black tree silhouettes and glistening snowy ground below.

Seven years before that — I sat on a rooftop in the Western Addition of San Francisco, four stories looking down on Eddy Street below — Fillmore Street to the West, city blocks of "The Projects" stretching East. I was an ambitious, aspiring journalist and reporter — no rest for the weary — but I would always take a break from writing ledes in my head to watch spot them in the dark night's sky with city sounds playing in the background as a spectacular soundtrack.

Five years earlier — A college student on a golden grassy hillside on a moonlit hike with a group of friends and college roommates. A backpack full of beer and weed. Talking about girls but really looking up and thinking about where I came from and where I was going.

The first time I ever paid notice to this particular constellation was in the backyard of my childhood home, in the winter of my thirteenth year, growing up in an East Bay suburb in the San Francisco Bay Area. My mom had just remarried. And she and my step-dad had a weekend rule that required the kids to find something to do out of the house. They'd lock all the doors around 10 a.m. and open them up quickly for lunch, then back out until dinnertime. The garage remained opened, and so often times I'd find refuge there, wasting the hours by pawing through boxes my mom had been dragging around for the past ten years since my grandfather died.

It contained the cache of artwork, writings, paintings, and sculptures accumulated by my family on my mom's side over the past century. Original Walt Disney celluloid animations fresh off the artists production room floor; paintings and mural concepts from my great aunt Moira and her friends from Works Progress Administration artists league in1930s San Francisco; hundreds upon hundreds of news clippings and original sketches from my grandpa's portfolio of columns and articles and illustrations from his time on staff at *The San Francisco Examiner, San Francisco Chronicle* and the New Yorker magazine. Soapstone sculptures he carved with a pocket knife, spraying interview subjects and colleagues with bits and shavings while they spoke.

Out of my four siblings, I might have been the most fascinated with this pile of stuff. To me it was evidence of something much bigger and more official than I had experienced before. A published and printed documentation of history through the eyes of my ancestors. Also, as the youngest of four, my mind had not yet been made up about the general state of life and things, which helped me be more open to these ideas. Whereas my brothers and sister had already concluded their world view, it was all new to me. All that seemed impossible, was possible.

And then I found Kevin's manuscript. Neatly packaged in an inch-thick black binder, hole-punched and collated direct from my grandpa's Royal typewriter. It begins with a hand-written timeline dating back to my family's ancestral roots in Ireland, around 1764. Almost a dozen pages of single-spaced text noting every birth and death and major life event for generations. The year my mom was born. The date in 1762, when great, great, great, great, great, great, great, grandpa Tom Dickey Wallace left Ireland for New Hampshire to start a new life with his young wife and kids.

It's amazing really when you think about it how we each got here: the string of unseemingly connected events. The happenstance meetings of people in obscure places. The relationships that failed and those that won out to establish their place in my family tree. Looking back you might think it was all just chance, but after 30 years making sense of it and pulling it all together into a 125-year narrative, it's much easier to see a more complex organism at work.

As the calendar year turns to 2020, the Pleiades rattle again through the universe with great force and vengeance. Just as this book was taking shape on my computer hard drive, a virus was spreading silently through the human population, infecting its way through towns and cities around the globe. Of all the patients infected with the coronavirus, or COVID-19, one percent will die, and 10 percent end up in the hospital. The virus had its sights set on more than 7 billion people distributed unevenly across the planet. Apply the odds and that's 700 million infected globally, 70 million hospitalized, and 7 million dead. As of this writing, it was unclear if mankind was prepared to beat the odds.

Now that you've gotten through the story, and have seen the evidence for yourself, you might forgive me for worrying that the reverberations from raising the ghosts in this story might have had something to do with raising a deadly virus from the dark. Like the "Tiki Necklace" episode of The Brady Bunch, did my digging up the past have something to do with the arrival of an earth-altering pandemic?

Probably not, but these days I've got a lot of time to let my mind wander. The six counties around the San Francisco Bay Area where we live ordered a Shelter in Place after midnight on Friday, March 13, 2020, and the forced solitude has givent me lots of time to think. It's also given me a lot of time to reflect on this multigenerational anthology of work.

For the few months leading up to isolation, I researched and reported on my family story through interviews and day-trips up and down the California coast, speaking with art experts and historians, taking photos, clipping news stories. The first person I met on my journey was an art collector named Terry Trotter, who shared an excitement for my discovery enough to also share his phonebook. That led me to the Crocker Art Gallery in Sacramento, where the great works from my family's dead contemporaries rest in peace.

It also led me to private art collectors familiar with my family's work, or at least its time and place. I had lunch at the exclusive Pacific Union Club atop Russian Hill in San Francisco with Charles Osborne, the grandson of S.F.B. Morse, who shared stories about the people and places he knew first hand growing up around his grandfather's Pebble Beach Resort and nearby Del Monte Hotel.

My search continued with a stop at the Montery Museum of Art, where I found a 15-foot oil-on-canvas mural painted by Moira. It was on long-term loan from the Monterey Unified School District, who commissioned it 100 years ago but later abandonded it in the 1980s to the museum's basement storage room.

Finally, it lead me to a much more difficult truth. At the heart of our universe is a stuggle over the human condition: a battle between good and evil, light and dark, self and selflessness. For decades I believed that my ancestors had discovered the secret to it all — and with that knowledge existed on an existential plane above the everyday world. But in my older age I've come to realize creating great art was just their way of triumphing over mental health and egotism.

The voices Grant attributed to "The Pleiades" that drove his life, other more conventional folk might call visual and auditory hallucinations. But the latter explanation doesn't pay the bills or ease the pain. My family's ability to turn their genius and madness into a mythical story of adventure and discovery makes it so much easier to endure, especially when people call it art and put it on a pedestal.

It turns out, the best artists are the ones who can translate their own mad visionary view of the world into words and pictures that speak more softly to those who can't see it for themselves. Consider this as you flip through the following portfolio of artwork.

Carmel Portraits
Original drawings by Moira Wallace

From a young age, Moira Wallace studied and practiced portrait art applying her intuition and masterful talents with pencils, pens, and brushes to capture the human spirit in the faces and expressions of her subjects. This collection of 29 portrait drawings and sketches on paper depict wealthy patrons, celebrities, and cultural icons of the 1920s and 30s who commissioned the young artist to capture their likeness at her family's home studio in Carmel, California, or at nearby Pebble Beach. It's presumed that some of these sketches were turned into matching oil painting, but none of those exist in the family collection.

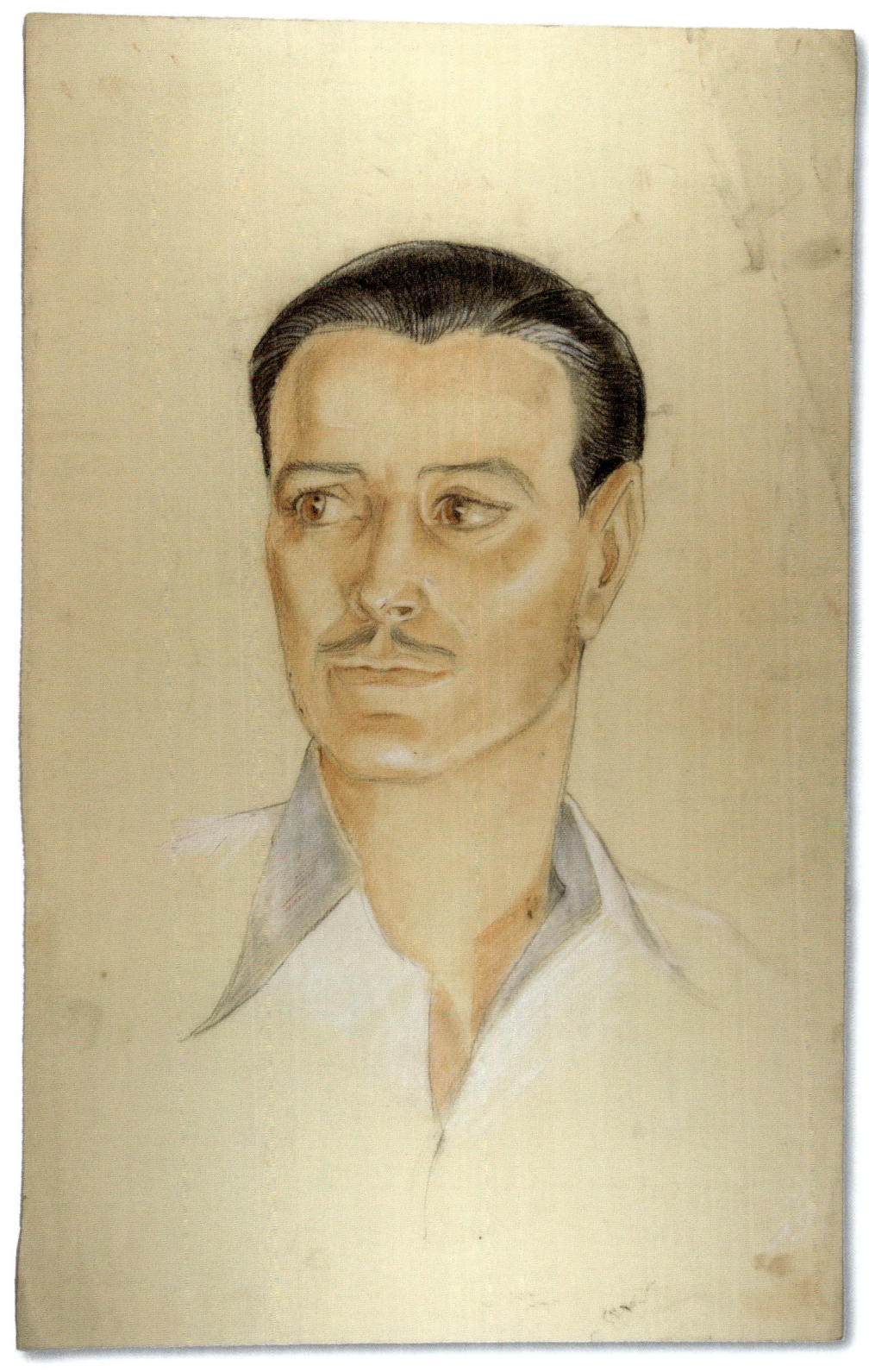

Clark Gable
by Moira Wallace
c. 1925–1931
Portrait

No artist signature
Unframed, Good Condition

Woman #1
by Moira Wallace
c. 1925—1931
Portrait

Signed by artist
Unframed, Good Condition

The Big Work

Girl #1
by Moira Wallace
1931
Portrait

Signed by artist; Dated by artist
Unframed; Good Condition

mw-0008
Woman #2
by Moira Wallace
c. 1925—1931
Portrait

Signed by artist
Unframed; Good Condition

Man #2
by Moira Wallace
c. 1925—1931
Portrait

No artist signature
Unframed; Good Condition

mw-0010
Man #3 "The Maje"
by Moira Wallace
c. 1925—1931
Portrait

No artist signature
Unframed; Good Condition

Man #4
by Moira Wallace
c. 1925–1931
Portrait

Signed by artist
Unframed; Good Condition

Man #5
by Moira Wallace
c. 1925–1931
Portrait

Signed by artist
Unframed; Good Condition

Man #5
by Moira Wallace
c. 1925–1931
771 Washington Rd North, Lake Forest

No artist signature; Original artist notation
Unframed; Good Condition

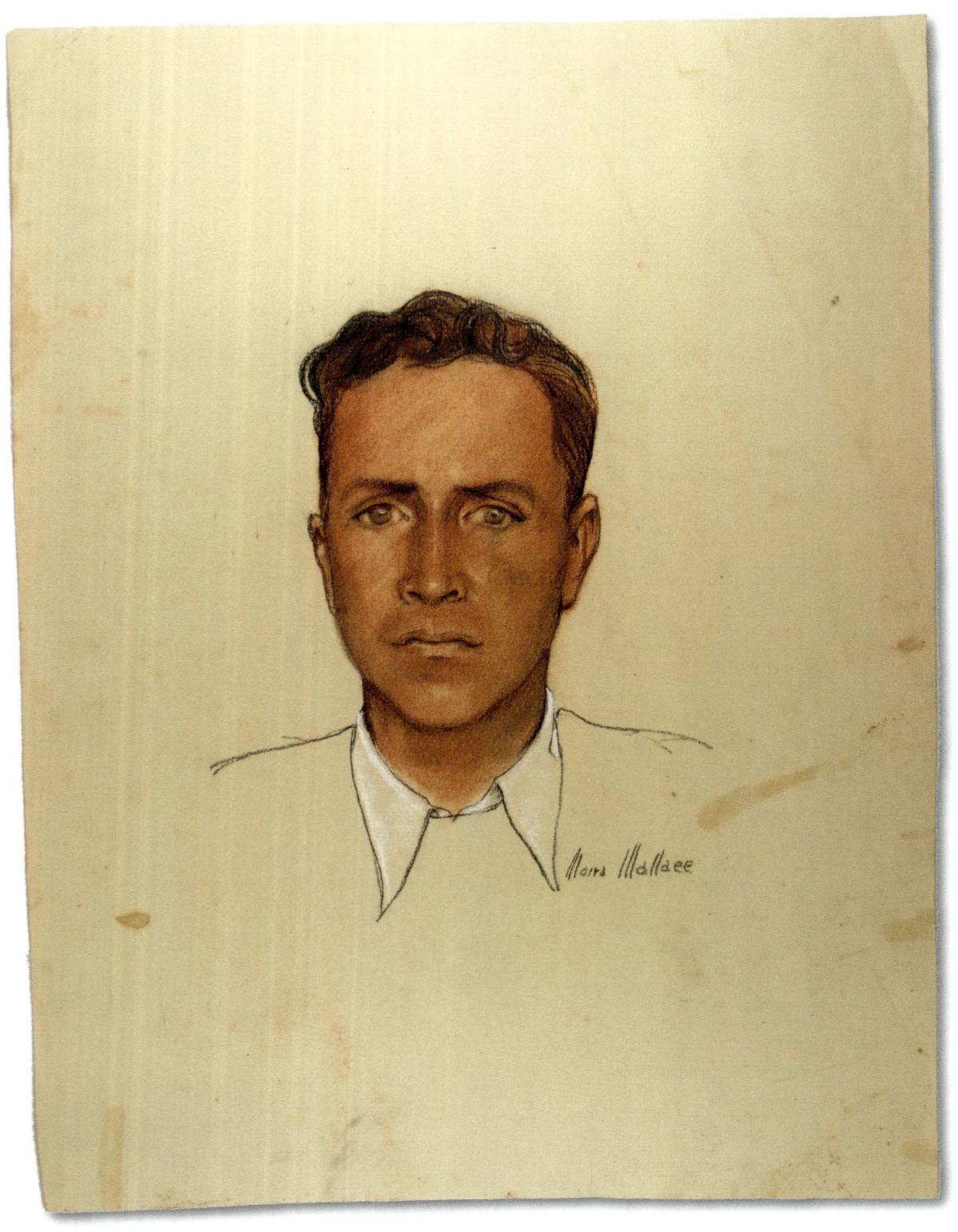

Man #6
by Moira Wallace
c. 1925—1931
Portrait

Signed by artist
Unframed; Good Condition

160

Man #7
by Moira Wallace
c. 1925—1931
Portrait

Signed by artist
Unframed; Fair Condition

mw-0007
Man #1
by Moira Wallace
c. 1925—1931
Portrait

No artist signature
Unframed; Good Condition

Man #8
by Moira Wallace
c. 1925—1931
Portrait

No artist signature
Unframed; Good Condition

mw-0017
Man #9
by Moira Wallace
c. 1925–1931
Portrait

No artist signatures
Unframed; Good Condition

Man #11
by Moira Wallace
c. 1925–1931
Portrait

No artist signature
Unframed; Good Condition

John Ward
by Moira Wallace
1928
Portrait

Signed by artist; Dated by artist
Original artist notation
Unframed; Good Condition

Jimmy Rand
by Moira Wallace
c. 1925—1931
Portrait

No artist signature
Unframed; Good Condition

mw-0020
Womand #3
by Moira Wallace
c. 1925—1931
Portrait

No artist signature
Unframed; Good Condition

Woman #4
by Moira Wallace
c. 1925—1931
Portrait

No artist signature
Unframed; Fair Condition

Man #10
by Moira Wallace
c. 1925–1931
Portrait

No artist signature
Unframed; Good Condition

Man #11
by Moira Wallace
c. 1925—1931
Portrait

No artist signature
Unframed; Good Condition

Woman #7
by Moira Wallace
c. 1925—1931
Portrait Sketch

Signed by artist
Unframed; Good Condition

Woman #7
by Moira Wallace
1930
Portrait Sketch

Signed by artist; Dated by artist
Unframed; Good Condition

Woman #6 by Moira Wallace
c. 1925–1931
Portrait Sketches

XX in. wide by XX in. tall

No artist signature
Unframed; Good Condition

Woman #8 by Moira Wallace
c. 1925—1931
Portrait Sketch

XX in. wide by XX in. tall

Signed by artist
Unframed; Good Condition

Carmel Block Prints
original works by Moira Wallace

Moira was introduced to block print under the tutelage of Mildred and Blanding Sloan, the husband-and-wife art luminaries in San Francisco who popularized the medium as the premiere block print artists of the 1920s and 30s. The couple serendipitously stumbled upon Moira working at her easel on the shore of the San Francisco Bay near Tiburon, immediately identify the young prodigy for her talent. As a student of Blanding, Moira produced a collection of linoleum block prints, several of which made it into print in Carmel's heritage local newspaper, the Carmel Pine Cone, known for publishing California's best-known artists and writers of the 20th century, from Ansel Adams to John Steinbeck.

Wait Adventure
by Moira Wallace
c. 1928
Linoleum Block Print

Signed by Artist; Original Artist Notation
Unframed; Good Condition

Rebellion
by Moira Wallace
1928
Linoleum Block Print
published in the Carmel Pine Cone, Aug. 1928

Signed by artist; Includes original published news clipping
Unframed; Good Condition

Prancing across Point Lobos
by Moira Wallace
c. 1925
Linoleum Block Print
published in the Carmel Pine Cone, Aug. 1928

Signed by artist
Unframed; Good Condition

Winged Centinal
by Moira Wallace
1928
Linoleum Block Print

Signed by Artist; Dated by artist
Original Artist Notation
Unframed; Good Condition

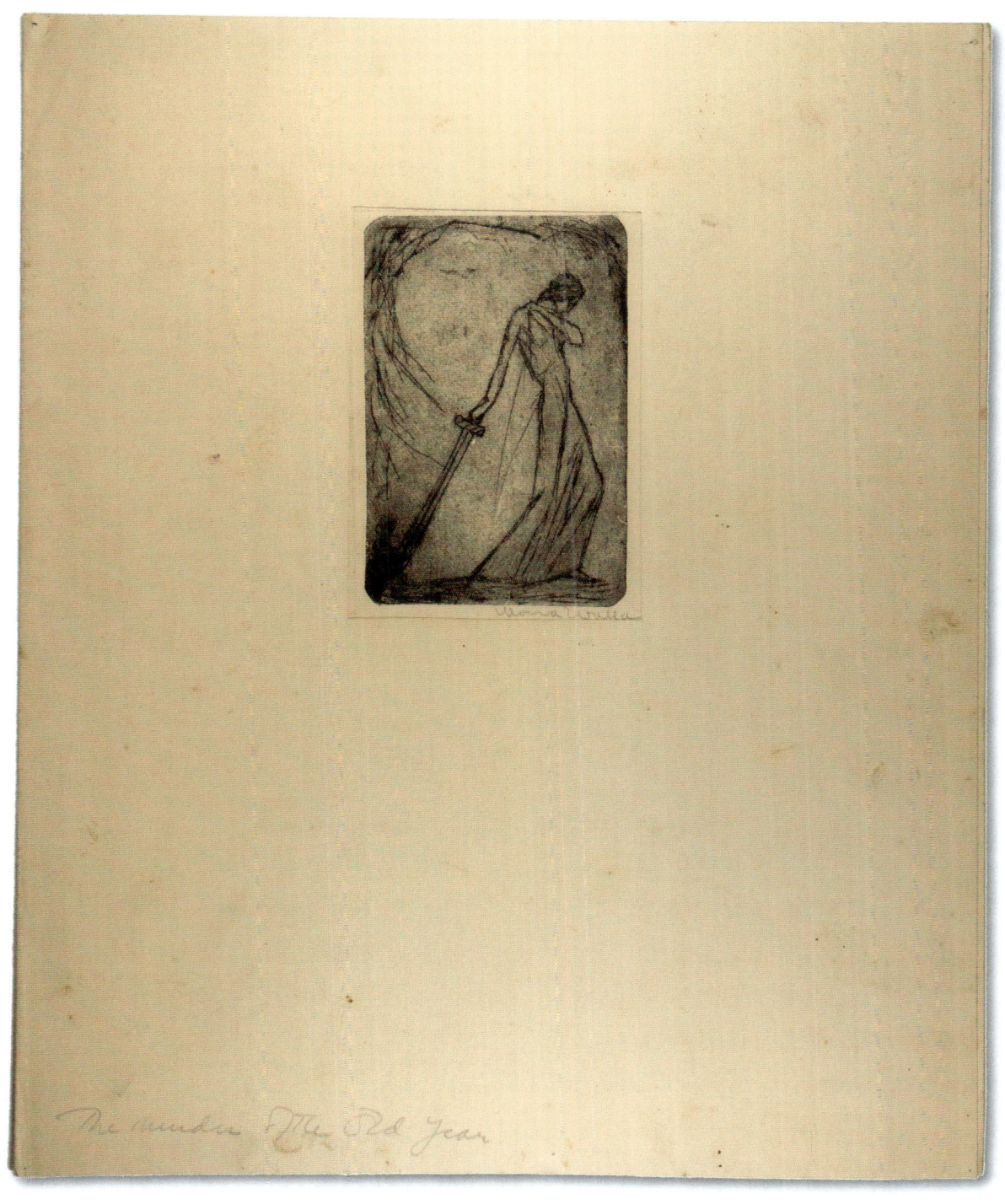

The Murder of the Old Year
by Moira Wallace
c. 1928
Linoleum Block Print

Signed by artist;
Original Artist Notation
Unframed; Good Condition

California Art and the New Deal
original works by Moira Wallace

This 80-plus piece art collection is the personal portfolio of Moira Wallace, carried around by the artist from city to city and home to home for nearly 50 years. The collection features a wide range of Moira's original artwork representing the most important eras of California art history: the Great Depression, The New Deal era, and Modernism after World War II. It includes costume and set designs for Walt Disney, commercial advertising sketches for a Los Angeles Billboard company, and a powerful collection of submissions to federally-funded mural competitions for the U.S. Post Office, the Monterey Unified School District, the San Francisco Department of Justice Building, and prestigious private San Francisco commissions.

Life Guard and the Mermaid
by Moira Wallace
c. 1926—1933
"Return to Moira Wallace care of Belle Bennett
6280 Temple Hill, Hollywood, California"

Signed by artist; Original artist notation
Unframed; Good Condition

Delilah
by Moira Wallace
c. 1925—1933
Costume comprised of flat silver and black metal links

Signed by artist; Original artist notation
Unframed; Good Conditionge

Angel with Wings
by Moira Wallace
c. 1926—1943
Illustration

No artist signature
Unframed; Good Condition

Egyptian Figures
by Moira Wallace
c. 1926—1943
Figure Sketches

No artist signature
Unframed; Good Condition

The Big Work

Bali Room Dancers
by Moira Wallace
c. 1926—1943
Figure Sketches

No artist signature
Unframed; Good Condition

mw-0042
Female Figure
by Moira Wallace
c. 1926–1943
Figure Sketch

No artist signature
Unframed; Good Condition

mw-0043
Dancing Woman
by Moira Wallace
1928
Dancer

Signed by artist, Dated by artist
Unframed; Good Conditionge

mw-0044
Unnamed Character
by Moira Wallace
c. 1926—1943
Costume Illustration

Signed by artist
Unframed; Good Conditionge

The Big Work

Salomé
by Moira Wallace
c. 1926—1943
Costume Illustration

No artist signatures; Original artist notation
Unframed; Good Conditionge

Wicked Witch
by Moira Wallace
c. 1928
Character Portrait

Signed by artist
Unframed; Good Condition

Wicked Witch B-Side
by Moira Wallace
c. 1928
Sketches on the back of Wicked Witch

No artist signature
Unframed; Good Condition

The Smoker
by Moira Wallace
c. 1928
Advertising Block Print
(matches sketches from Wicked Witch b-side)

No artist signature
Unframed; Fair Condition

Marionettes
by Moira Wallace
c. 1926—1943
Thought-Sketch for Fabric Design

Signed by artist; Original artist notation
Unframed; Good Condition

Beach Breeze
by Moira Wallace
c. 1925—1933
Commercial Illustration

No artist signature
Unframed; Good Condition

Sketch for Shampoo
by Moira Wallace
1929
Commercial Illustration

Signed by artist; Original artist notation
Unframed; Good Condition

Roaring 20s
by Moira Wallace
c. 1925—1943
Small Watercolor

No artist signature
Unframed; Fair Condition

Evening Gown
by Moira Wallace
c. 1925—1943
On Delicate Paper

Signed by artist
Unframed; Good Condition

Woman
by Moira Wallace
c. 1925–1943
Watercolor

No artist signature
Unframed; Good Condition

Isolde
by Moira Wallace
1925—1943
Watercolor

Signed by artist; Original artist notation
Unframed; Good Condition

Balarina No. 2
by Moira Wallace
c. 1925—1943
Wax Pencils

Signed by artist
Unframed; Good Condition

202

Prodigal Prunella
by Moira Wallace
c. 1925—1943
Charcole Sketch

Signed by artist; Original artist notation
Unframed; Good Condition

Balarina No. 1
by Moira Wallace
c. 1925–1943
Oil on Hardboard

No artist signature
Unframed; Good Condition

The Big Work

Resting Ballarina
by Moira Wallace
c. 1925–1943
Water Color Figure Sketch

Signed by artist
Unframed; Good Condition

Woman with Urn
by Moira Wallace
c. 1924
Watercolor

Signed by artist
Unframed; Good Condition

206

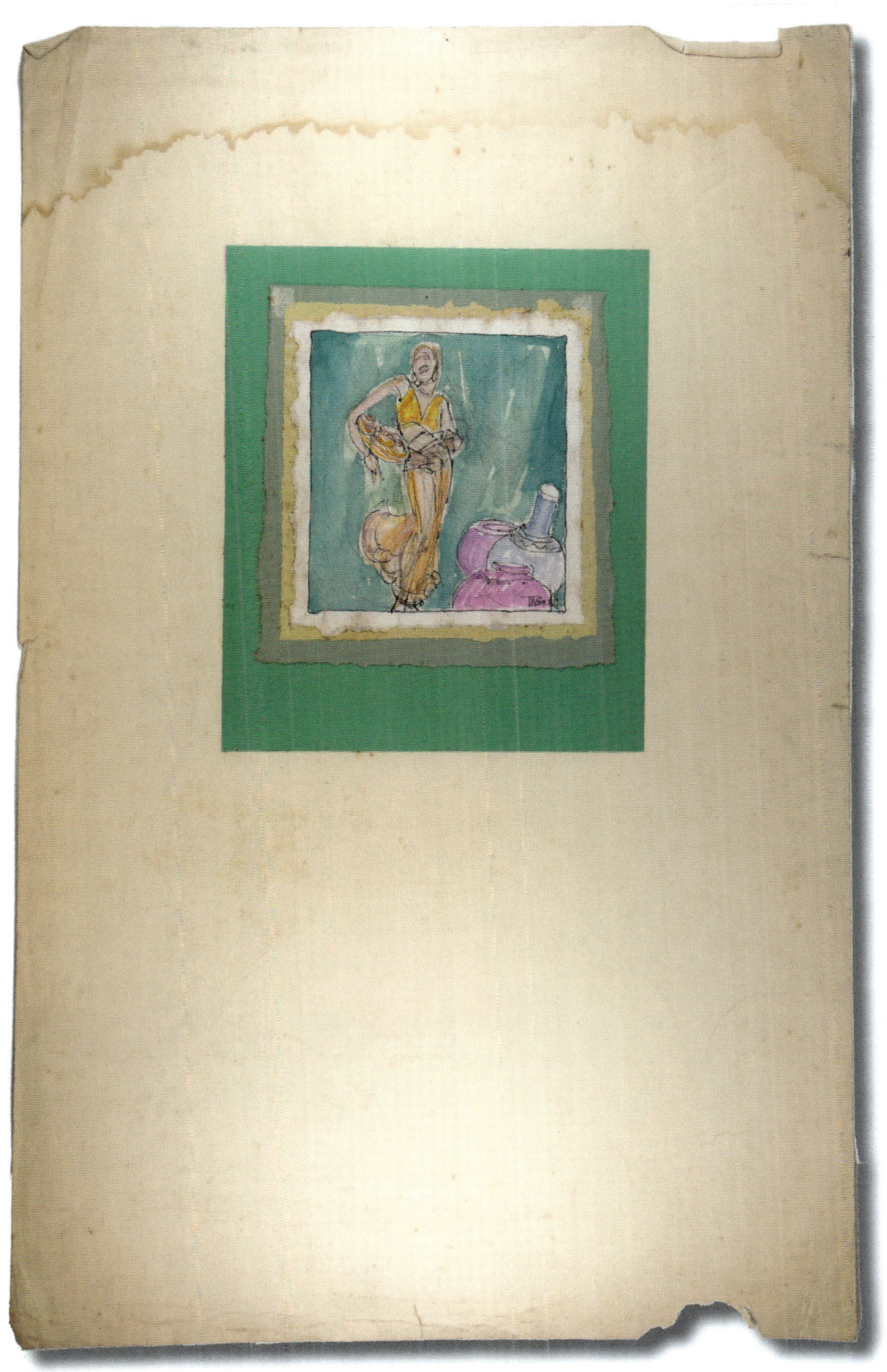

Woman with Basket
by Moira Wallace
c. 1924
Watercolor

Signed by artist
Unframed; Good Condition

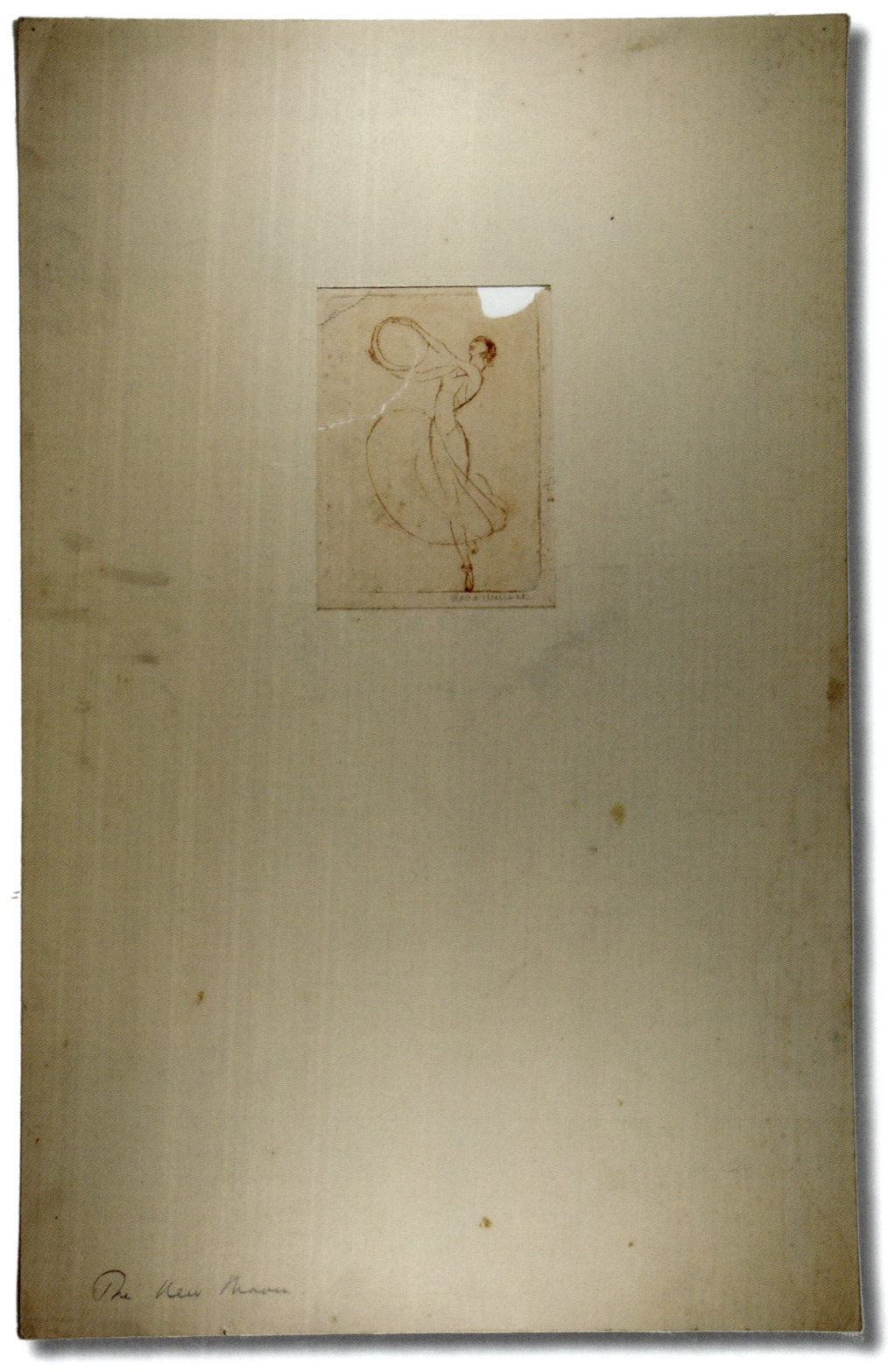

The New Moon
by Moira Wallace
c. 1926—1943
Delicate Paper

Signed by artist; Original artist notation
Unframed; Major damage

Boy Kevin
by Moira Wallace
c. 1924
Watercolor

Signed by artist
Unframed; Good Condition

Oasis
by Moira Wallace
c. 1924—1935
Watercolor on Hardboard

No artist signature
Unframed; Good Condition

The Big Work

The Garden of Eden
by Moira Wallace
c. 1924
Watercolor and Gouache

No artist signature
Unframed; Good Condition

Shephard No. 1
by Moira Wallace
c. 1926—1943
Watercolor and Gouache

Signed by artist
Unframed; Good Condition

Shephard No. 2
by Moira Wallace
c. 1926–1943
Watercolor and Gouache

No artist signature
Unframed; Good Condition

Starfall
by Moira Wallace
c. 1926–1943
Watercolor and Gouache

No artist signature
Unframed; Good Condition

The Big Work

Dancer
by Moira Wallace
c. 1926—1943
Charcole Figure Drawing

Signed by artist
Unframed; Good Condition

Cliff Hanger
by Moira Wallace
c. 1926–1943
Charcol Sketch

No artist signature
Unframed; Good Condition

The End of Dreams
by Moira Wallace
c. 1926–1943
Short Description

Signed by artist
Unframed; Good Condition

At Sea
by Moira Wallace
c. 1926–1943
Charcol Drawing

No artist signature
Unframed; Good Condition

The Big Work

He has Risen
by Moira Wallace
c. 1926–1943
Charcol Drawing

Signed by artist
Unframed; Good Condition

Chained Angel
by Moira Wallace
c. 1926–1943
Charcol Drawing

No artist signature
Unframed; Good Condition

The Big Work

Fallen Angel
by Moira Wallace
c. 1926–1943
Charcol Drawing

No artist signature
Unframed; Good Condition

Woman at Point Sur Lighthouse
by Moira Wallace
c. 1937
Block Print in the collection of the
Fine Arts Museum of San Francisco #FA9642

No artist signature; Registered in the GSA database
Unframed; Good Condition

Family
by Moira Wallace
c. 1937
Block Print in the collection of the
Fine Arts Museum of San Francisco #FA9642

No artist signature; Registered in the G&A database
Unframed; Good Condition

March Wind
by Moira Wallace
c. 1926–1943
Three scenes, woman blowing in the wind.

Signed by Artist
Unframed; Good Condition

The Big Work

mw-0079
Fantasy Animal Kingdom
by Moira Wallace
c. 1926—1943
Watercolor and Charcol

No artist signature
Unframed; Good Condition

Carnival Mural Bar Sketch
by Moira Wallace
c. 1926—1943
Short Description

No artist signature
Unframed; Good Condition

Sketch for Screen Mark Hopkins Bar
by Moira Wallace
1934
Short Description

Dated by artisted; Signed by artist
Unframed; Good Condition

African Village
by Moira Wallace
c. 1926—1943
White Paint on Black Slate

Signed by artist; Original artist notation
Unframed; Good Condition

Olympus from Debussy Nocturn Story of the Siren
by Moira Wallace
c. 1926—1943
Mural Sketch

Signed by Artist
Unframed; Good Condition

Mission Village Life
by Moira Wallace
c. 1934
Original Mural (photo) and Artist Sketches
for the Monterey Unified School District

No artist signature; Artist notes and sketches in margins
Unframed; Good Condition

Protection of the Child Through Child Labor Laws
by Moira Wallace
c 1938
The the Department of Justice
Mural Competition

No artist signature; Original typed placard
Unframed; Good Condition

Protection of the Child Through Child Labor Laws
by Moira Wallace
c 1938
The the Department of Justice
Mural Competition

No artist signature; Original typed placard
Unframed; Good Condition

mw-0089–mw-0091

Design for San Pedro Post Office Mural #2 A, B, and C
by Moira Wallace
c 1936
To be painted in oil
by Moiral Wallace Harnden
241 Greenwich
San Francisco

Original Handwritten Placard
Unframed; Good Condition

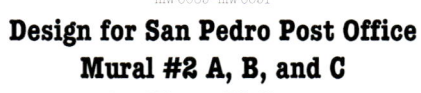

The Big Work

235

A-Side: Mural Sketch Unknown
B-Side: Portrait #84.B
by Moira Wallace
c. 1936
Sketch for unknown mural comptetion.
Portrait of a woman on the back
with the lable #84.B.

No artist signature
Unframed; Good Condition

Illustrating the World in Color

Art and illustrations by Kevin Wallace

Kevin Wallace revered his older sister Moira, but when it came to art he adopted a style of his own. "Sometimes colorful, sometimes black and white" describes not only the tones of his artwork and illustrations, but also the overtones of their contents and captions. Kevin mostly drew about the daily lives of San Francisco's residents and businesses, often pairing his illustrations with columns and articles for the city's newspapers. He tried endlessly to break through while on staff a *The New Yorker*, but never had an illustration make it to the magazine. Meanwhile, he put just as much effort into the hand-drawn postage-stamped postcards he mailed to his teenage daughter away at summer camp.

The Big Work

kw-0003
Couple
by Kevin Wallace
c. 1942—1979
Watercolor and Colored Pencil

No artist signature
Unframed; Good Condition

Sunset on the Golden Gate
by Kevin Wallace
c. 1942–1979
Watercolor and Colored Pencil

No artist signature
Unframed; Good Condition

The Big Work

Fisherman's Wharf
by Kevin Wallace
c. 1942–1979
Charcole and Colored Pencil

No artist signature
Unframed; Good Condition

Washington Square Park
by Kevin Wallace
c. 1942–1979
Final Version

Signed by Artist
Framed; Good Condition

The Big Work

"Washington Square Park, which is not square
and has a statue of Ben Franklin,
is in North Beach, which is not a beach."
- Kevin Wallace

kw-0006
Washington Square Park
by Kevin Wallace
c. 1942—1979
Draft Version

No artist signature
Unframed; Fair Condition

kw-0008
Central Park
by Kevin Wallace
c. 1942–1979
Watercolor and Colored Pencil

NO artist signature
Unframed; Good Condition

The Big Work

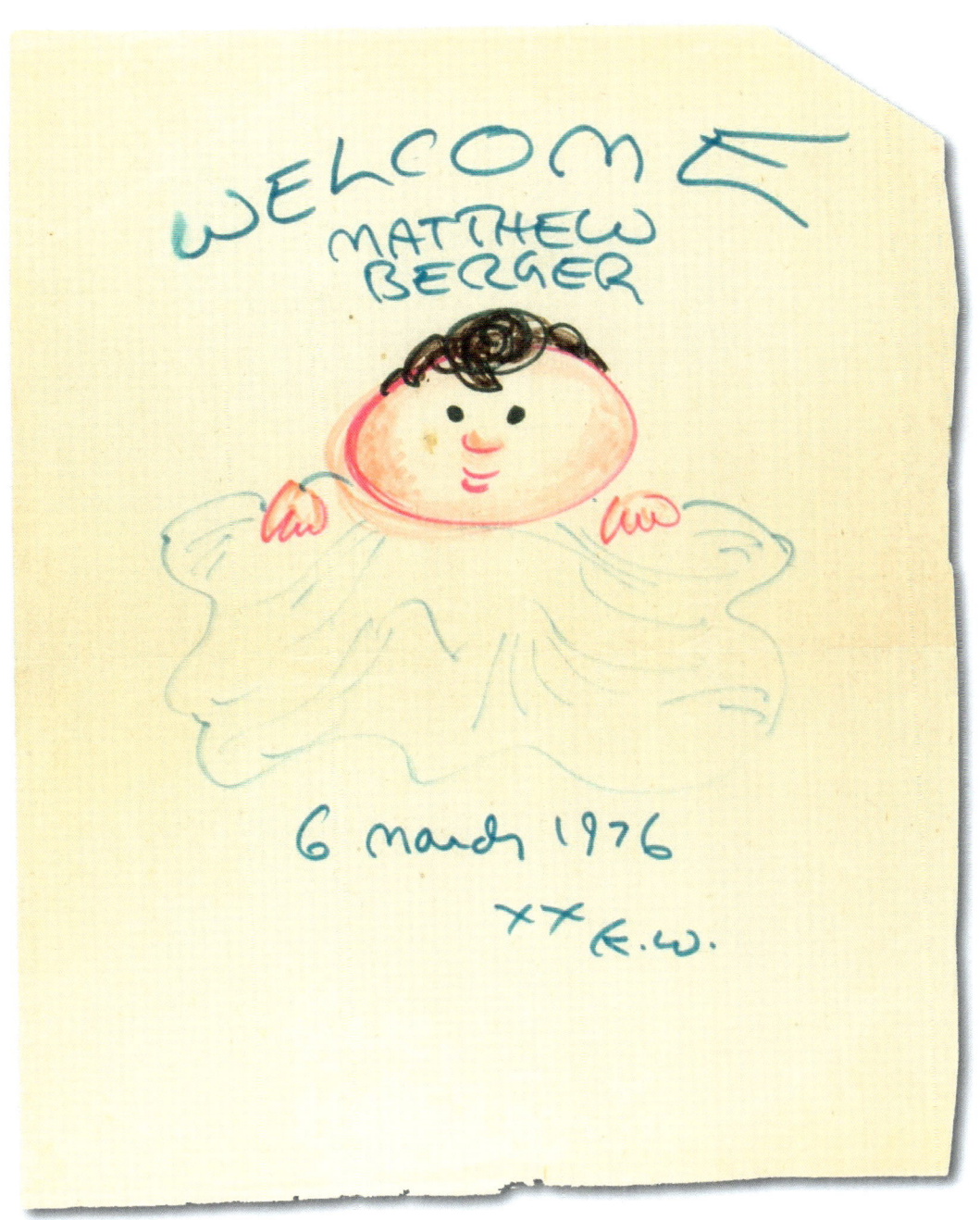

Welcome Matthew Berger
by Kevin Wallace
6 March 1976
XX K.W.

Signed by artist; Original artist notation
Unframed; Good Condition

Summer Camp Letters to his Dauther
by Kevin Wallace
1958–1959

Mailed to Miss Deirdre Wallace

SIgned by artist
Notated by artist

  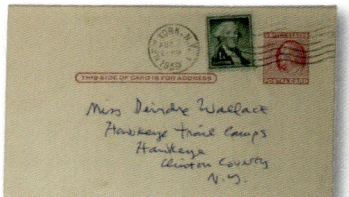 

  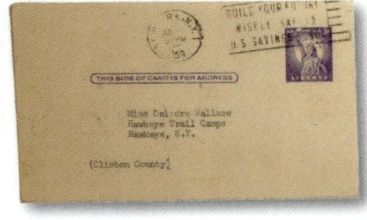 

"Picture of Helen and Me-Too missing you and Brian."

"Breakfast Scene, N.Y.C. (Love, Daddy)"

"Scenic New York City: Fifth Avenue. Love Kev"

"Dear Deirdy: This is part of the mess on my desk—I must clean it up—Have fun—Love—Daddy"

"Looking down on a mountain lake I saw last night—Can you figure it out? Love, Daddy"

Dear Deirdie: This is how the start of my trip Wednesday looked from the plane. See Brian's card for the end of it. Love, Daddy"

"I keep thinking about you. Love, Daddy"

The Berger Kids
by Kevin Wallace
1979 Personalized Illustrations

No artist signature; Notated by artist
Unframed; Good Condition

Inquisitive and chatty Is social expert Matty.

Graceful as her granny Is skiing hot-shot Tanny.

Nimble, fast & tricky Is sledding artist Nicky.

Brightest in the galaxy Of trumpet stars is Alexie.

Humorist, Humanist, Nudist

Original sketches and news illustrations by Kevin Wallace

You might think Kevin Wallace moonlighted as an editorial cartoonist for *Playboy* magazine alongside his *Chronicle* and *Examiner* work when you examine the reems of sketches he left behind in a shoebox alongside his archive of published newspaper clippings. Kevin endlessly drew characters in everyday situations, street scenes, and sometimes engaged in compromising positions with delivery men. He sketched blue-collar workers, philosophers and street musicians, scholars and actors, house wives and retirees, and left behind a rich record of San mid-century American history and humanity.

Woke Garden of Eden
by Kevin Wallace
c. 1942—1979
So God created men Folks in his own image...
male Person and felmale Person created he them.

Signed by artist; Original artist notation
Unframed; Good Condition

249

Rapids
by Kevin Wallace
c. 1942–1979
Pen and paper sketch

No artist signature
Unframed; Good Condition

'Caddyshack'
by Kevin Wallace
c. 1942–1979
Pen and paper sketch

No artist signature
Unframed; Good Condition

Fairy Tales No. 1
by Kevin Wallace
c. 1942–1979
Triumphs of Western Man: Dalliance with Dragons is Discouranged
(Bayou Tapestry, L'Oeuvre Musee"

Signed by artist; Original artist notation
Unframed; Good Condition

The Big Work

Fairy Tales No. 2
by Kevin Wallace
c. 1942—1979
People Section

Signed by artist; Original artist notation
Unframed; Good Condition

Three Kings of NYC
by Kevin Wallace
c. 1942—1979
Pen and paper sketch

Signed by artist
Unframed; Good Condition

The Big Work

AC Transit
by Kevin Wallace
c. 1942–1979
Pen and paper sketch

No artist signature
Unframed; Good Condition

Sketches No. 101
by Kevin Wallace
c. 1942–1979
Pen and paper sketch

No artist signature
Unframed; Good Condition

The Big Work

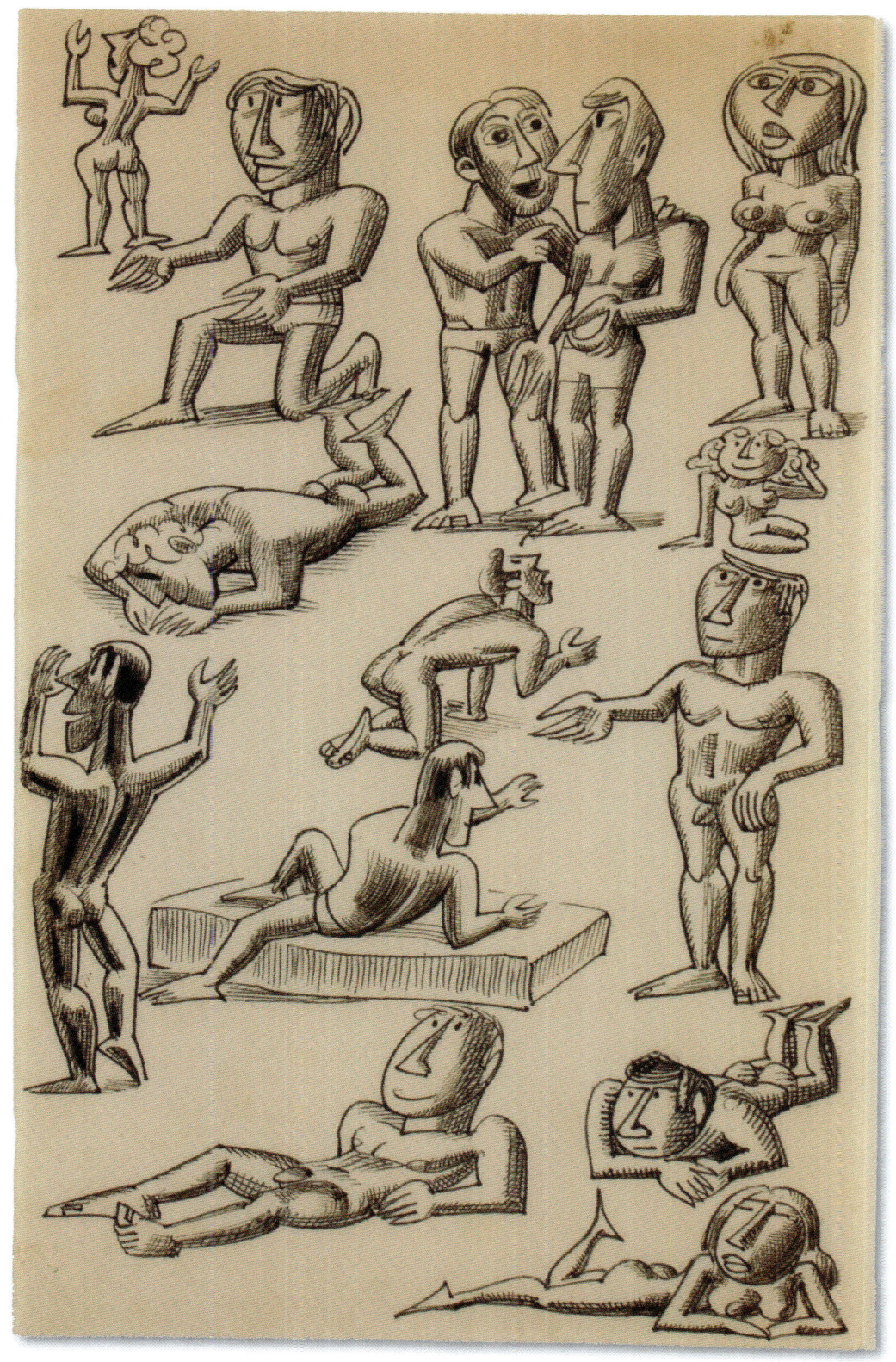

Sketches No. 102
by Kevin Wallace
c. 1942–1979
Pen and paper sketch

No artist signature
Unframed; Good Condition

kw-0038–kw-0043

Sketches No. 103
by Kevin Wallace
c. 1942–1979
Pen and paper sketches

No artist signature
Unframed; Good Condition

The Big Work

kw-0044–kw-0047
Sketches No. 104
by Kevin Wallace
c. 1942—1979
Colored Pen and paper sketches

Signed by artist
Unframed; Good Condition

kw-0048–kw-0055
Sketches No. 105
by Kevin Wallace
c. 1942–1979
Pen and paper sketches

No artist signature
Unframed; Good Condition

Sketches No. 106
by Kevin Wallace
c. 1942–1979
Pen and paper sketches

No artist signature
Unframed; Good Condition

Sketches No. 107
by Kevin Wallace
c. 1942–1979
Pen and paper sketches

No artist signature
Unframed; Good Condition

Sketches No. 108
by Kevin Wallace
c. 1942—1979
Pen and paper sketches

No artist signature
Unframed; Good Condition

Sketches No. 109
by Kevin Wallace
c. 1942–1979
Pen and paper sketches

No artist signature
Unframed; Good Condition

The Big Work

kw-0073–kw-0080
Sketches No. 110
by Kevin Wallace
c. 1942—1979
Pen and paper sketches

No artist signature
Unframed; Good Condition

kw-0081–kw-0087
Sketches No. 111
by Kevin Wallace
c. 1942–1979
Pen and paper sketches

No artist signature
Unframed; Good Condition

Sketches No. 112
by Kevin Wallace
c. 1942–1979
Pen and paper sketches

No artist signature
Unframed; Good Condition

Sketches No. 113
by Kevin Wallace
c. 1942–1979
Pen and paper sketches

No artist signature
Unframed; Good Condition

The Big Work

kw-0093- kw-0094
Sketches No. 114
by Kevin Wallace
c. 1942—1979
Pen and paper sketches

No artist signature
Unframed; Good Condition

269

kw-0095–kw-0103

Sketches No. 115
by Kevin Wallace
c. 1942–1979
Pen and paper sketches

No artist signature
Unframed; Good Condition

The Big Work

kw 0104–kw 0111
Sketches No. 116
by Kevin Wallace
c. 1942–1979
Pen and paper sketches

No artist signature
Unframed; Good Condition

271

Cemetary
by Kevin Wallace
c. 1942—1979
Pen and paper sketches

Initialed by artist
Unframed; Good Condition

The San Marcos, Phoenix
by Kevin Wallace
c. 1942—1979
Black Paint White Chalk

Initialed by artist; Original artist notation
Unframed; Good Condition

Phoenix from South Mountain Park

c. 1942—1979

Black Paint White Chalk

Initialed by artist; Original artist notation
Unframed; Good Condition

The San Marcos
c. 1942—1979
Black Paint White Chalk

Initialed by artist; Original artist notation
Unframed; Good Condition

The Berkeley Benefactor

Select oil-on-canvas paintings by Madeline Thomas Langworthy (1893-1980)

Madeline Thomas Langworthy was the mother of Helen Wallace, who married Kevin just after America won the Second World War. "Tommy" as she was better known by her freinds and family, was born in New York City on July 24, 1893, married a physician and hospital equipment inventor, and became widowed after the tragic murder of her husband by a patient. After her husband's death, Tommy followed Helen to U.C. Berkeley, built a house above campus on Panoramic Way, and set off on a life traveling the world collecting fine art and artifacts from under-represented artist communities, including carved masks from the First Nations near Alaska, Native American baskets from California, and Navajo rugs from the Southwest. Their influence is seen across her original oil paintings through color inspiration, and still-life cameos.

The Big Work

Deirdre Reading
by Madeline Thomas Langworthy
c. 1950-1960
Oil on Canvas

Signed by artist
Framed; Good Condition

John F. Kennedy at Cal Berkeley
by Madeline Thomas Langworthy
1962
Oil Painting depicting JFK's speech
at the Cal Memorial Stadium on March 23, 1962.

Signed by artist
Framed; Good Condition

mtl-0004
Developing a Matisse Habit
by Madeline Thomas Langworthy
c. 1951
Oil Painting depicting the
1951 Matisse exhibit at the New York MOMA.

Signed by artist
Framed; Good Condition

Still Life No. 1
by Madeline Thomas Langworthy
c. 1939
Oil on Canvas

Signed by artist
Framed; Good Condition

Still Life No. 2
by Madeline Thomas Langworthy
c. 1939
Oil on Canvas, exhibited
at the 1939 World's Fair on Treasure Island

Signed by artist
Framed; Good Condition

The Campanili
by Madeline Thomas Langworthy
c. 1939
Oil on Canvas

Signed by artist
Framed; Good Condition

Porch View of the Bay
by Madeline Thomas Langworthy
c. 1939
Oil on Canvas

Signed by artist
Framed; Good Condition

Fall L:eaves
by Madeline Thomas Langworthy
c. 1939
Oil on Canvas

Signed by artist
Framed; Good Condition

The Fire Trail
California Live Oaks
by Madeline Thomas Langworthy
c. 1939
Oil on Canvas

Signed by artist
Framed; Good Condition

New England Folk Art
by Madeline Thomas Langworthy
c. 1940-1960
Oil on Canvas

Signed by artist
Framed; Good Condition

Still Life
by Madeline Thomas Langworthy
c. 1940-1960
Oil on Canvas

Signed by artist
Framed; Good Condition

Cats No. 1
by Madeline Thomas Langworthy
c. 1948
Oil on Canvas

Signed by artist
Framed: Good Condition

The Big Work

Cats No. 2
by Madeline Thomas Langworthy
c. 1948
Oil on Canvas

Signed by artist
Framed: Good Condition

Red Tabby
by Madeline Thomas Langworthy
c. 1948
Oil on Canvas

Signed by artist
Framed: Good Condition

The Big Work

Paco
by Madeline Thomas Langworthy
c. 1948
Oil on Canvas

Signed by artist
Framed; Good Condition

mtl-0017

Baby Deirdre
by Madeline Thomas Langworthy
c. 1948
Oil on Canvas

Signed by artist
Framed; Good Condition

The Big Work

Lap Cat
by Madeline Thomas Langworthy
c. 1939
Oil on Canvas

Signed by artist
Framed; Good Condition

mtl-0019
Kevin
by Madeline Thomas Langworthy
c. 1948
Oil on Canvas

Signed by artist
Framed; Good Condition

The Big Work

Urania P. Cummings
by Madeline Thomas Langworthy
c. 1950
Oil on Canvas

Signed by artist
Framed; Good Condition

West Indies to North Berkeley

Original oil-on-canvas paintings by Urania P. Cummins

Madeline Thomas Langworthy shared her easel with a West Indies artist named Urania P. Cummins, who moved to San Francisco in 1922, worked for Madeline as a domestic helper, and grew to become close friends and companions in their old age. Between work, Urania joined Madeline at the easel overlooking a panoramic view of the Bay Area from atop the Berkeley hills. Urania was born in St. Thomas, Virgin Islands, and her paintings bring the colors and scenese of her hometown to life. In an October 1971 recorded interview, Urania said this of her passion for becoming an artist: "I'll tell you it was like a dream come true... Being among the artist people, you forget about yourself."

The Big Work

Palm Tree Trail
by Urania P. Cummins
c. 1950
Oil on Canvas

Signed by artist
Framed; Good Condition

The Big Work

Palm Tree Grove
by Urania P. Cummins
c. 1950
Oil on Canvas

Signed by artist
Framed; Good Condition

Artichoke Flower
by Urania P. Cummins
c. 1950
Oil on Canvas

Signed by artist
Framed; Good Condition

West Indies Sea Fishing
by Urania P. Cummins
c. 1950
Oil on Canvas

Signed by artist
Framed; Good Condition

Tommy's Personal Collection

original art by Various Artists

Madeline Thomas Langworthy, aka Tommy, was just as much a collector of art as she was a maker of it. Her personal collection of paintings, prints, and cultural artifacts was impressive and diverse. The following pieces from her collection includes mostly of oil on canvas paintings by American and European artists from the mid-century, including Matisse and Orosco, to Southern depression-era artist Staurt R. Purser. Perhaps the most notable item in her collection: a Renoir oil painting that hung above our family mantle for decades. This painting has never been officially authenticated, but why would Tommy have a fake Renior?

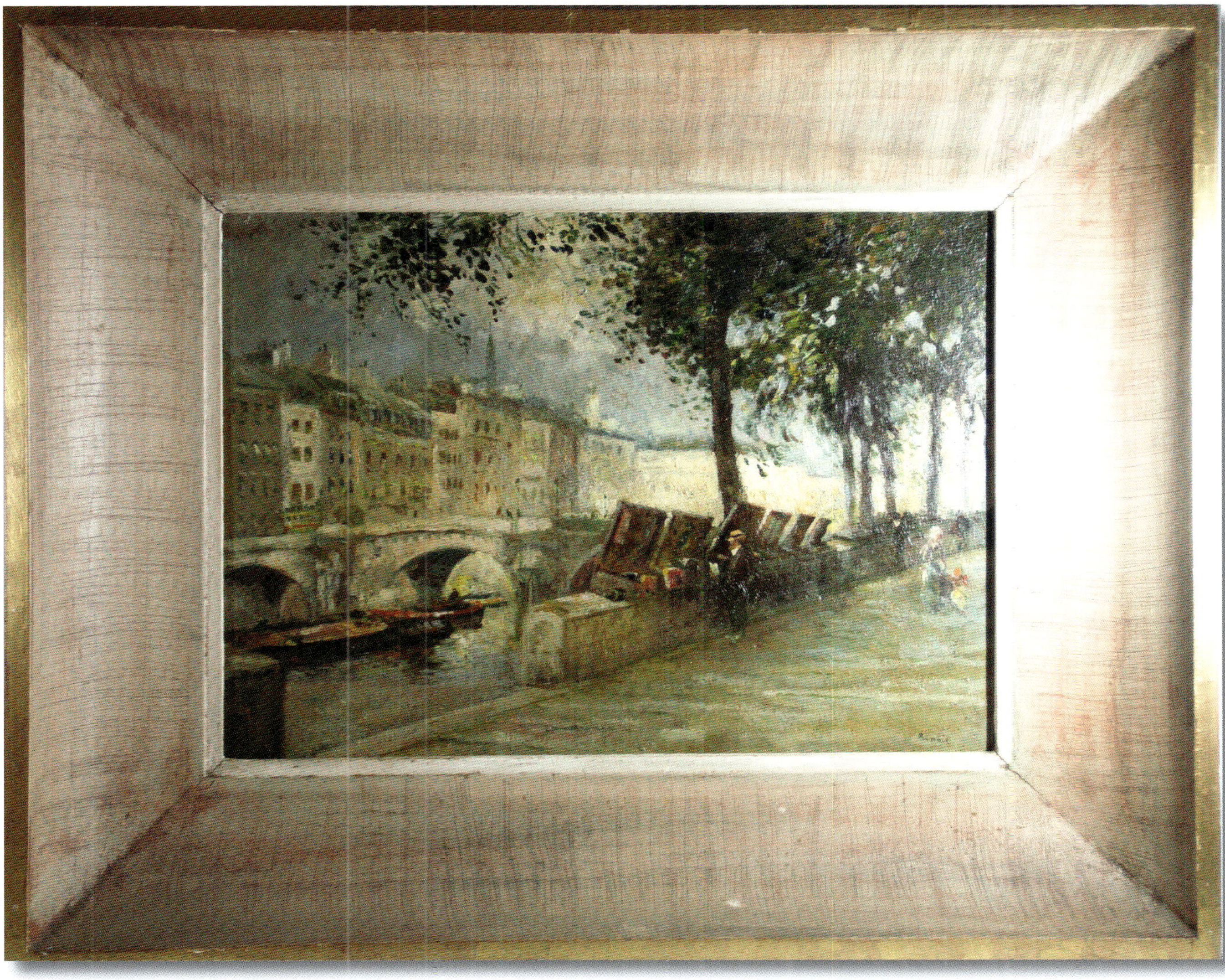

mtl-0020

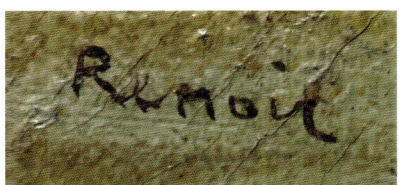

"The Renior"

by Pierre-Auguste Renoir

Comes with a bill of sale from a Washington State gallery.

Signed by artist

Framed; Good Condition

Farm Landscape (front)
Southern Black Church (back)
by Robert S. Purser
c. 1929

Two Sided Oil on Canvas
(back and front side)

Signed by artist
Framed; Good Condition

The Big Work

Railroad Bridge
Unknown Artist
Oil on Canvas

No artist signature
Framed; Good Condition

Dia de Los Muertos
Jose Clemente Orozco
Exhibited in the 1953 memorial exhibit
at the San Francisco Museum of Art

Signed by artist
Framed; Good Condition

Cyprus Bog
Unknown Artist
c. 1948
Oil on Canvas

No artist signature
Framed; Good Condition

The Big Work

mtl-0026
Lake View
Wally Walter
1949
Oil on Canvas

Signed by artist
Framed; Good Condition

About the Authors

Kevin Wallace (1918 - 1979) is an American journalist, writer, and illustrator, who spent most of his career pairing his wit and artistic talents as an editorial cartoonist and city writer for the *San Francisco Chronicle* and rival *Examiner* newspapers.

In the 1940s, Kevin joined the *New Yorker Magazine* as a staff writer for the "Talk of the Town" column, writing the occasional feature story on luminaries like Ansel Adams and Walt Disney. After 10 years in New York, Kevin returned to San Francisco to finish out his career at the *Chronicle*, sketching the people and places of his hometown.

Matt Berger (1976 - present) is the grandson of Kevin and a writer and producer in Silicon Valley, Calif. Forty years after his grandfather's death, Matt set out to resurrect Kevin's unpublished memoir, authenticate the stories, and compile it all with context alongside his family's paintings, portraits, drawings, and historical records.

The Big Work

www.thebigwork.com